THE INSTITUTE OF CHARTERED SHIPBROKERS

The Institute of Chartered Shipbrokers is the only internationally recognised professional body representing shipbrokers, ship managers and agents throughout the world.

With 24 branches in key shipping areas, 3,500 individual and 120 company members, joining ICS represents a commitment to maintaining the highest professional standards across the shipping industry worldwide.

In today's world it is essential for reasons of

- competitiveness
- efficiency and
- safety

that all key players understand the contractual relationships between themselves.

Staff with ICS qualifications subscribe to a common worldwide standard of professional competence and conduct. They have a thorough understanding of all aspects of shipping including law, insurance and economics and by doing so can communicate effectively with specialist professionals.

"ICS is the only source of professional and vocational qualifications in shipping. Take it from us, all other things being equal, the ICS qualified candidate will get the job."

Phil Parry, Managing Director, Spinnaker Consulting

Companies employing ICS qualified staff can be confident that they have played their part in ensuring that professionalism, industry knowledge and risk awareness are of paramount importance to their Board and management.

To find out more about ICS and membership either as an individual or company, please contact us at:

85 Gracechurch Street
London EC3V 0AA
UK
T: +44 (0)20 7623 1111
F: +44 (0)20 7623 8118
E: info@ics.org.uk

www.ics.org.uk

PREFACE

Professional education through TutorShip distance learning courses

The Institute of Chartered Shipbrokers (ICS) is the professional body for all concerned in the business of commercial shipping. Passing its examinations and being elected to membership (MICS) provides a successful candidate with the only internationally recognised qualification for shipbrokers.

The complete syllabus covers the following subjects:

Introduction to Shipping
Legal Principles in Shipping Business
Economics of Sea Transport and International Trade
Shipping Business

Dry Cargo Chartering
Ship Operations and Management
Tanker Chartering
Ship Sale and Purchase
Liner Trades
Port Agency

Shipping Law
Financial and Management Accounting
Logistics and Multi-modal Transport
Marine Insurance

The Institute believes it is essential that a qualified shipbroker has a thorough knowledge of certain profession-specific subjects plus a sufficient knowledge of the law, insurance, economics etc so that they can communicate with a specialist professional. This results in less confusion, misunderstanding and hopefully less contractual risk. Professionally qualified personnel are consequently ideally placed to undertake the key executive roles in the shipping service sector.

The true value of these course books is only gained if the student enrols on the TutorShip distance learning programme and all TutorShip Courses are accredited by the O.D.L.Q.C. (the Open and Distance Learning Quality Council). We would suggest that there is nowhere better to turn to than ICS TutorShip courses for preparing yourselves for a highly successful career in the shipping profession.

We further recommend these books for practitioners and those already working in the Shipping Industry and allied trades. They will ensure you are kept abreast of developments as well as acting as useful everyday knowledge based texts for every aspect of this 'shipping business'.

Further details can be found at www.ics.org.uk

SHIP SALE AND PURCHASE

'rogramme

Shipbrokers

Shipbroker A person having one of several occupations, chartering agent or owner's broker, negotiating the terms of the charter of a ship on behalf of a charterer or shipowner respectively; sale and purchase broker negotiating on behalf of buyer or seller of a ship; ship's agent, attending to the requirement of a ship, her master and crew while in port on behalf of the shipowner; loading broker, whose business is to attract cargoes to the ships of his principal.

Published and Printed in England by
Witherby & Co. Ltd., 32-36 Aylesbury Street, London EC1R 0ET

Published for the Institute of Chartered Shipbrokers
First Published 2006

ISBN 13: 978 1 85609 280 7
ISBN 10: 1 85609 280 1

British Library Cataloguing in Publication Data

Ship sale and purchase
1. Ships – Purchasing – Law and legislation
2. Ships – Registration and transfer
I. Institute of Chartered Shipbrokers
343'.07862382

ISBN 1856092801

Notice of Terms of Use

While the advice given in this document ("document") has been developed using the best information currently available, it is intended purely as guidance to be used at the user's own risk. No responsibility is accepted by the Institute of Chartered Shipbrokers (ICS), the membership of ICS or by any person, firm, corporation or organisation [who or which has been in any way concerned with the furnishing of information or data, the compilation or any translation, publishing, supply or sale of the document] for the accuracy of any information or advice given in the document or any omission from the document or for any consequence whatsoever resulting directly or indirectly from compliance with or adoption of guidance contained in the document even if caused by a failure to exercise reasonable care.

Published and Printed by
WITHERBY & COMPANY LIMITED
32–36 Aylesbury Street,
London EC1R 0ET, England
Tel No. 020 7251 5341 Fax No. 020 7251 1296
International Tel No. +44 20 7251 5341 Fax No. +44 20 7251 1296
E-mail: books@witherbys.co.uk Website: www.witherbys.com

[5850]

CONTENTS

		Page
	PREFACE	iv
1	**THE SHIP**	1
1.1	Introduction	1
1.2	Size and Tonnage	1
1.3	Cargo Categories	4
1.4	Ship types	5
1.5	Bulk Cargo Carriers – Tankers	5
1.6	Tankers and Oil Pollution	10
1.7	Bulk Carriers – Dry Cargo	11
1.8	General Cargo Ships	12
1.9	Refrigerated Cargo Ships	13
1.10	Container Ships	14
1.11	Ro-Ro Cargo Ships	15
1.12	Passenger Ships	15
1.13	Miscellaneous	16
1.14	Types of Machinery	18
1.15	General Arrangement Plans	19
1.16	Self-Assessment and Test Questions	20
2	**SHIP REGISTRATION**	21
2.1	The Need for Registration	21
2.2	The Growth of "Open" Registries	22
2.3	The Current Scene	23
2.4	The Positive and Negative Elements of Flags of Convenience (FOC's)	23
2.5	The Response by Traditional Maritime Nations	25
2.6	Ship Registration and the Ship Sale and Purchase Broker	26
2.7	Self-Assessment and Test Questions	26

3 CLASSIFICATION 27

3.1 Classification Societies 27

3.2 Other Functions of Classification Societies 31

3.3 Tonnage Measurement Regulations 33

3.4 Practical Application for the Sale and Purchase Broker 34

3.5 Classification Society Records 34

3.6 Self-Assessment and Test Questions 35

4 THE SHIP SALE (PART 1) 37

4.1 The Offer 37

4.2 The Structure of an Offer 38

4.3 Inspection and Inspection of Records 40

4.3.1 Records Inspection 41

4.3.2 Reply Time for Inspection of Vessel and Records 41

4.4 Delivery – Where and When? 41

4.5 Dry-docking or Diver's Inspection 42

4.6 What is Included in the Price? 43

4.7 Bunkers and Lubricating Oils 43

4.8 Buyer's Crew on Board before Delivery 44

4.9 Same Condition as When Inspected 44

4.10 English Law/Arbitration London 45

4.11 With Class Maintained Free of Recommendations and Free of Average Damage Affecting Class 45

4.12 The Offer and Counter Offer 46

4.12.1 The First Counter Offer 46

4.13 Self-Assessment and Test Questions 48

5 THE SHIP SALE (PART 2) 49

5.1 Introduction 49

5.2 Concluding the Sale 49

5.3 Signature on Contracts 58

5.4 Other Sale Contract Forms 58

5.5 To Sum Up 58

5.6 Brokers' Commissions 59

5.7 Self-Assessment and Test Questions 59

6 DEMOLITION 61

6.1 Introduction 61

6.2 The Ship-Breaker's Work Place 61

6.3 The Basic Principles of a Demolition Contract 62

6.4 Selecting the Right Buyer 63

6.5 The Sale Contract 64

6.6 Other Sale Forms for Demolition 66

6.7 The Demolition Market 67

6.8 Self-Assessment and Test Questions 68

7 FINANCE, NEWBUILDINGS AND INSURANCE 69

7.1 Introduction 69

7.2 Funding the Purchase from Own Resources 69

7.3 Borrowed Money 69

7.4 Incentives to Borrowers and Lenders 71

7.4.1 Shipbuilding 71
7.4.2 Leasing 73
7.4.3 Other Methods of Finance 73

7.5 Newbuildings 73

7.5.1 The Sale Contract 74

7.6 Insurance 75

7.7 Insurance for the S & P Broker 76

7.8 Self-Assessment and Test Questions 76

8 LEGAL ASPECTS OF SHIP SALE AND PURCHASE 79

8.1 Introduction 79

8.2 The Ship Sale and Purchase Broker 79

8.3 The Broker's Commission 80

8.4 The Law and the Saleform 81

8.4.1 When Does a Binding Contract Exist 81
8.4.2 Identifying the Parties 81
8.4.3 The Price and Payment 82
8.4.4 Inspections 82
8.4.5 Cancelling Date 82

8.5 Spares, Bunkers etc. 83

8.6 Maritime Liens and Encumbrances 83

8.6.1 At Place of Delivery 84
8.6.2 Default by Either of the Parties 85

8.7 Dispute Resolution 85

8.8 The S & P Broker's Role When Principals are in Dispute 86

8.9 Ethics Among S & P Brokers? 87

8.10 Self-Assessment and Test Questions 87

9 THE MARKETS AND THE PARTIES INVOLVED 89

9.1 Introduction 89

9.2 Shipowner Personalities 89

9.3 Dry Bulk Carriers 90

9.4 General Purpose Ships 92

9.5 Small Ships 92

9.6 Passenger Ships and Ferries 93

9.7 Obsolete Tonnage 93

9.8 Who Should an S & P Broker Know? 93

9.9 What Should an S & P Broker Know? 95

9.10 Test Questions 95

10 DOCUMENTATION AND SHIP VALUATION 97

10.1 Part One – Documents and Procedures on Delivery 97

10.2 Part Two – Ship Valuations 100

10.3 Self-Assessment and Test Questions 102

APPENDICES 103

MOCK EXAMINATION 159

COURSE GUIDE 163

Chapter 1

THE SHIP

1.1 INTRODUCTION

The Sale and Purchase Broker is concerned – as an intermediary – with the selling and buying of ships and anyone intending to pursue a career in this area of shipping business, or to understand how it operates, must have a strong knowledge base in respect of the product being sold. A proper understanding of ship details is therefore an essential part of the Sale and Purchase Broker's armoury. It is important to understand fully and to memorise what is meant by the following.

1.2 SIZE AND TONNAGE

A ship can have five different tonnage measurements and it is vital when comparing one vessel with another that the same tonnage measurements are used. Most of the following measurements can be found on the ship's plans. Tonnage can be expressed in long tons (2240 lbs.) or metric tonnes (1,000 Kg). Tonnages are:

i) **Deadweight (dwt)**. The weight of cargo, stores, fuel, passengers and crew carried by the ship when loaded to her maximum permissible draught in salt water.

   The abbreviation dwat will often be encountered as it stands for deadweight all told this is to differentiate it from dwcc which refers to deadweight cargo capacity.

ii) **Gross Tonnage (GT).** The use of the word "tonnage" here is really a misnomer. The word originates from the days when the most convenient way to measure a ship was to calculate how many "tuns" it could carry. A tun was, and indeed still is, a standard sized barrel of 252 gallons (approx 1145 litres) in which all manner of cargo was carried in the days of sailing ships.

   The word became changed to "ton" with the passage of time but **gross tonnage** is essentially a measure of **volume**. Originally Gross tonnage was calculated at 100 cubic feet to the ton but, under the International Convention on Tonnage Measurement of Ships 1969 which came into full force in 1994, Gross Tonnage is defined broadly as the capacity in cubic metres of all the spaces within the hull, and of the enclosed spaces above the deck available for cargo, stores, fuel, passengers and crew with certain exceptions. A Gross Ton is between 2.5 and 3 cubic metres; there is a scale depending upon the ship's size which determines exactly which figure of cubic metres shall be used to calculate the **GT.**

iii) **Net Tonnage (NT).** Is based upon the same scale as for gross tonnage as defined above but it is the interior volume less deductions for crew, engine, propelling and navigating spaces. It can be considered as a crude measurement of the revenue earning capacity of the ship. NT shall not be less than 30% of the GT.

   GT and NT are not accurate measures of a ship's carrying capacity, a better method is the measure of grain and bale cubic (see later). However, GT and NT are favoured by many port authorities as a convenient measure upon which to base port dues. GT is also used when seeking to enhance the sheer size of a passenger/cruise liner

iv) **Light Displacement or Lightweight (ldt).** The actual weight of the vessel in long tons or tonnes. It includes full equipment plus the weight of the machinery, boilers, and spare parts, but excludes bunkers, cargo, dunnage, provisions, water and other consumables.

This is **a very important measurement** for ship sale and purchase brokers because it is a measure of the actual weight of metal (mainly steel) which is a vital figure when a ship is being sold for demolition.

v) **Displacement.** This represents the total weight of the ship and everything on board. The volume of water displaced will vary according to whether it is salt water or freshwater but not enough to make much difference. This tonnage is **not** used for merchant ships but **always** for warships.

Capacity

Another important measurement of merchant ships is that of the actual volume of the holds. This is because many cargoes are so light that the ship can be physically full before being loaded down to her permissible draught. There are two such measurements, Grain capacity and Bale capacity which can be expressed in cubic metres or cubic feet.

Grain capacity is the volume of cargo spaces measured to the outside of frames, to the top of ceiling and to the top of beams, including hatchways (insulated spaces are not included). NB the word "ceiling" in maritime terms means the **bottom** of the hold, **not** the part overhead.

Bale capacity extends to the inside of cargo battens and to underside of beams. The names become self explanatory when one considers the fact that a bulk cargo such as grain can flow around beams and frames and fill every part of the hold whereas cargo which comprises individual pieces (such as bales) will not be able to flow into spaces between frames etc.

T.E.U. This is the customary method of referring to the carrying capacity of a container ship; the initials stand for Twenty Foot Equivalent Units. Despite widespread standardisation of metric measurements in the maritime world, because containerisation began in the USA, which still retains pre-metric standards of measurement, freight containers are referred to in feet and inches. Except for specialist units, containers are either 20 feet or 40 feet long by 8 feet wide and 8 feet 6 inches high. Thus a 20 foot container is one teu and a 40 foot container, two teus. Occasionally one may encounter reference to FEUs (forty foot equivalent units).

Lane Metres (LM) This is the manner in which ships designed to carry wheeled cargo are measured. These include car carriers and Roll-on Roll-off (RoRo) ships and as the name implies, it is measure of the length of the lanes in the cargo decks. In the case of car carriers one would need also need to know the headroom to get a meaningful measure of the ship's carrying capacity.

Freeboard

Reference has already been made to "permissible draft" (this may also be spelled **draught**) but it is the **freeboard** with which the international safety authorities are concerned. Freeboard is the vertical distance between waterline and the uppermost continuous deck equipped with permanent means of closing all openings which are exposed to the elements. The waterline is that which is dictated by the **load line.**

Load Line

By international convention, all merchant ships must be marked with a load line. The upper edge of this line indicates the maximum permissible draught. The load lines – known as the **Plimsoll Mark** – are set off amidships, on both sides of the ship, at specified distances below a deck line thus:

Diagram 1.1

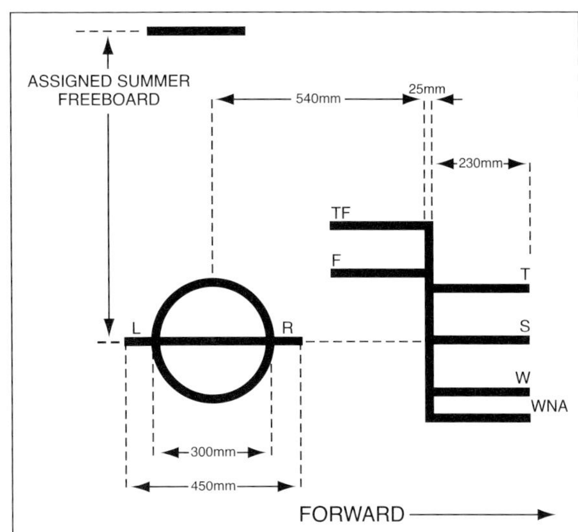

TF = Tropical Fresh Water F = Fresh Water T = Tropical S = Summer W = Winter WNA = Winter North Atlantic (Except where stated the marks refer to normal salt sea-water)

The reason for the variations is that the more severe the expected weather, the greater the amount of freeboard that is needed for safety. Thus WNA (Winter North Atlantic) being the area of the most treacherous weather is where the greatest freeboard is required.

The upper edge of the summer line, if continued, passes through the centre of the load line disc and is the basic line.

On the line you will see the initials LR which relate to the classification society which surveyed the ship to determine the positioning of the mark. In this case the LR relates to Lloyds Register, but there are many more such as AB (American Bureau), BV (Bureau Veritas), RI (Registro Italiano) and so on.

Light Draft (draught)

The vessel's draft at light displacement is called "light draft".

Suez and Panama Canal Tonnage.

Both of these authorities have their own rules for the measurement of gross and net tonnage and ships using the canals are charged on these tonnages.

Moulded Depth

The vertical distance amidships from the top of the keel to the top of the upper deck beam at the side.

Overall Length (l.o.a.)

The extreme length of the ship. When the overall length is followed by the notation (BB) it indicates that the ship has a bulbous bow and the overall length includes that bow.

Length B.P (between perpendiculars)

The distance on the summer load waterline from the fore side of the stem to the after side of the rudder-post, or to the centre of the rudder stock if there is no rudder-post.

Extreme Breadth

The maximum breadth to the outside of the ship's structure and in paddle ships includes the paddle boxes.

Moulded Breadth

The greatest breadth amidships from heel of frame to heel of frame.

Scantlings

All structural parts such as frames, beams, shell plating, bulkheads used in the construction of ships are covered under this heading. The classification societies have fixed rules and tables for the construction of steel ships, which must be observed by shipbuilders in order to obtain the required certificates.

Air Draft

This is an unofficial measurement but one that S & P Brokers may encounter. It is the measurement from the waterline to the ship's highest point (usually the top of a mast). Its importance comes into effect in trades which involve negotiating waterways where bridges may be a problem.

1.3 CARGO CATEGORIES

A general understanding of different cargo categories and the cargo-handling modes should be considered before a study is made of the various types of merchant ships involved in their carriage.

Cargo categories may be defined as follows:

i) **GENERAL CARGO** – diverse types and forms of cargo (which may be carried simultaneously or alternatively depending upon the ship's trading pattern). General cargo often involves manufactured or semi-manufactured goods.

ii) **CONTAINER CARGO** – cargo carried in purpose-built cargo containers constructed according to ISO container standard dimensions and strength requirements

iii) **RO-RO CARGO** – general cargo which can be loaded/unloaded to or from cargo decks; in/on wheeled vehicles; cargo loaded or unloaded by wheeled transport (e.g. fork lift trucks, tractor units).

iv) **BULK CARGO** – liquid or loose cargo (of a homogeneous nature) which is not in any form of packing within the ship's tanks/holds.

Cargo Handling Modes may be defined as follows:

LIFT-ON/LIFT-OFF – the loading/unloading of dry cargo by the ship's own derricks/cranes, or by shore-based cranes or gantries.

ROLL-ON/ROLL-OFF – the loading/unloading of cargo by way of the ship's doors/ramps (and in conjunction with shore-based cargo handling facilities).

PUMP-ON/PUMP-OFF – the loading/unloading of liquid cargo by way of shore based/ship based pumping and pumping equipment. Almost invariably the shore facilities pump the cargo IN and the ship pumps the cargo OUT.

FLOAT-IN/FLOAT-OUT – the loading/unloading of floating cargo by way of either the ship's bow door or the ship's stern door/ramp, whilst the ship is in a semi-submerged state.

FLOAT-ON/FLOAT-OFF – the loading/unloading of floating cargo to/from the ship's weather deck cargo space whilst the ship is in a semi-submerged state.

SPECIALISED HANDLING – with the growth of modern technology a wide variety of highly specialised equipment has evolved which may include one or more of the main modes of cargo handling. For example, coal and ore may be discharged by an "Archimedes Screw" device which feeds a conveyor belt. Bulk grain may be discharged by suction or by a system of dredger type buckets feeding a conveyer into the grain elevators. Some modern bulk carriers designed for a particular trade (e.g. coal) are "self-unloaders" having the discharging equipment as part of the on-board equipment.

1.4 SHIP TYPES

Refer to **Appendix 1** and locate the profile of each of the ships described below. In some cases the sketches include arrows showing the manner in which the cargo is loaded.

When considering ship types it is important to have a clear mental picture of the vessel concerned and the best way to do this is to develop the skill of producing sketches. The basic points to display in such a sketch can be seen from the following outline.

Diagram 1.2 – A Basic Ship Type

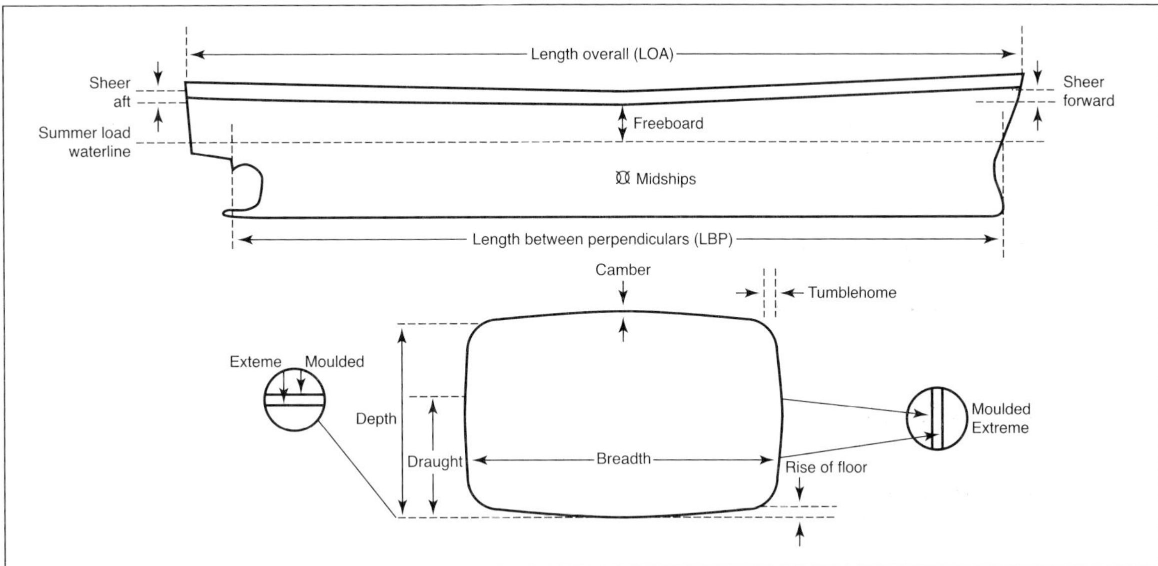

1.5 BULK CARGO CARRIERS – TANKERS

Tankers are designed for the carriage of oils, chemicals, liquefied gases, edible liquids (e.g. vegetable oil, wine, orange juice etc) fresh water and other liquids. They are almost invariably described in terms of deadweight tonnage (dwt) because this is the basis on which they are chartered.

The cargo-handling mode for tankers is pump on/pump off. Almost invariably shore pumps are used for loading and the ship's own pumps for discharging, this is because pumps are far less efficient 'sucking' than they are pushing.

Tanker types include **Oil Tankers** – for the carriage of crude oil, refined petroleum products and similar flammable liquids. The pattern of the oil trade is for the **crude oil** to be loaded near the point of production (the oil wells) and taken to refineries near the areas of consumption. It has, therefore been possible for oil companies to take full advantage of economies of scale in connection with the size of crude carriers and S & P brokers will encounter the term VLCC (Very Large Crude Carrier) and ULCC (Ultra Large Crude Carrier). Both VLCCs and ULCCs can sometimes be described as "Capesize" because they are too large to transit either the Panama or the Suez Canals and thus have to be routed round Cape of Good Hope or Cape Horn.

Diagram 1.3 – A Typical Tanker Configuration

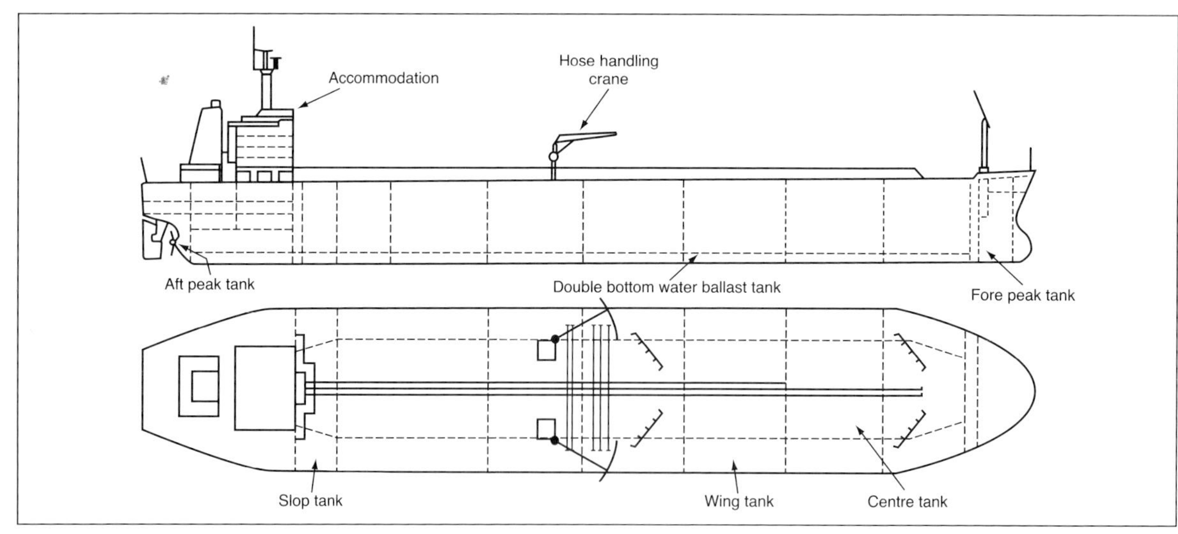

A typical modern Capesize tanker will be **double-skinned,** have all machinery and accommodation aft, a small crane amidships to handle the hoses used for load/discharge and a small crane aft to load stores.

The cargo space will be divided athwartships, typically into five compartments each of which is in turn divided by the two longitudinal bulkheads which run the length of the ship; this effectively provides fifteen tanks. The several tanks each connected by pipelines to the discharging manifold, enables the cargo to be loaded and discharged evenly. If some tanks were emptied completely whilst others left full there would be bending stresses to the hull which could prove catastrophic.

In addition to cargo tanks there will be segregated ballast compartments; much of the ballast water is carried in the double bottom and in the side spaces. The segregation ensures that no oil becomes mixed with ballast water so that there is no risk of pollution when discharging ballast. Ballast water has to be taken on/discharged, evenly across the ship, in the same way as cargo in order to avoid undue stresses. Ballast is essential on the non-cargo part of the voyage in order to bring the ship deep enough in the water to be stable and for the propeller to be submerged,

Between the cargo section and the accommodation/machinery space there will be a **cofferdam**. This ensures complete separation of the cargo with its potential for inflammable gases, from the living quarters as well as providing space for the **cargo pumps**.

ULCC – Ultra large crude carriers are in the region of 350,000 dwt or larger. The largest ever built was a little over half a million tonnes deadweight; many naval architects designed tankers larger still, even up to one million tonnes but they were never seriously considered by the trade.

VLCC – Very large crude carriers range from 200,000 to 300,000 dwt and these are the archetype Capesize class.

Typical dimensions of a VLCC would be:

Length overall (LOA) 330/340 metres
Breadth 58 metres
Draft 20/21 metres
Deadweight 300,000 tonnes
Service speed 15/16 knots
Fuel consumption 50/55 tonnes per day

Suezmax – 100,000 to 160,000 dwt with dimensions which enable it to transit the Suez Canal (but not the Panama Canal). This size is often referred to as a "**million barrel tanker**" because although in the chartering and S & P world tankers are referred to in deadweight tonnes, the oil itself is referred to in barrels (bbls). This dates back to the days when a barrel was the only way of transporting liquids and this is still the unit used when buying and selling oil. A barrel in this context is 42 US gallons (approx 160 litres) and crude oil is usually traded in lots 500,000 bbls. Crude oils vary considerable in their specific gravities so that it is not possible to say what the weight of a barrel of oil will be but a very rough figure is six barrels to a tonne.

Despite its name, tanker traffic through the Suez Canal is not so great as may be expected because many Mediterranean destinations are now reached by pipelines and the economies of scale that are achieved with Capesize tankers often produce a lower delivered cost, bearing in mind that Suez Canal Dues have to be paid on that route.

A Suezmax tanker would have the same basic configuration as a VLCC but typical dimensions would be:

Length overall (LOA) 275 metres
Breadth 45 metres
Draft 16/17 metres
Deadweight 140/145,000 tonnes
Service speed 14/15 knots

Panamax – 55,000 to 70,000 dwt able to transit the Panama Canal fully laden. The restrictions of the Panama Canal are because, unlike Suez which travels through flat country, Panama has to negotiate a difference in land height of approximately 26 metres which is achieved by locks. It is the size of these locks that governs the size of ships which can pass through the canal.

A typical Panamax tanker's dimensions would be:

Length over all (LOA) 225/275 metres
Breadth 32 metres
Draft 12/13 metres

Handysize – a loose expression covering ships from 30,000 up to 100,000 more used in the products trades than in crude oil business

Aframax – although originally, AFRAMAX was 79,999 dwt it is now applied to ships between 70,000 and 119,999 dwt. Aframax tankers usually have a speed around 14/15 knots

AFRA is the acronym for Average Freight Rate Assessment. These are rates assessed periodically by the London Tanker Brokers Panel at the behest of the major oil companies. The majors use AFRA as a source of unbiased "market" rates when they buy oil from each other. Other organisations also use them for different purposes. As you would expect, the larger the ship the lower the rate per ton and one such cut off size is 80,000 dwt thus a ship of 79,999 dwt is the maximum size in that bracket. Some people have referred to AFRAMAX as another form of "paragraph ship".

Although Aframax ships have been included here in the crude section, the term refers only to the size and such ships may be found in the products trade (clean and dirty – see below) even in the chemical trades.

Crude Carriers Generally Tankers are invariably built with their machinery and accommodation all aft. The tanks themselves are sub-divided into several sections both fore and aft and athwartships. This serves three purposes, first, it gives structural strength to the ship. Secondly having many small compartments the free-surface effect is minimised; were there one large tank, if the ship heeled over the weight of liquid moving to the lower side would cause the ship to capsize. A third benefit is that should there be more than one consignee, the different parcels can be kept separate.

All the tanks are linked by a system of **pipelines** which enable the cargo to be transferred between the tanks and the load/discharge **manifold** which is the link between the ship and the shore tanks.

There is a **cofferdam** (a separate compartment) immediately aft of the tanks one purpose of which is to ensure complete separation of the inflammable cargo from the accommodation/machinery space. The cofferdam also contains the **pumproom** which serves a complex arrangement of pipelines serving all the tanks and the discharging manifold. It is common now for the pumps to be steam-turbine driven.

Many tankers are also equipped with **heating coils** to ensure that the cargo does not become too viscous to be pumpable

By international convention, all tankers have **segregated ballast tanks** (SBTs) to ensure that ballast water no longer enters the cargo tanks which would cause oil residues to be dumped in the sea when ballast is pumped out.

Because crude oil has all the different fractions from light unstable gases to thick tarry material, any empty space in a tank would soon be filled with a mixture of gas and air – an explosive combination. The same risk applies when the cargo has been discharged but oil residues remain. To obviate risk, the empty space is filled with an inert gas which is usually generated from the engine exhaust suitably treated. The treatment device and the pipeline system is called the **Inert Gas (IG) system**.

After normal discharge, the sides and bottoms of the tanks are coated with oil residues which, in the past, were cleaned with water sprayed around the tank by a device rather like a giant lawn sprinkler (A Butterworth system). This produced an oil/water emulsion which had to be separately dealt with by the refinery. More recently it was discovered that by using some of the ship's own oil cargo under pressure, a satisfactory cleaning result could be obtained. Therefore most crude carriers today are equipped with a **Crude Oil Washing** (**COW**) system.

Do not overlook that new tankers are **now built with double skins** and eventually all tankers, with a few rare exceptions will all be of this configuration.

Diagram 1.4 – A Double Bottom Configuration

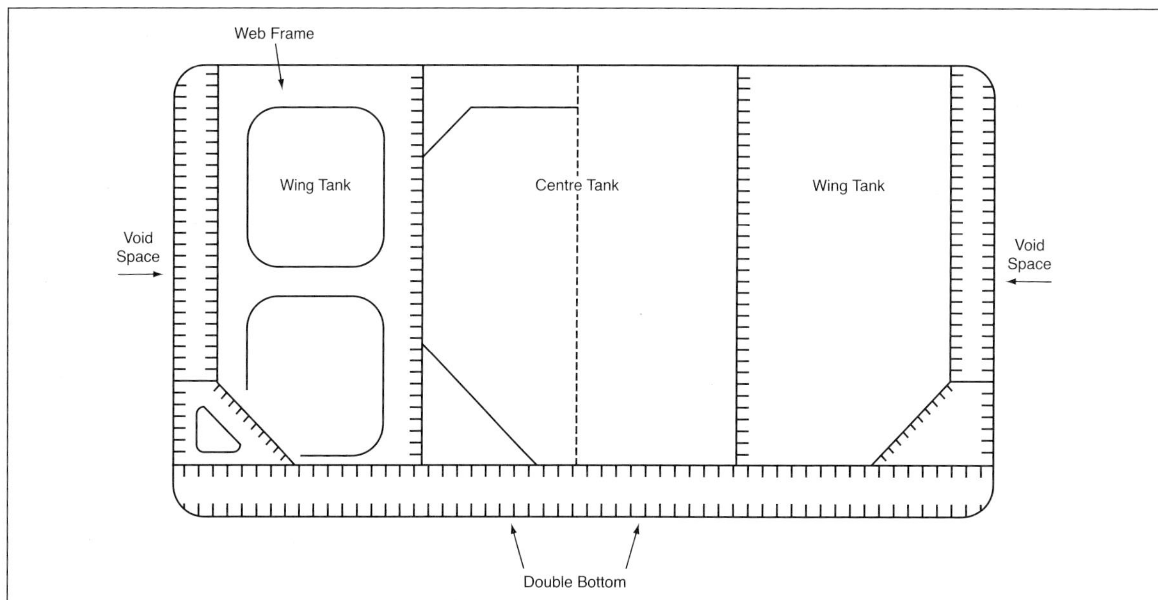

Diagram 1.5 – A Product Carrier

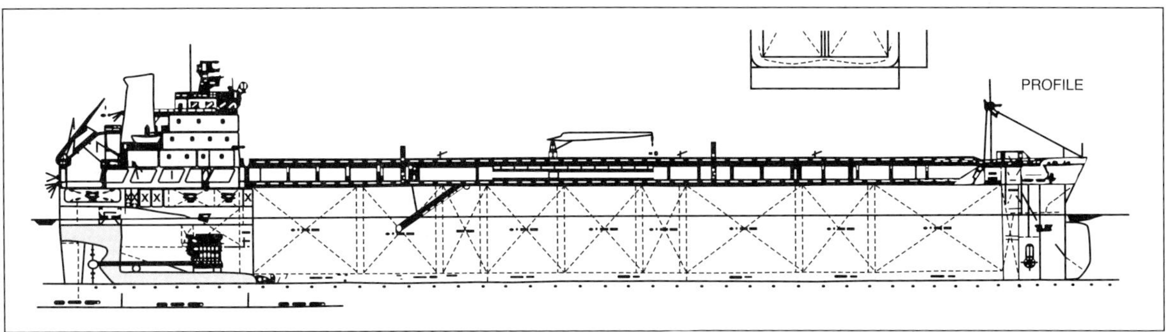

The sizes of tankers designed for carrying **refined petroleum products** vary widely depending upon the trade for which they are intended. 45,000 dwt is a fairly common size for this trade although up to 100,000 is not unusual.

S & P Brokers will encounter the expressions "clean" and "dirty" as descriptions of product carriers; this indicates the type of trade the ships have been in. Gasoline (petrol), kerosene (paraffin) and other light coloured products are referred to as "clean" whilst dark coloured products, such as heavy fuel oil, are "dirty"; tankers regularly in the dirty trades usually have heating coils. Although it is possible to clean a tanker from dirty to clean, it is an expensive business and seldom happens.

Almost all the cargoes carried in product tankers are intended for use without further refining thus cleanliness and avoidance of contamination is important. For this reason it is common, especially for ships designed for clean products, to have the tanks **coated** with an epoxy (inert plastic) coating to avoid any cargo contact with bare steel and to make cleaning easier. Tank cleaning in product carriers is by high pressure washing with water; there is no equivalent of COW in product carriers.

Product carriers, especially those in the clean trades, are able to segregate grades of cargoes; the ability to carry four separate grades is common.

Chemical tankers – Crude oil yields many more materials than those simply used for burning; there are a wide variety of by-products many of which have fire hazards in excess of those of gasoline and similar flammable liquids, or significant hazards in addition to or other than flammability such as reactivity, corrosive or toxic properties. The tanks of chemical carriers are invariably treated with some form of **coating** so that the cargo never comes into contact with the bare steel.

The coatings vary because no one coating is impervious to all the likely cargoes. S & P Brokers intending to specialise in the chemical tanker trades should acquaint themselves with the different types of coating and the cargoes for which they are intended. A principal would not thank a broker for wasting time proposing ships with a coating incompatible with the buyers intended business.

Some chemical cargoes are aggressive to any form of coating and so demand **stainless steel** tanks. Many chemical cargoes can be rendered unusable by the smallest degree of contamination so modern chemical carriers have a separate pump for each tank.

Parcel Tankers are a highly specialised ship designed, as the name implies, for the carriage of several part cargoes or "parcels", usually of chemicals or products of a high degree of purity demanding scrupulous care in handling to ensure there is no contamination. The segregation of the tanks and pumping systems is of a particularly complex. Four pump rooms would not be unusual and in many cases the pumps (hydraulically driven) will be submerged in the tanks themselves.

Diagram 1.6 – A Typical Parcel Tanker

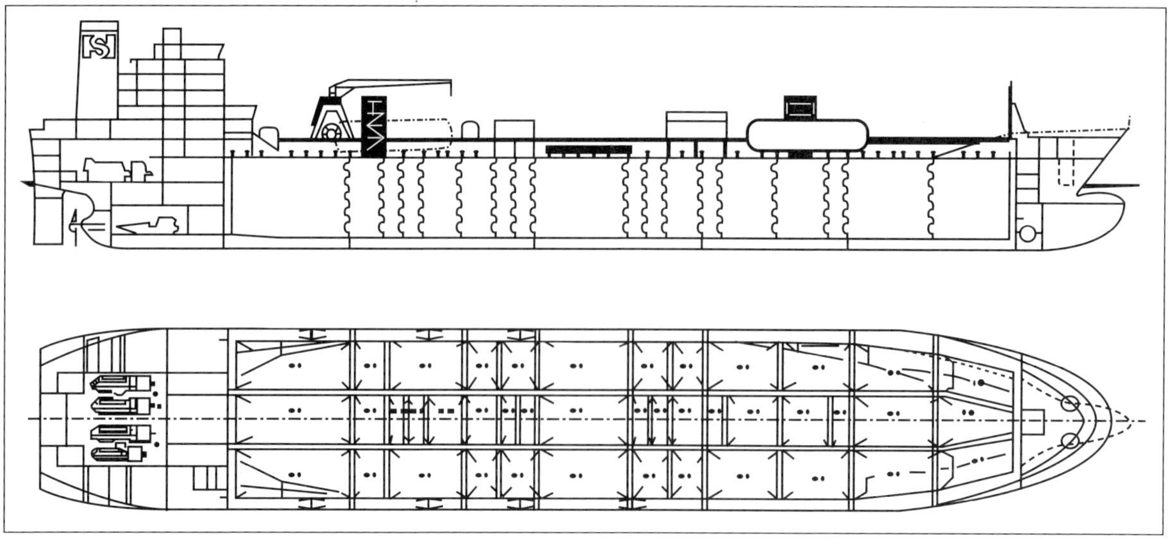

Liquefied Natural Gas (LNG) Carriers – as the name implies, LNG is gas as is found in its natural state. This is mainly methane and is used as a fuel. In some cases (e.g. the North Sea) natural gas is pumped straight from the gas wells to the gas mains for home and industrial heating. To be transportable in liquid form, LNG has to be refrigerated down to minus 160° C. This involves special tanks, often of spherical design, quite separate and insulated from the ship's hull which would become brittle at such low temperatures.

Liquid Petroleum Gas (LPG) Carriers – LPG is found within crude oil deposits and is also a product of the refining of crude oil. Mainly butane or propane it will be familiar to smokers as fuel in cigarette lighters or to campers in their portable cooking stoves, there are, of course, many other industrial uses for LPG.

LPG carriers are of various designs, some carry their cargo under pressure to keep it in liquid form, others semi-refrigerated/semi-pressurised or fully refrigerated. The design depends upon the type of cargo for which the ship is intended.

Other Bulk Liquid Carriers are designed for specific tasks including some special chemicals, acids, vegetable oils, fruit juice, wine etc and in many of these cases the containment system does not form part of the hull structure (independent tanks).

1.6 TANKERS AND OIL POLLUTION

The majority of tanker owners are highly responsible people and their trade association – INTERTANKO – has made an undisputed claim that do-it-yourself motor enthusiasts cause more pollution with their discarded engine oil than is caused by INTERTANKO members. The fact is, however, when a loaded tanker does become a casualty the oil pollution causes considerable environmental damage.

Most tankers were originally designed for the carriage of their cargoes in a containment system which forms part of the hull structure (integral tanks), the arrangement of which depends upon the nature of the cargo itself. However, with the world's greater concern about pollution of the oceans and coastlines by spilled oil, tankers are now being built with **double hulls** so that if the outer hull is pierced through collision or grounding, the oil does not leak out.

As long ago as 1990 The United States of America introduced their Oil Pollution Act 1990 **(OPA90)** which act insists upon all tankers entering their territorial waters being double hulled. This was in reaction to several serious oil spills but in particular the "**Exxon Valdez**" which grounded in Prince William Sound. Alaska and spilt many thousands of tonnes of crude oil, resulting in colossal clean-up costs. OPA90 also demands that ships trading with the USA have to have Certificates of Financial Responsibility **(COFRs)** which ensure that any ship causing pollution will have the financial capability to pay the clean-up costs.

Nine years later, the 24 year old Maltese flagged *"Erika",* on a voyage from Rotterdam to Leghorn in Italy, broke in two in a storm off the coast of France dumping about 14,000 of her 37,000 tonnes cargo of heavy fuel oil. Heavy fuel oil can be an even worse pollutant than crude oil because the former is extremely sticky and hard to clean up. Much of the spilt oil reached the coast of Brittany causing massive pollution, not only to pleasure beaches but more especially to shellfish stocks which were a major source of local income.

This casualty caused a widespread international reaction with blame being aimed in turn at the shipowners (a one-ship company), the French charterers (TotalFina), the flag state (Malta), the ship's classification society (Registro Italiana), even the International Association of Classification Societies (IACS) whose purpose in life is to monitor those classification societies who are their members.

In the end the role of "class" was held by many to be most culpable. There was also, of course, considerable concern expressed as to whether Port State Control was as effective as it should be and this particularly exercised the minds of the European Union. The EU started talking in terms of copying the USA and introducing anti-pollution regulations unilaterally,

In the event the members of the International Maritime Organization **(IMO)** took up the challenge and agreed to introduce a revised Regulation 13G of Annex I of the Marine Pollution Convention **(MARPOL).** The Marpol convention had already introduced rules concerning ships having segregated ballast tanks (SBTs). Previously, tankers when needing stability on the ballast run, would simply flood some of the tanks. This meant that when the ballast water was discharged it would take with it considerable quantities of oil residues. SBTs ensure that ballast tanks never contain oil, only water, so that there is little or no pollution when ballast water is discharged prior to loading.

The latest revised convention decrees that, by the year 2015, all single hulled tankers (with a few special exceptions) will have to be scrapped. The trade refers to **2015** as the "**drop-dead phase-out date**". To ease the impact there was a phase-out schedule which started in 2003 when tankers built before 1973 had to go. Then in 2004 those built in 1974 and 1975 had to be scrapped and so on until by 2015 all the single hull tankers will be gone.

There is little doubt that this programme will have a considerable impact on the tanker chartering markets because many hundreds of tankers (one estimate is 2200) will have to be scrapped. It will obviously also have an influence on the prices quoted by shipyards for the replacements and by breakers being offered the single hulled ships for demolition. Just what the impact will be is the subject of countless articles in the shipping press but perhaps only time will tell.

1.7 BULK CARRIERS – DRY CARGO

These are ships designed specifically for the bulk carriage of loose dry cargo of a homogeneous nature such as coal and grain from Australia and the USA. Dry cargo bulkers do not reach the exceptionally large sizes common in the tanker trades. All ships within the bulk carrier category are single decked with machinery and accommodation aft. They have wide hatches to allow direct vertical loading without the need for "trimming" (levelling the top of the cargo-mound). The interior of the holds are unobstructed to allow free use of grabs for discharging. Space for ballast water is in "wing" tanks, tanks with a triangular cross-section along the bottoms of the holds and under the deck to give a "hopper" effect which also aids easy discharge. Ballast tanks are thus deployed along the whole length of the ship so that excessive bending stresses can be avoided at any stage from empty, through partially loaded/discharged to empty of cargo. High capacity ballast pumps and a comprehensive ballast pipe-line system aids in this procedure.

The hopper shaped holds in bulkers also provide a safety feature in the carriage of grain cargoes because the wing tanks reduce the free surface at the top of the load: grain can flow like a liquid under the stress of a ship rolling.

A Buyer who contemplates using a bulker in the iron ore trade as well as, say, coal and grain should ensure that the ship is properly strengthened because iron ore is an unforgiving trade.

The cargo-handling mode for bulk-carriers is lift on/lift off, usually by grabs except for grain which more generally involves conveyors and/or suction for loading/discharging. The larger classes of bulk carrier are almost invariably **gearless**, as they depend upon the fast shore-based equipment for loading and discharging. The exception is a class of sophisticated specialist ships which have conveyor systems on board and are known as "self unloaders"

Capesize Bulk Carriers. These are ships in the 120,000 dwt plus range; 200,000 dwt is currently about the maximum. As their name implies they are too large to negotiate the Suez or Panama canals and their routing has to be via either the Cape of Good Hope or Cape Horn.

Panamax Bulk Carriers – are in the 60/80,000 tonne range and are a popular size because as the name implies, such vessels are designed to carry the maximum amount of cargo within the constraints imposed by the locks in the Panama Canal.

Handymax Bulk Carriers – is the name used to relate to ships in the 40/60,000 tonne range.

Handy size Bulk Carriers – the name tends to cover anything from a thousand or two up to 40,000 dwt. Many of these ships have their own cargo gear.

Diagram 1.7 – Typical Handy Size Bulk Carrier

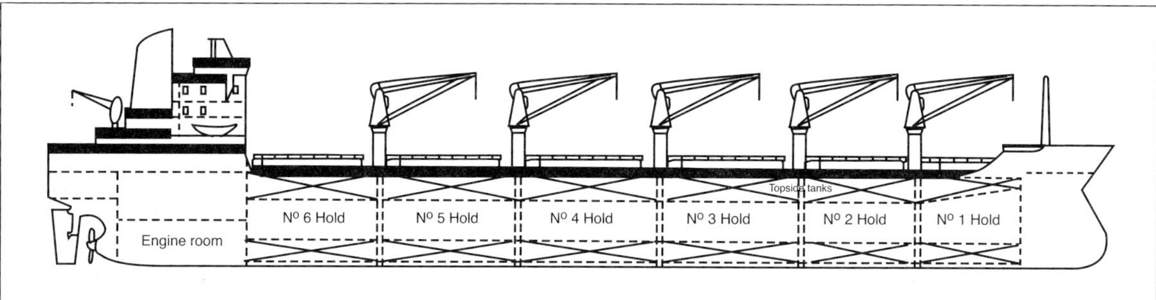

Ore Carriers are designed with centre holds (and wing ballast tanks) and weather deck hatches specifically for the bulk carriage, in centre holds only, of ore. Because of the density of metallic ores, such ships have a relatively low cubic capacity but because of the rough treatment that the loading and grab discharge can inflict, ore carriers may be of a more robust construction than a bulk carrier design for less heavy cargoes

Ore/Oil Carriers and Ore/Bulk/Oil Carriers are designed with combined topside and hopper tanks and are strengthened for the carriage of ore, and with additional facilities for the alternative (but not simultaneous) bulk carriage of oil and other liquid cargo (the cargo handling mode for which is pump on/pump off).

1.8 GENERAL CARGO SHIPS

These are designed with holds and weather deck hatches for the carriage of diverse types and forms of cargo. These are the ships which are generally referred to as **tramps.** The cargo handling mode is lift on/lift off.

Features may include one or more of the following:

- Holds divided by one or more tween decks with openings giving access to the lower spaces.
- Cargo carried on the weather deck/hatch covers.
- Facilities pertaining to the carriage of specific types of cargo (e.g. heavy lift derrick/crane, container securing arrangements, hoistable vehicle decks, deck pens for livestock, etc.).
- Strengthening for the carriage of heavy cargo.
- A part of refrigerated cargo space for the carriage of perishable cargo.
- The carriage of liquid cargo (usually vegetable oil) in specially designed holds/tanks.
- Additional cargo handling by way of side doors/side loader.
- Additional cargo handling by way of weather deck ramp.
- Additional cargo handling by way of stern (quarter) door/ramp to the tween deck (and where additional cargo segregation is provided by hinged door openings).
- The simultaneous or alternative carriage of bulk cargo and other forms of cargo.
- Accommodation for up to 12 passengers, the maximum permitted without special facilities.
- Alternatively they may be designed as **passenger/general cargo** ships having additional facilities for the carriage of more than 12 fare-paying passengers, all of whom are accommodated in cabins (berthed).

Diagram 1.8 – Typical General Cargo Ship

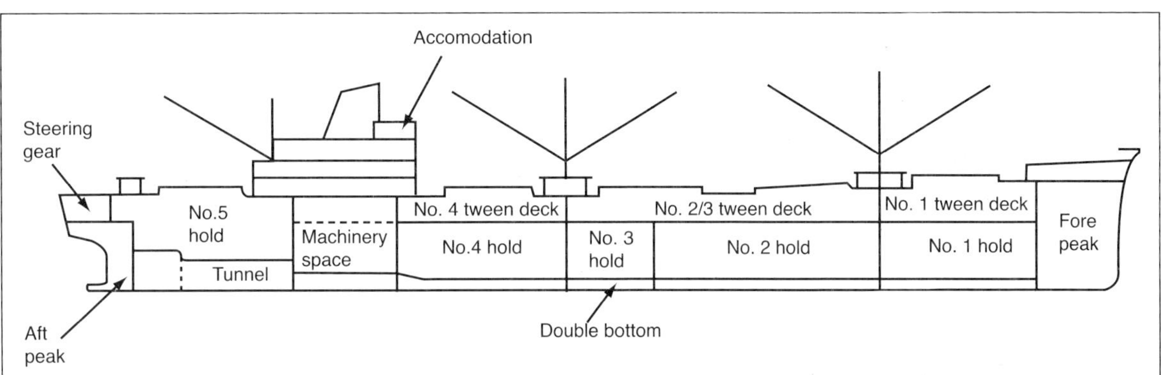

1.9 REFRIGERATED CARGO SHIPS

Included in this category are ships having a fully refrigerated cargo space, comprising multi tween-decked holds, specifically for the carriage of perishable cargo.

The cargo-handling mode may be lift on/lift off (by way of weather/tween deck hatches) or alternatively, cargo handling is by way of a side loading system. With the advent and wide use of refrigerated containers, fully refrigerated ships now tend to be confined to special trades.

Other features may include one or more of the following:

- Additional cargo handling by way of side doors.
- The additional carriage of (refrigerated) liquid cargo in specially designed holds/tanks.
- The alternative carriage of other (non-refrigerated) types and forms of cargo.

Diagram 1.9 – Typical Reefer ship

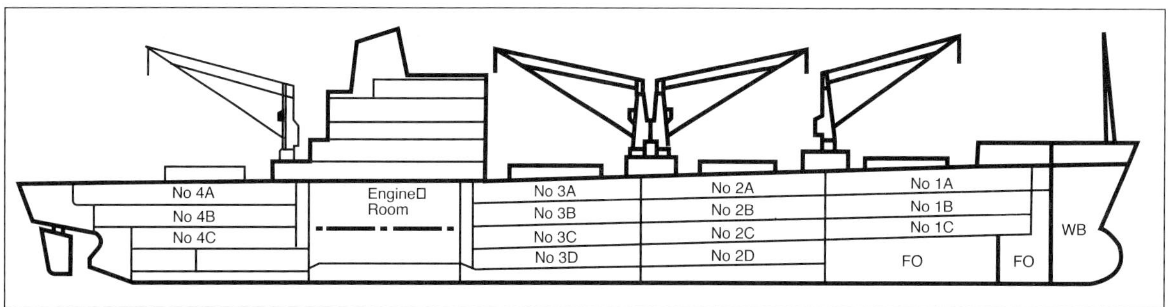

1.10 CONTAINER SHIPS

These are designed with holds and weather deck hatches specifically for the carriage of containers

The cargo-handling mode is lift on/lift off and other features may include holds with cellular guides (and weather deck mounted guides) to facilitate the positioning of the containers and their restraint during transit. The most recent designs are hatchless to facilitate uninterrupted cell guides.

Most large container ships have facilities for refrigerated containers either with their own cooling machinery needing an electric supply or with vents which may be connected to the ship's own refrigerating plant.

The size of container ships is seldom referred to in tonnage terms but in the number of containers that can be carried. Cargo containers are of internationally agreed standard dimensions with their lengths being either 20 feet or 40 feet. Ships capacities are therefore referred to as **TEUs (twenty-foot equivalent units)** thus one 40 foot container is two teus.

The larger container carriers, 4000 teu, 6000 teu even 8000 teu that are used on major routes are invariably gearless, depending upon sophisticated shore cranes for loading and discharging. Even larger ships are in the design stage but bringing them into service will depend on several factors not the least of which is the operators' confidence in sufficient cargo being available on each sailing to utilise their extra capacity. Such confidence will have to be strong enough to warrant the extra building costs because 8000 teu ships have pushed the ability to be driven by a single engine/single screw to the limit; installing two engines significantly increases the capital cost. Furthermore such ships will be too wide for existing shore gantries so that terminal operators would have to invest heavily in new berth configuration.

Diagram 1.10 – Containership Typical Layout

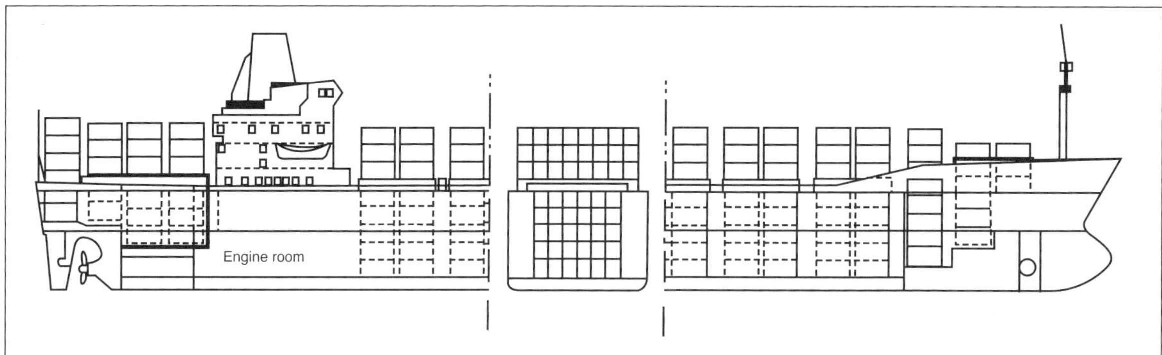

As well as thinking "larger", shipowners are now thinking "faster" and a new design of 40 knot 1400 teu ship is now a reality with proponents of this service intending to offer a seven-day door-to-door transit time Europe/East Coast USA.

Containers destined for smaller ports are transhipped into **feeder ships** which are often around 1500 teu but can even be as small as 200 teu. The smaller feeders tend to serve unsophisticated ports and such small container carriers often have their own lifting gear so that they can operate in ports that have no cranes.

1.11 RO-RO CARGO SHIPS

Diagram 1.11 – Typical Ro-Ro ship

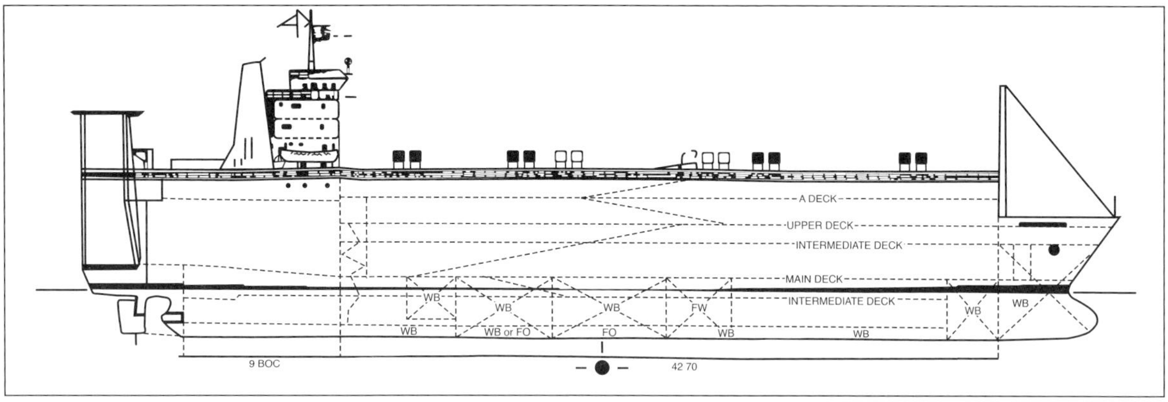

These are designed with decks specifically for the carriage of road vehicles/trailers, and cargo in pallet form or in containers loaded/unloaded by wheeled transport. The cargo-handling mode is roll on/roll off.

Ro-Ro ship features may include one or more of the following:

- The carriage of cargo on the weather deck by way of an internal ramp/lift, side ramp, or lift on/lift off.
- The additional carriage of other (specified) types and forms of cargo in holds/tanks under the main (ro-ro) deck and accessed by way of deck panels.
- Facilities pertaining to the carriage of specific types of cargo (e.g. hoistable vehicle decks, deck pens for livestock, etc.).
- The additional cargo-handling mode of lift on/lift off to/from the main (ro-ro) deck by way of weather deck hatches, and where any additional cargo segregation is provided by hinged or hoistable deck panels.
- There are also Passenger/Ro-Ro Cargo ships which have the additional facilities of more than 12 fare paying passengers (including the drivers of vehicles), all (or most), of whom are accommodated in cabins (berthed).
- A Ro-Ro Container ship is designed with an aft section of that of a Ro-Ro Cargo ship and a segregated fore section of that of a Container ship for the carriage of containers (throughout), or containers and other ro-ro cargo (including road vehicles/trailers and new unladen road vehicles).
- A specialised type of Ro-Ro is the Pure Car Carrier. Features of this type of ship may include a superstructure (garage) section comprising multi-decks of light construction for the additional carriage of new unladen road vehicles.

1.12 PASSENGER SHIPS

The top of this range of ships are the **Cruise Liners** many of which are built in European shipyards and this activity has been responsible for their survival since these yards can no longer compete with the Far East in the production of run-of-the-mill cargo ships. European know-how in the luxury hotel building industry is as much demanded for these vessels, as is the normal run of naval architecture.

Less luxurious passenger liners intended for the few remaining scheduled services are designed with multi-decks (and superstructure multi-decks) specifically for the carriage of more than 12 fare-paying passengers and where all of the passengers are accommodated in cabins (berthed).

Other features may include one or more of the following:

- The additional carriage of a limited amount of cargo in one or more holds.
- The carriage of passengers in dormitory type accommodation.

Included in this category are:

Passenger Ferries which have one or more decks (and superstructure decks) specifically for the carriage of more than 12 fare paying passengers and engaged on a regular scheduled service (of relatively short duration), and where there is either no cabin accommodation for the passengers (unberthed) or not all of the passengers are accommodated in cabins where cabins are provided (berthed or unberthed).

General Cargo/Passenger Ferries which have the same function as a Passenger Ferry but with one or more holds for the additional carriage of general cargo (the cargo handling mode for which is lift on/lift off).

Vehicle Passenger Ferries have a similar function to Passenger Ferries but with one or more cargo decks for the additional carriage of passenger and freight road vehicles (the cargo handling mode for which is roll on/roll off, and where the vehicles belonging to the passengers are driven on/driven off by the passengers themselves).

Features may include the additional carriage of a limited amount of other types of ro-ro cargo and the alternative (out of season) service mode of cruising.

Train/Vehicle/Passenger Ferries have a similar function to a Vehicle Passenger Ferry but with a separate (or the only) cargo deck fitted with fixed rails for the simultaneous carriage of passenger/freight railway vehicles (the cargo handling mode for which is roll on/roll off).

1.13 MISCELLANEOUS

Vehicle Carriers are designed with hull/superstructure multi-decks of light construction specifically for the carriage of new unladen road vehicles. The cargo-handling mode is roll on/roll off. Features may include certain deck strengthening for the simultaneous carriage of heavier cargo and the alternative carriage of other (specified) types of cargo. Vehicle carriers may be referred to as Dedicated (or Pure) Car Carriers (DCCs or PCCs) or Dedicated or Pure Car and Truck Carriers (DCTCs or PCTCs)

Livestock Carriers are designed with hull/superstructure multi-deck pens and sanitation arrangements specifically for the carriage of livestock. The cargo-handling mode is such that livestock is walked on and walked off, via ramps, to and from containment areas.

Livestock carriers are vitally important to Islamic countries whose faith demands that animals have to be slaughtered according to strict codes close to the point of consumption.

Fishing Vessels designed for fishing operations which include Trawlers, Factory ships, Live Fish carriers. Whale catchers and Whale Factory ships are still occasionally encountered despite the international conventions restricting the killing of whales.

Offshore Vessels which include the following:

- Supply ships designed with a weather deck cargo space specifically for the carriage of stores and cargo to offshore oil and gas exploration/production installations.

- Support ships which are of similar design to support ships but are fitted for support activities which include well stimulation, pipeline/cable trencher support, well maintenance, search and rescue. Additional activities may include anchor handling, fire fighting, oil dispersal, standby-safety, etc.
- Drilling ships for offshore oil/gas drilling operations.
- Pipe-laying ships for pipe laying/repair operations associated with offshore oil/gas production.
- Offshore well-production ships designed for the extraction, processing and storage (in integral tanks) of oil from offshore wells.

Tugs are designed for the towing (and pushing) of ships, non self-propelled units, or other floating structures. Additional activities may include salvage, fire-fighting, ice-breaking, oil dispersal, etc.

Some pusher tugs are designed for the pushing of barges and pontoons, widely used in such rivers as the Rhine (Germany) and the Mississippi (USA).

Dredgers are designed for the raising of spoil from the sea-bed by means of a cutter suction, grab, bucket or ladder with the spoil then deposited into its cargo space or the cargo space of another ship (or non self-propelled barge unit) alongside, for subsequent discharge elsewhere.

Many dredgers are employed for the purpose of maintaining or deepening ports and their approaches or deepening canals. Others are used for the specific purpose of collection of sea-bed sand and stones for use as building or land reclamation material.

Hopper dredgers have a similar function to a dredger but are arranged so that the spoil is deposited into hoppers within the ship for subsequent discharge elsewhere through the bottom of the ship by means of doors/valves or by means of a split hull separation. Hopper ships are used to support dredgers by carrying dredged spoil or other waste material in hoppers within the ship and its subsequent discharge through the bottom of the ship by means of doors/valves or by means of split hull separation.

Sludge carriers carry liquid waste (sludge) in integral tanks for subsequent discharge through the bottom of the ship by means of valves.

Incinerator ships are designed for the burning of toxic waste at sea but they are now being withdrawn from service in most areas due to the environmental concerns with emissions.

Barges are non self-propelled units designed for the carriage of cargo in holds/tanks. The units are designed to be towed or pushed (Tug or Pusher Tug) or may be moored for the purpose of storing cargo.

Types of barges include general cargo (often called "lighters"), container, bulk liquid and hopper designs. Each of these is used for a specific purpose as their names imply.

Landing Craft are designed to run on to a beach or shore ramp prior to loading/unloading of various types of cargo.

The cargo handling mode is roll on/roll off from the single cargo deck by way of a bow ramp to the shore.

Other features may include the carriage of liquid cargo in under deck tanks, deck pens for the carriage of livestock and an additional roll on/roll off facility by way of a stern ramp.

Deck Cargo Ships are designed with a weather deck cargo space only for the carriage of various types of (non perishable) cargo.

The cargo handling mode may be lift on/lift off and/or roll on/roll off by way of a deck ramp.

They may be strengthened for the carriage of heavy cargo and for the carriage of large/awkward cargo.

Semi-Submersible Cargo Ships are deck cargo ships with the additional handling mode of float on/float off for the carriage of floating cargo. These ships have an array of ballast tanks and heavy-duty pumps.

Heavy Lift Cargo Ships are designed specifically for the lifting and carriage of heavy and/or large/awkward cargo in a cargo space below the weather deck (or on strengthened weather deck covers). The cargo-handling mode is lift on/lift off.

Features may include one or more of the following:

- The additional cargo handling mode of roll on/roll off/to/from the cargo space by way of a stern/door ramp.
- A weather deck linkspan/hydraulic roadway arrangement and lift to the cargo space below the weather deck.

Semi-Submersible Heavy Lift Cargo Ships have the additional cargo mode of float in/float out (or float on/float off from the weather deck covers) for the carriage of floating cargo.

Barge Carriers are designed with holds or decks specifically for the carriage of barges (lighters). Such vessels are often referred to as **LASH (Lighter Aboard Ship)** ships or **BACAT (Barge Aboard Catamaran)**

Barges can be either hoisted at the stern and stowed in the holds or on the weather deck by way of a gantry crane or can also be hoisted by way of a stern elevator and stowed on the decks by wheeled transport or may be semi-submersible to allow the lighters to float on and off.

1.14 TYPES OF MACHINERY

Main propulsion

Almost all merchant ships are now propelled by diesel engines which can best be described as like giant truck engines. The smallest of these are fuelled by diesel oil (the very smallest by gas-oil which is even lighter than diesel). The improved design of diesel engines which began about half a century ago enabled such engines to accept heavier fuel-oils until the present day when most large diesel engines can be run on oil that at one time was only considered suitable for burning under the boilers of steam engines. The advantage of these developments is that as a general rule the heavier (thicker) the oil the cheaper the cost.

A description of the main machinery is always part of the particulars of any ship being proposed for sale and S & P Brokers quickly become familiar with the major manufacturers of marine engines and in time will tend to have a view as to their relative good/bad points.

Engine power is usually referred to in terms of Brake Horsepower (BHP) and often this is followed by its equivalent in kilowatts (kW). 1000kW = approx 1400 bhp.

Ship particulars will also include reference to speed and fuel consumption and generally this will refer to a number of tons of fuel-oil per day (usually detailing the grade of oil) and then, in older ships, will refer to a much smaller quantity of diesel oil. The reason for this is that, when burning heavy fuel oil, some machinery has a rather sluggish response to demands for changes in revolutions and so diesel oil is used for manoeuvring in and out of port.

The development in diesel engine technology has now advance to the extent that more modern ships do not need to switch to diesel for manoeuvring, the machinery is now versatile enough that everything can be done on heavy fuel oil.

In older ships diesel oil is also used for the **generators** which supply all the ship's needs for electricity. Large ships have two or often three electricity generators because modern vessels have such a heavy dependence on electric power, that lack of it would be intolerable. More modern ships now have generators which run on the same heavy fuel oil as the main engines.

Machinery is not confined to the engine room as, except for gearless bulk-carriers and container ships, there is **cargo handling equipment** to be considered. Tankers require **cargo pumps** as almost invariably liquid cargo is pumped IN to the ship by shore pumps but the ship's pumps are used to pump the cargo OUT. Such cargo pumps are of a capacity that, regardless of the ship's size, she can discharge all her cargo well within the short time allowed for this purpose. Cargo pumps are normally sited in a segregated pump-room which is vital if they are electrically driven when there would otherwise be a fire risk.

Dry cargo ships may have a wide variety of cargo handling gear. The simplest, in general-purpose ships, will be **winches and derricks** which in the past were driven by steam but now electric motors are more usual. More sophisticated ships will have **cargo cranes** which can operate more quickly than derricks.

Geared container ships may use cranes or the larger ones may have **gantries** which are a miniature version of the shore gantries used in container ports.

Self-unloading bulk carriers will have a complex system of conveyors to move the cargo out of the holds and on to the quay.

Other machinery on deck will include **windlasses**, the devices used to haul on mooring cables, and/or hoist anchor chains. In larger ships there are passenger lifts (elevators) to move quickly from deck to deck.

The propulsion machinery may be supplemented by **bow-thrusters** and sometimes also **stern-thrusters**, small electrically driven propellers in athwartship tunnels used when manoeuvring in port, allowing the ship to swing without needing any forward speed which would otherwise be necessary to activate the rudder. These devices will often enable even very large ships to berth without having to employ tugs.

Anti-pollution legislation increases the demand for specialist machinery, the most universal being **ballast pumps** which are often designed to move dirty ballast water into oil/water separators to ensure that no oil is ever pumped into the ocean.

Large ships, especially passenger liners, must have facilities for **sewage treatment** which mimics the sewage disposal plants on shore.

1.15 GENERAL ARRANGEMENT PLANS

There are, of course, several different types of plans involved in the life of a ship but the one which S & P Brokers are most likely to encounter is the General Arrangement Plan. As its name implies, such a plan includes details of the hull shape, decks, holds, hatches and the main equipment. It invariably includes a deadweight scale which shows the draft the ship will draw at every stage from empty to fully laden. Study **Appendix 2** which is a replica of a General Arrangement Plan; an actual plan is, of course, much larger measuring as much as 2 metres x 1 metre in some cases and contain much more information than shown in the appendix. The real thing will include many dimensions and invariably has a deadweight scale which shows the ship's draft at any deadweight. Students visiting ships will almost always see a framed copy of the General Arrangement plan hung on the same level as the officers' cabins.

1.16 SELF-ASSESSMENT AND TEST QUESTIONS

Attempt the following and check your answers from the text:

1. Define what is meant by:
    a) Deadweight tonnage
    b) Gross tonnage
    c) Net tonnage
2. How are grain and bale cubic capacity assessed?
3. Why are ships sold for scrap on their light displacement tonnage?
4. What is the usual cargo-handling system for tankers?
5. Why is this the usual method?
6. How is grain usually loaded/discharged?
7. What is meant by "Air Draft"?
8. What do the initials Ro-Ro stand for?
9. What is the size range of ULCCs?
10. What do the expressions "clean" and "dirty" mean in tanker terms?
11. Where did the "Exxon Valdez" spill her oil?
12. What cargo was the "Erika" carrying?
13. What has been the effect of the recent oil pollution disasters?
14. What is the customary way of referring to the size of container ships?
15. What is the size range of "Panamax" ships?
16. What is the largest size tanker in service today?
17. Where are many cruise liners now built?
18. Why is 8000 teus likely to be the largest size for the foreseeable future?

Having completed Chapter One, attempt the following and submit your essay to your Tutor.

Choose three different types of ship and outline those main characteristics of each type that you would need if you intended proposing them to prospective buyers. Illustrate your answers with sketches.

Chapter 2

SHIP REGISTRATION

2.1 THE NEED FOR REGISTRATION

Ships, like human beings, must have a name and in addition must also have an established identity, port of registration and nationality before setting forth on the oceans of the world. The owners must declare to the Registrar of Shipping, or other appropriate authority, their interest according to the flag under which the vessel in question is intended to trade. Details of the ship with plans and other data will be filed and when formalities are completed and the ship's tonnage verified by a government surveyor the owners will receive a Certificate of Registration. On this certificate will appear the official number allotted to the ship together with her port of registry, details of tonnage and construction with the name(s) of her Owner(s). The Registration Certificate is the most important of the ship's papers and must be kept aboard in the custody of the Captain. **Appendix 3** is an example of a British Certificate of Registry.

A ship on the oceans of the world is considered part of the territory of the country under whose flag she sails. Her name must appear on both sides of her bow and also at her stern where the **port** of registry must also appear. Traditionally also the merchant marine flag of the country of registration is flown at the stern. However, the certificate of registry is the only acceptable evidence of identity and its production to persons at sea or ashore entitles those on board to the protection and assistance from her country and its representatives. It follows that even in time of war, provided she is not violating neutrality or trying to run a blockade she is entitled to full protection under International Law and should be free from seizure or arrest. A ship which is not officially registered and without identity papers would be regarded as 'stateless' and even liable to be regarded as a pirate ship, registration of merchant tonnage being compulsory throughout the world. There may be exceptions in the case of small coasters and fishing vessels which never venture out of territorial waters or small pleasure boats in private ownership. These minor categories can be exempt from compulsory official registration dependent on the laws of individual countries.

There is no conformity of qualification required for the bodies or persons who are entitled to register ships under, and claim the protection of, a particular country. It follows that the degree of control over shipowners and the conditions under which their ships trade differs in severity from flag to flag. Not only does this apply to their civic and tax liabilities but also in regard to manning levels, living conditions and general maintenance of the ships themselves. The extremes lie between, on one hand, those flags whose only requirement is a modest registration fee in return for a listing in the national register and the painting of the shipowner's name on the office door of an attorney and on the other hand, the demands and regulations of the traditional maritime nations.

Genuine maritime nations require that the Owners have a permanent place of business within the national territory and also that none but nationals of the country under which the ship is to be registered appear as owners.

Originally, as an example, none but British subjects were permitted to register the ownership of merchant ships in their own names under the Red Ensign. Now, with the open borders of the European Union, a citizen of any of the EU member countries may register under British Flag if they so wish and have established an office in the UK. Nationals of other countries may share in the ownership by investment in Limited Companies or other corporate bodies provided such companies have their place of business in the territory where the ships are registered.

It is a tradition going back to the days of the merchant venturers that ownership of a British ship is considered to be divided into 64 individual shares. In this manner merchants would club together to finance a shipowning enterprise. It follows that a single person who owns an entire ship will be registered as the possessor of 64/64ths. As, however, it is almost invariable for a British ship to be owned by a limited company the 64th rule is now hardly relevant although reference to it may still be encountered. The port of registry may not be the same as the business address of the Owners who may have their place of business anywhere within the United Kingdom. In such cases the port of registry will probably be the one most frequently used by the ship or alternatively a commercial port with a long maritime tradition.

Other maritime countries have their own rules, laws and traditions in connection with registering ships. An S & P Broker will be expected to be an expert in such matters so that the active practitioner in the S & P market must make him or her self well acquainted with the regulations in the countries where clients, or potential clients, reside.

2.2 THE GROWTH OF "OPEN" REGISTRIES

Traditional maritime nations have tended to impose stringent safety levels upon ships registered under their flags. These include regulations as to the numbers as well as the proficiency of all shipboard personnel. In many cases these regulations have been heavily reinforced by powerful trades unions who also impose wage levels. Furthermore, many of those same nations have a high rate of taxation so that the combination of these factors has made registration under a traditional flag less popular.

Many years ago, a handful of countries established far less stringent maritime laws, little or no taxation beyond the actual cost of ship registration and a nationality qualification which demanded nothing more than a small brass plate on the entrance to an attorney's office. The benefits of such legislation rendered trading under these flags beneficial to owners to such an extent that they are now a major force in world shipping.

Some countries were so keen to establish a national merchant fleet that they went beyond simply attracting registration and ensured preference for cargo being given to locally registered ships.

No matter how eager one may be to own and operate ships, the profit motive is of primary importance and a Shipowner will naturally consider the incentives available when deciding under which flag his vessel should trade to his greater advantage.

A problem always facing shipowners is the difference between the cost of living, and hence wage levels, in one country as compared with another. Furthermore, high cost countries tend to have powerful trades unions. To attract seafarers, a Shipowner in a high cost country will be expected to match shore-based wages which will result in a wage bill far higher than that of a low-cost country. Thus ships owned in high-cost countries become uncompetitive in the international market of shipping business. The United States was among the earliest to encounter this problem.

Since the early years of the 20th century there have been close links between the US and the republic of Panama and thus the first open registry country to be placed with full international legal recognition was that of **Panama** in the 1920s. The incentive was cheap labour and in 1939 a treaty was signed between the United States and Panama whereby profits from shipping were exempted from taxes which made it attractive for American owners to take advantage of freedom of employment while obtaining tax benefits. Panama's neutrality during time of war was an additional encouragement for shipowners, not only from the United States but also world wide, to trade under the Panamanian flag.

Honduras was similarly attractive at that time being within the Western Hemisphere and therefore considered safe for US investment. Over 100 vessels which were American controlled traded under the Panamanian and Honduran flags during the second World War.

Liberia, a state in West Africa originally created in 1847 as a new homeland for freed American slaves, was the third of the original trio of free flags. Liberia's close links with the USA made it another country especially favoured by American Shipowners.

Because of the relaxed regulations and minimum taxation, these countries, and most of those that followed their traditions became known as **flags of convenience**. They attracted many Shipowners whose own national flag became uncompetitive due to regulation, taxation and local wage levels. Unfortunately flags of convenience (FOCs) not only attracted genuinely reliable Shipowners whose only motivation was remaining competitive, the relaxed attitude of such FOC countries to safety regulations also attracted owners who had no compunction about operating dangerously sub-standard ships. It became quite common for such Owners to establish a separate limited company for each of their ships, thus making legal action against them a hopeless task. The use of these flags by unscrupulous Owners has severely damaged the reputation of flags of convenience.

A brief history of the growth of the open registry phenomenon will be found in **Appendix 4.**

2.3 THE CURRENT SCENE

The list of countries offering flag of convenience registration is now almost endless. In addition to the original Panamanian, Honduran and Liberian flags one can now add:

> Costa Rican, Cypriot, Haitian, Lebanese, Marshall Islands, Omani, San Marinese, Sierra Leonian, Somalian, Vanuatuan and many more.

Inevitably the question is why have open registries grown so rapidly during the last five decades? The reason is that open registries, following the pattern of Panama and Liberia, who deliberately established laws to provide all the necessary fiscal incentives, encouraged shipowners to register their vessels under their flags. More important, the incentives are continuously being reviewed to suit the current market situation and thereby encourage shipowners to register ships under these flags.

Some of these incentives are:

1. No taxes on profits; no fiscal control. Only tax is a subscription tax per net registered ton.
2. No labour restrictions. Employment is global and therefore wage rates flexible.
3. Limited liability.
4. No political restrictions on freedom of trade
5. Very flexible corporate laws.
6. Easy financing because of simple mortgage laws.
7. No risk of political instability or nationalisation.
8. Minimum safety laws and regulations. In the past, lack of control and inability to enforce safety standards was a key feature of open registries.

The growth of open registries, particularly Panama and Liberia was a direct result of the policy of these countries to attract shipping investment. This, plus the overall global economic growth in world trade, especially in the movement of bulk cargo, provided shipowners who were non-nationalistic with a commercial incentive which the traditional maritime nations laws did not.

2.4 THE POSITIVE AND NEGATIVE ELEMENTS OF FLAGS OF CONVENIENCE (FOCs)

Shipping is probably the most international of all industries. A charterer seeking a ship to carry his cargo places his business on a market which is so world-wide that economists describe it as the nearest one can get to **perfect competition**.

Thus a ship with a low wages bill, little or zero taxation on income and a minimum of regulation on its operations will be able to offer a substantially lower rate than a ship whose Owner has to pay wages to match a high standard of living ashore, is taxed on profits as well as contributing to social security benefits and has its operations dictated by government edict plus trade union restrictions.

This prompts the question, why are not all ships registered under flags of convenience?

It has been said that:

"There are no bad flags, only bad shipowners"

and there is no doubt that many excellently maintained ships with full complements of competent officers and crew are trading under flags of convenience. The sad fact remains, however, that the relaxed control of many FOCs attract Owners of severely sub-standard ships and even if were a fact that these are in the minority they have brought the whole range of flags of convenience into disrepute.

Reaction against FOC ships comes in several forms. Some port authorities claim to distrust tonnage measurements of FOC ships and demand either a local tonnage certificate to be obtained which would cost the shipowner time as well as money, or alternatively the ship has to pay an increased level of port dues.

Perhaps a greater resistance to flags of convenience comes from the trade unions. The transport unions of most traditional maritime countries are affiliated to the **International Transport Workers Federation (ITF)**. The ITF is renowned for targeting ships with crews from less developed countries whose wage levels matching those ashore are far lower than those of industrialised countries. Such ships are almost always flying a flag of convenience and the ITF demands that the owners sign wage agreements with their crew at a much higher level. Until such an agreement is signed the ships is "blacked" very effectively because most of the labour (dockers, tug crews etc) are in unions affiliated to the ITF so that the ship is immobilised.

The ITF claims that its motivation is to improve the lot of crews from less developed countries but this is not the true case because the crews, without any intervention from the ITF, enjoy a standard of living which compares very favourably with any work ashore in their own countries. In their more honest moments the ITF admits that its objective is to discourage the employment of seamen from less developed countries and to have shipowners revert to employing crews from the industrialised countries.

At government level, many countries now impose **Port State Control**. This expression arises from the basis that, in an ideal world, the country of registration would impose **Flag State Control.** The world is not ideal in this respect and so the object of Port State Control is for the country at which the ship arrives to have the power to immobilise that ship if surveyors find that levels of safety, seaworthiness and/or crew welfare fall below minimum standards. Such a ship remains immobilised until the defects are put right. Most victims of such control tend to be flying the most relaxed of the flags of convenience.

The FOC countries themselves have not been idle and several of the more reputable now impose many of the safety measures imposed by the international conventions devised by the **International Maritime Organization (IMO)**; Liberia claims to be the leader among the FOCs in this regard.

The IMO is a branch of the United Nations with its headquarters in London whose main concerns are for seafarers' safety and restriction of marine pollution. These include the original convention on **Safety of Life at Sea (SOLAS)**, more recently agreement was reached on the **International Convention on Standards of Training, Certification and Watchkeeping (ITCW)** and the most recent has been the **International Ship Management Code (ISM)**. The IMO's activity in pollution prevention was the **MARPOL** convention which has since been reinforced by various other pieces of legislation not the least of which was the enactment in 1990 by the United States of the **Oil Pollution Act (OPA90)** which introduced the **double hull** requirement.

Despite measures taken to discourage registration under FOCs, there are more ships registered under Liberian flag than any other, with Panamanian a close second. Cyprus, whilst among the top ten flags of convenience, argues that it ensures strict compliance with international safety conventions by all the ships on its register.

It is worthy of note that Greek shipowners were at one time among the largest users of flags of convenience particularly during the time of military rule in that country. In more recent years, with the return to democracy, the Greek government recognised that their nationals were the world's most prolific shipowners and accordingly modified their fiscal regulations radically. This has resulted in the Greek national flag being well up in the world's top ten merchant fleets close behind Liberia and Panama.

2.5 THE RESPONSE BY TRADITIONAL MARITIME NATIONS

It will have been noted that in this Chapter the expression "Open Registries" was initially used but then all further references were to Flags of Convenience; this is because there is **another form of open registry**.

Some of the industrialised nations have not been idle in trying to retain national merchant fleets despite the competition from FOCs. They have devised systems of registration which retain the essential elements of such things as safety but with a more relaxed attitude to the nationality of crews and the levels of taxation.

Countries like the United Kingdom are particularly well placed in this regard because some overseas territories, such as Bermuda and Gibraltar, still retain colonial status. This enables ships to register in such countries, fly the British merchant shipping flag (the Red Ensign) but not be subject to United Kingdom financial and other restraints. In terms of complying with international safety standards, such registrations are equal to those of the UK itself but operating costs are considerably lower.

Closer to the UK mainland and probably unique are Britain's "Crown Dependencies". These are the **Channel Islands**, Jersey, Guernsey, Alderney and Sark which are located off the north-west coast of France and the **Isle of Man** in the Irish Sea equidistant from England, Scotland and Ireland. These territories have self-governing status in all matters except international relations and defence.

The **Isle of Man** has recently become particularly popular among British shipowners as a means of **"flagging out"** but still retaining the British Flag; notable among such companies is BP the major oil company. In many cases, the owners register their ships in the Isle of Man but only contract with Manx companies for crew matters, retaining all other aspects of ship management themselves. One typical fleet of British mini-bulk carriers switched to Isle of Man flag and re-recruited most of the original crews. The Owners pointed out that simply being able to close down the department that dealt with the crews' income tax, social security payments and family allotments as well as saving the actual cost of social security payments themselves was the difference between profit and loss for the fleet.

Perhaps because it has its colonies and dependencies, the United Kingdom has not yet adopted a scheme similar to some other European countries which have followed a different path, They have established **"open registries"** which enable ships to retain the national flag, still adhere to international safety standards but avoid the restrictions as to the nationality of the crew members. **Norway**, a traditional shipowning nation, has been particularly successful with their **Norwegian International Ship Register (NIS)** which was launched in 1987 and has had the effect of the Norwegian flag moving into the top ten merchant fleets of the world.

The European Commission had plans to establish a European Union register and flag but this has not yet found great favour among shipowners.

Another attempt to make the national flag more acceptable has been the way several European countries are tackling the problem of taxation. They have done this by introducing a **"tonnage tax"** which is a low rate of tax based upon the size of the fleet regardless of the income the ships generate. Tonnage tax systems already operate in the **Netherlands, Norway** and **Germany**, is under serious consideration in **Denmark** and **Finland** and has now come into force in the **United Kingdom;** experts predict that the introduction of this new tax system will double the size of the UK merchant fleet. An additional dimension to the UK tonnage tax is that shipowners electing to adopt the system must recruit one new trainee every year for every 15 officers employed. This condition should also ensure a substantial increase in the number of British seafarers.

2.6 SHIP REGISTRATION AND THE SHIP SALE AND PURCHASE BROKER

The services of an S & P Broker may well be required in assisting in or even taking a leading part in arranging for a client's newly purchased ship to be registered under the flag of the Buyer's choice. Intending practitioners in sale and purchase broking should, therefore, ensure that they know to whom they apply and what will be required for registering a ship.

Total familiarity with the procedure for registering under the national flag of the Broker's own country is an obvious essential. More difficult might be finding out how to arrange registration under one of the FOCs and a broker's personal address book should include a contact for all the likely flags that clients may seek to use. In most cases the first contact will be through the Embassy, High Commission or Consulate of the country concerned, although a search through the Internet could save much time.

2.7 SELF-ASSESSMENT AND TEST QUESTIONS

Attempt the following and check your answers from the text:

1. Which was the first Flag of Convenience?
2. Why were FOCs especially popular with US owners?
3. What is bad about FOCs?
4. Which were the first three flags of convenience?
5. Which is now the largest?
6. Why do many Shipowners register under FOCs?
7. What is the name of the United Nations body concerned with safety?

Having completed Chapter Two attempt the following and submit your essay to your Tutor.

Take an imaginary ship-purchase client domiciled in a country of your choosing and write a letter to him discussing the respective merits of registering under his national flag as compared with those of an "open" register; conclude your letter with a recommendation.

N.B. The Institute's Qualifying Examinations test a candidate's ability to communicate effectively as well as testing knowledge of the subject of the question. Occasionally this will require the answer to be in the form of a letter, memo, report or other means of communication and it is important to ensure that such instructions are properly followed.

Chapter 3

CLASSIFICATION

3.1 CLASSIFICATION SOCIETIES

The previous Chapter explained how a ship had to be **registered** in order to have an identity. In addition, ships have to be **classified** because international convention demands that an approved classification society must verify that the ship is in a sound seaworthy condition. This is, of course, vital to a prospective buyer.

Almost every maritime country has its own Classification Society; inevitably they vary in quality but those which reach an internationally agreed standard of reliability have this affirmed by their being accepted for membership of an organisation known as the **International Association of Classification Societies (IACS).** IACS is a corporate body based in London which is recognised by the **International Maritime Organization (IMO**) the maritime arm of the United Nations; IACS enjoys observer status at IMO meetings.

Current full members of IACS are:

Lloyd's Register of Shipping (LR)
American Bureau of Shipping (AB)
Bureau Veritas (BV)
China Classification Society (CCS)
Det Norske Veritas (NV)
Germanischer Lloyd (GL)
Korean Register of Shipping (KRS)
Nippon Kaiji Kyokai (NK)
Polish Register of Shipping (PRS)
Registro Italiano Navale (RINA)
Russian Maritime Register of Shipping (RS)

The Associate members currently are:

Croatian Register of Shipping (CRS)
Indian Register of Shipping (IRS)

There are many more other organisations which go by the description "classification society" and which range from small private companies to subsidised or governmental offshoots which do not yet (and perhaps never will) reach the standards required by IACS.

The status of the society with which a ship is classified is a matter for careful consideration by a prospective buyer and ship S & P Brokers need to be fully informed on this subject. It is especially important to keep a watch on the shipping journals in order to note any changes in IACS membership.

Although most classification societies are non-profit making they have to remain financially viable which inevitably means some degree of competition among them to attract shipowners to their register. One of the principal problems IACS has to deal with is ensuring that competition amongst societies does not lead to a lowering of standards.

Recent catastrophic oil spills, which have arguably been due to the ship in question being in a seriously sub-standard condition, have led to court action being taken against the classification society involved. Affected parties, such as fishermen and holiday resorts claim that the damage from the spill would not have occurred had the classification society not failed in its duty to demand that defects should be put right in order for the ship to retain class.

In most countries ships are compelled by law to be classified by a recognised society for the purposes of safety, insurance, etc. Several countries go so far as to sub-contract the registration of the ship and the issuance of safety certificates to a classification society.

To understand the development of classification societies, a brief history of Lloyd's Register provides a useful guide, Lloyds being the premier Classification Society in the world.

Shipowners, Shippers, Captains and Insurers were accustomed to meet in the early Seventeenth Century in Edward Lloyd's Coffee House for the purpose of doing business. Lloyd's Coffee House eventually became a formal society concerned with the insurance of ships and their cargoes. From these beginnings emerged both Lloyds of London – the insurance organisation – and eventually also Lloyds Register of Shipping. Although they both sprang from the same roots they are **now totally separate entities.**

Incidentally, the enterprising Edward Lloyd has another claim to fame because, as early as 1694, he produced a newsletter entitled "Lloyds's News" which is reputed to be the second oldest newspaper in existence. In 1734, the title changed to "Lloyd's List" and it is under this banner that it has been published ever since.

Prior to 1760 there was no Register of vessels and because of marine casualties, it was suggested that there should be a proper Register which would be acceptable to all interested parties and that ships should be surveyed by experts in order to be listed in the register.

The first Register of Vessels was therefore produced in that year and was recognised as the birth of Lloyd's Register of Shipping. Sadly, the 1760 Register is no longer in existence but the 1764 Register can be viewed to this day.

Originally, the hulls were classed A E I O U according to the merit of their construction and continuing soundness. Equipment on such vessels was described as G M or B which stood for Good, Middling or Bad, and by examining the lists of vessels, an Underwriter could assess the premiums he should charge in order to insure either a vessel or her cargo.

This system of grading existed until 1775 when equipment was then described as 1, 2 or 3, and so, for the first time the expression "A1 at Lloyd's" came into existence.

In 1797 a dispute over classification methods prompted Shipowners to publish their own book which appeared in 1799 and remained a rival register until 1834 when a common problem of finance brought about a reconciliation which resulted in the official formation of Lloyd's Register of Shipping.

Over the years, the format of the Register has changed from the age of wood construction in the 18th century to wood and iron ships in 1866 and the first all-welded vessel in 1920.

Similar changes have taken place in propulsion systems from sail only to sail and steam, steam only fuelled by coal, steam fuelled by oil, steam turbines, and eventually the almost universal adoption of diesel engines. Gas-turbines have been experimented with but gained little popularity outside fast ferry services although a generation of gas-turbine powered super-fast container ships are now well beyond the planning stage. Nuclear powered ships have been built but their use has tended to be restricted to ice-breakers and warships. At least one nuclear powered merchant ship was actually built but the capital cost was beyond commercial limits and in any case many ports were too afraid of anything nuclear to accept them.

All classification societies publish their own register of ships that they have classified but **Lloyd Register**, which is currently published in four volumes, is unique in that it publishes details of **all ships** over 100 tons regardless of the society with which they are classified. Supplements are issued monthly giving an up date on all changes to the Register since publication.

Appendix 5 is a copy of the guide to abbreviations with which every copy of Lloyds Register is supplied.

Appendix 6 contains the column headings in the Register in several languages.

Appendix 7 is a copy of a typical page from the LR and, for comparison, **Appendices 8 and 9** are copies of pages from Germanischer Lloyd and the English edition of France's Bureau Veritas Register respectively.

Lloyd's Register produces many other publications for the shipping industry and among those which are particularly useful to S & P Brokers include:

List of Shipowners: This contains details of 40,000 Owners, Managers and Managing Agents worldwide, providing details of their addresses, telephone, telex and fax numbers together with brief but informative fleet details cross-referenced to the *Register of Ships*.

Maritime Guide: A unique collection of diverse maritime information, with sections covering such items as port facilities, call signs, shipbuilders, shipbreakers, postal and communications addresses and a gazetteer with maps.

Register of Offshore Units, Submersibles and Diving Systems: This contains sections listing mobile drilling rigs, submersibles, selected work units and diving systems (where classed with or certified by Lloyd's Register). Also details for owners of equipment in these sectors.

Merchant Shipbuilding Returns: A quarterly statistical summary of world shipbuilding for all self-propelled ships of 100 gross tonnage and above which are under construction or on order. Tables include analyses by country of build, size, ship-type, registration and progress.

Annual Summary of Merchant Ships Completed: A statistical summary of world shipbuilding based on the same criteria as the *Merchant Shipbuilding Return*, with tables covering completions and launches by country of build, size ship-type and registration.

Casualty Return: An annual statistical summary which includes all merchant ships totally lost or reported broken up during the calendar year, individual ships are also listed with brief details of casualty or disposal. A further section lists ships sold for breaking up.

Shipyard Orders Weekly Report: A list of confirmed orders reported during the week showing selected items of information. Also included are lists of reported cancellations and completions.

Lloyd's Register is a non-profit distributing organisation, governed by a Board of Governors and a General Committee with its Head Office in the City of London and many National and Area Committees in different countries. Represented among the Committees are the Corporation of Lloyd's, Underwriters, P & I Clubs together with specially elected members. The Technical Committee comprises representatives of Shipbuilders, Marine Engineers, Electrical Engineers, Steel Makers, Engine Builders, makers of the other component parts of a modern ship and Government organisations.

The day-to-day affairs are controlled by a Management Committee chosen from the senior members of its staff who co-ordinate the activities of some 4,500 employees in 120 countries.

The objective of all classification societies is, however, the same and that is to ensure that those who gain their livelihood at sea, travel in ships as passengers or entrust their merchandise to the care of a Shipowner shall have safe transit as far as is humanly possible. It is equally important that underwriters shall be able to assess with reasonable accuracy the risks involved against the hazards of maritime adventures and so provide adequate insurance cover.

It follows that if these objectives are to be attained ships must be built and designed on a sound basis to the highest techniques and specification according to the prevailing time of construction. Furthermore, they must be maintained in first class condition throughout their life span and should never be put to sea with defects or un-repaired damage which may affect their class. Ballast arrangements and cargo stowage must never impair stability and a ship must never sail with a greater weight than is permitted according to her tonnage mark.

Over the years international and national legislation has proliferated with the object of improving safety standards but it is to Lloyd's Register of Shipping that credit is due for being the first organisation to impose such rules. As far back as 1835, Lloyd's Load Line Rules came into being for the express purpose of ensuring against overloading. This preceded by 41 years the *Merchant Shipping Act of 1876* which Mr. Samuel Plimsoll steered through the British Parliament and which made the marking of maximum load-line compulsory.

Ships are classed for a period of four or five years with their machinery and equipment on the understanding that provided there is adequate maintenance, there should be no major failures during the period considered safe for the vessel to ply its trade.

The main part of the Classification concerns the hull with the propulsion machinery, electrical systems and other materials used in construction being taken into account.

For full Classification, a ship and its machinery should be built in accordance with the Society's Rules, from materials from an approved steel works under the survey of one or more of the Society's Surveyors.

For a new ship seeking classification, the plans must be submitted prior to commencement of building and examined to ensure that they conform to the Society's Rules. The plans are then used by the attending Surveyor to ensure that the vessel is built to the standard required by the Classification Society and that after working tests all equipment and the vessel itself comply with the Rules laid down. A similar close inspection is undertaken in the case of a ship seeking to change its classification from one society to another; such a change of society is not unusual when a ship changes ownership and the work will inevitably involve the S & P Broker.

In the case of Lloyds Register, the highest possible category is given to those ships which are, in effect continuously surveyed whilst being built. Those ships 'built under Lloyds Special Survey' will have a symbol similar to the Maltese Cross placed before the 100A1 in the register book (often referred to as "Plus 100A1" when spoken).

The precise explanation of the symbols in the Register which combine to make up the +100A1 are:

+ (the Maltese Cross)	This distinguishing mark denotes that the ship was constructed under the Society's special survey, in compliance with the societies rules.
100	Character figure assigned to ships considered suitable for sea going service
A	Character letter assigned to ships which have been constructed or accepted into class in accordance with the Society's rules and regulations and which are maintained in good and efficient condition
1	This character figure is assigned to: (a) ships having on board in good and efficient condition, anchoring and/or mooring equipment in accordance with the Rules. (b) ships classed for special service. for which no specific anchoring and mooring Rules have been published, having on board, in good and efficient condition, anchoring and/or mooring equipment considered suitable and sufficient by the Society for the particular service

A similar system is employed by all the other major classification societies, using different symbols.

The Rules require that certain items are inspected at prescribed intervals but all items must have a major survey once every four or five years with annual surveys being mainly concerned with the ability of the hull and deck to maintain a water tight 'envelope' to protect the cargo.

At regularly prescribed intervals the ships must enter dry-dock for the inspection of all underwater parts including tail-shaft, rudders, propellers, side valves, etc. Alternatively, this work (except for the tail-shaft) may be carried out by suitably qualified divers in which event the inspection has to be conducted in an approved location.

With the rapid changes in technology, it follows that Rules are often revised and updated. Suggested changes may come from industry or may be made by the Societies Surveyors for consideration by the Technical Committee which represents all branches of industry. The safety factor of any amendment is of prime consideration and a consultative exercise is therefore undertaken to ensure that no Rule is introduced which would hazard the vessel or require solutions which were beyond the means of the industry.

All the major Classification Societies now have all their data in computerised form so that instant access to up-to-the-minute information is available to the Society's staff almost anywhere in the world.

Societies' Rules have to embrace, in addition to ships, such things as floating docks, inland waterway vessels, mobile and offshore units, submersibles, diving systems, yachts, small craft and the carriage of all the commodities carried in bulk such as oils, liquid gas, ore, grain, refrigerated stores, etc.

Should a vessel sustain damage of a serious nature, a Classification Society Surveyor must inspect the vessel. He may insist upon certain repairs without which the ship's class will be withdrawn. Alternatively he may make recommendations which usually demand that certain repairs are carried out within a given period.

NB. The question of damage affecting class and recommendations by classification societies will be referred to fully in the Chapter dealing with sale contracts.

Mention has been made of inspection every four years. The initial four year period can be extended to five by carrying out a modified survey at the end of the four year period or an Owner may opt to keep his vessel under continuous survey whereby instead of carrying out a major survey once every four years, the vessel is examined incrementally throughout the survey period.

An Owner is provided regularly with a computerised listing which indicates the survey situation and what outstanding work is to be done or must be undertaken at the next major survey.

Classification societies now provide certificates for many other things besides ships including, for example **Containers** and in the case of Lloyd's Register an initial approval scheme was introduced in 1967 and the first type approval certificate was issued in 1968. Their Container Certification scheme, which covers the approval of all types of containers including refrigerated and tank containers for the carriage of liquid cargoes, is co-ordinated from the Croydon office of Lloyd's Register Industrial Services.

3.2 OTHER FUNCTIONS OF CLASSIFICATION SOCIETIES

Most Classification societies have an **International Conventions Department** which carries out statutory surveys exclusively on behalf of the government of the state where the vessel is registered. In this regard there are about 120 governments assigning a variety of certificates for compliance with International conventions and hence the title of this department.

The purpose for which such departments are probably most used is concerned with the **International Convention on Load Lines, 1966** (which came into force in July 1968) and almost all work concerned with the assignment of load lines is done by classification societies. In general, the freeboard convention ensures that a ship is not overloaded, it provides a watertight containment system and ensures that the vessel has an adequate margin of reserve buoyancy. It also requires a suitable range of intact stability.

A load line certificate is issued for a period of five years and requires an annual survey of hatches, ventilators, closing appliances, etc. For specialised type ships (bulk carriers and tankers) the assigning authority must also be satisfied that the damage stability is satisfactory. Refer back to **Chapter 1 Diagram 1.1** to see the way the society appends its initials to the Plimsoll mark.

Almost all certificates issued by classification societies are concerned with **International Conventions for the Safety of Life at Sea (SOLAS).** There have been four SOLAS Conventions, 1929, 1948, 1960 and 1974, each in turn updating and improving the safety aspects, first of all for passenger vessels and later dry cargo ships and tankers.

Among the safety certificates issued by classification societies are:

Cargo Ship Safety Construction Certificate. Under the terms of the 1960 and 1974 Conventions, any cargo ship of 500 tons gross and over, engaged on international voyages is required to be issued with a "Cargo Ship Safety Construction Certificate". Before this can be issued a survey of the hull, machinery and equipment must be carried out in order to ensure compliance with the requirements of the Conventions. About 80 countries have authorised Classification Societies to undertake these surveys and issue the Certificate on their behalf.

Cargo Ship Safety Equipment, Safety Radio Certificates, Survey of Radio and Radar Installations. The 1960 and 1974 Conventions require that all cargo ships of 500 tons gross and over, engaged on international voyages be provided with a Cargo Ship Safety Equipment Certificate.

Passenger Ship Safety Certificates. Many leading maritime nations also undertake the initial and periodical inspection and survey of passenger ships for the issue of a Passenger Ship Safety Certificate following compliance with the requirements of the 1974 SOLAS Convention. Governmental administrations may authorise Classification Societies to conduct these surveys on their behalf and issue certificates after a satisfactory report although this is exceptional.

International Convention for the Prevention of Pollution from Ships, 1973, as modified by the Protocol of 1978 relating thereto (MARPOL 73/78)
This Convention which came into being on 2nd October 1983 aims to minimise and eventually to eliminate completely pollution of the seas. The Regulations are grouped in five Annexes namely Oil, Noxious liquid substances in bulk, Harmful substances in packaged forms, Sewage and Garbage.

All ships engaged in international trade are required to have on board the International Pollution Prevention Certificate.

Chemical tankers and other ships engaged in the carriage of noxious liquid substances in bulk must have an International Pollution Certificate for the Carriage of Noxious Liquid Substances or for chemical tankers in order to comply with the **IMO Code for the Construction and Equipment of Ships Carrying Dangerous Chemicals in Bulk** This code is mandatory and requires that the design, construction, equipment and operation of ships carrying noxious liquid substances and dangerous chemicals in bulk shall be such as to minimise the uncontrolled discharge of the cargo into the sea.

The **IMO Code for the Construction and Equipment of Ships Carrying Liquefied Gases in Bulk** is more commonly known as the (International) Gas Carrier Code, i.e. without the word "liquefied" and it requires that the design, constructional features and equipment of new ships shall be such as to minimise the risk to the ship, its crew and the environment having regard to the nature of the products carried.

The ISPS Code

Or to give it its full name, the **International Ship and Port Facilities Security Code**. This is a part of the **SOLAS** convention devised by the **IMO** as a response to concerns over security and terrorism.

From a ship sale and purchase perspective, it must be noted that as with the **ISM** certificate approval is given to the managing companies procedures and has nothing to do with the construction or physical condition of the ship in question. If a ship is being sold then almost certainly the ship management company and crew will also change and the **International Ship Security Certificate (ISSC)** will have to be returned to the approving RSO. The new shipowner will then have to re-apply to the same RSO for a new ISSC to be issued or if the flag state has been changed to the RSO that has been approved by that particular Government.

However lack of history can cause a problem so it might be useful to have the background knowledge of why the ISPS Code came into being.

The ISPS Code came into force on 1st July 2004. The code was very much a reaction to the terrorist attacks on New York in September 2001 but it does include elements of two other problems - piracy and stowaways – that have been of concern for many years in the shipping industry.

As the full name suggests the ISPS code works on two levels - ships (covers all ships over 500 GT) and ports. Governments and maritime administrations must appoint **Recognised Security Organisations (RSOs)** to certify the security arrangements that have been made in ports, on ships and in the shore offices of shipping companies. Exactly what sort of organisation can become an RSO is entirely at the discretion of national governments. Within the UK, only the **Maritime and Coastguard Agency (MCA)** has the power to vet ships but many flag states have delegated the work to classification societies while Panama has awarded a monopoly to a specialist security company founded by former US intelligence and military people.

To comply with the code, ships and ports have to be subjected to a risk assessment after which a security plan is drawn up. The plan is then reviewed by the RSO and after a successful inspection and audit of the port or ship, a certificate will be issued. After the coming into force of the code, port states will be able to deny entry to any ship which does not have certificate, as well as ships coming from ports which have not been certified as complying with the code.

On a practical level both ports and ships will operate on a three-stage security alert with the precautions taken dependant on the security threat assessed. This would mean that for the most part both would operate at the lowest level until some intelligence received makes a higher level desirable.

3.3 TONNAGE MEASUREMENT REGULATIONS

Classification Societies are also authorised by many governments to carry out tonnage measurement surveys and issue Tonnage Certificates on their behalf.

The International Convention on Tonnage Measurement of Ships 1969 came into force on the 18th July 1982, and is applicable to ships under the flag of contracting parties to this Convention.

Certain administrations such as the canal companies have developed their own systems of measurement based loosely upon one or more of the main systems of measurements. Lloyd's Register is among the societies authorised to prepare and issue Suez and Panama Canal Tonnage Certificates.

3.4 PRACTICAL APPLICATION FOR THE SALE AND PURCHASE BROKER

Each Classification Society issues and publishes its own register book and these are the essential tools of the S & P Broker. For this reason, no Sale and Purchase office is complete without possession of at least one register of a member of IACS.

Lloyd's Register is particularly useful because it contains details of all known self propelled sea-going merchant ships in the world with a gross tonnage of 100 and above, whether they are classed with Lloyd's or not.

Each Classification Society records ship details in its own individual format. Symbols vary and some provide details which will not be found in other registers. What is important is that the S & P Broker should be fully conversant with the layout and information available in the register in his possession so that the details he requires can be obtained with speed and accuracy.

The more information about a vessel the better for obtaining the interest of a prospective client. Not all details will appear in a Classification Society Register; an obvious example being the latest speed and consumption of a vessel. These can only be obtained from an Owner's office and if required checked with log books aboard the ship. Ship plans can also only be obtained from an Owner and these will usually be required should the prospect of a sale become more serious.

Initially, the following information is essential when placing a ship on the market for sale:

1. Type (ie Tanker, Bulk Carrier/Dry Cargo etc)
2. Deadweight
3. Year built
4. Shipbuilder's name including name and location of yard
5. Class/survey position
6. Number of decks/tanks
7. Type and number of holds/hatches (dry cargo ships only)
8. Number of derricks/cranes (dry cargo ships only)
9. Capacity (grain/bale/insulated/liquid cargo space/teus etc.)
10 Make and type of main engine
11. Horse power (BHP) of engine
12. Speed and consumption.

Most of the foregoing details can be obtained from Lloyd's Register which allows 7 columns for each ship (look again at **Appendices 6 and 7**).

In the case of a ship to be sold for demolition, the following information is required by a scrap yard:

1. Light displacement – this indicates the amount of scrap metal the ship contains. Light displacement must be clearly stated in terms of long or metric tons.
2. Materials of working and spare propellers (i.e. bronze and iron).
3. If a spare propellor and/or tailshaft is included in the sale

3.5 CLASSIFICATION SOCIETY RECORDS

It is rare for a vessel to be purchased for further trading without inspection of the records.

The records that are kept by the Classification Society provide a history of the ship since being classed by that Society. Records of all the special surveys, notations and recommendations will be noted and recorded by a prospective Buyer so that when the physical inspection of the vessel occurs, any areas where recurring problems exist may be given special attention.

S & P Brokers are not expected to be qualified engineers, naval architects or technical men. They do not therefore inspect ship records on behalf of their clients nor do they inspect ships for the purpose of giving an expert opinion. It is part of their function to facilitate inspection of records and ships on behalf of their clients and this they may do with the consent of a Seller. Classification Societies will not authorise inspection of a ship's records without permission from the Owner of the vessel. It is therefore part of an S & P Broker's function to arrange such inspections when a request has been made.

If a Buyer does not have a person available to inspect records or a vessel, the S & P Broker should be in a position to suggest the names of qualified consultants to act on behalf of a Buyer. The Broker must however be careful to suggest names rather than recommend any particular one for the obvious reason that should inspection of records or ship not be carried out efficiently, to the detriment of his Principal, the Broker will not be laid open to any negligence claims that might ensue which will then properly be directed at the consultant concerned.

Classification Society registers and records play an important part in the process of buying and selling ships. Students should, therefore, endeavour to study one or more registers in order to understand the information they contain and where it can be found

3.6 SELF-ASSESSMENT AND TEST QUESTIONS

Attempt the following and check your answers from the text and/or appendices:

1. How does Lloyds Register book differ from other registers?
2. What does the expression "plus 100 A1" mean?
3. What is th name of the Italian classification society
4. What is meant by GL against a ship's classification?
5. What is the nationality and abbreviation of Bureau Veritas?
6. What size must an ocean going self-propelled merchant ship be in order to appear in today's Lloyd's Register?
7. Who may inspect the Classification Society's records prior to a ship being purchased?

Having completed Chapter Three attempt the following and submit your essay to your Tutor.

Imagine you are trying to obtain the interest of a prospective client in the purchase of a ship. What information would you seek to obtain from a Classification Society register about the ship in question and why?

Chapter 4

THE SHIP SALE (PART 1)

4.1 THE OFFER

This Chapter examines the terms of a firm offer to purchase a ship together with some of the potential implications and problems.

There is no set pattern in putting forward an offer to purchase because this is dependent upon the requirements of the individual Buyer and also on the particular ship which is to be purchased. There are, however, certain features which any offer must contain and as the eventual deal will be based upon one of the standard forms such as the **Norwegian Saleform**, it is usual to follow the same logical sequence as in such a form. Standard Saleforms will be dealt with in the next Chapter.

The vast majority of work carried out by S & P Brokers involves the sale of second hand ships intended for further trading. As with any contract, there has to be an **offer**, a **consideration** (the price to be paid for the ship) and an **acceptance**. In real life this will involve negotiation – that is to say by offer and counter offer. These will continue until the two parties to the deal, the Buyer and the Seller, are satisfied they have obtained the best transaction for their particular interests on the prevailing market. The negotiations will then usually conclude by reaching an agreement on principle terms "subject to contract details" when it will normally be the task of the Seller's Broker to draft a written contract for approval and eventual signature.

An S & P Broker (the Seller's Broker) appointed to sell a ship will circulate its details. At one time these would have been the subject of particulars widely circulated by mail to a comprehensive list of S & P Brokers and each Broker tended to have an easily identified "particulars sheet". Mail has, however, been almost completely overtaken by electronic communication. Telex was the first to replace the postal system but fax became more convenient and now more widely than anything else is the use of e-mail which is proving to be the ideal medium for "putting a ship on the market".

It is usual for the opening offer to be made by the Broker acting for the intending Buyer and the offer will be based upon details which have been provided by the Seller's Broker.

When an offer is put forward, provided it is sufficiently interesting to the Seller, it will merit a counter offer; it would be rare indeed for the first offer to be accepted outright. It is important to bear in mind that, although one uses the expression "counter offer", legally each counter offer is actually saying "I decline your offer and now make you the following firm offer". Even if negotiations have reached the stage where, for convenience, the loose expression used when making the counter offer is "accept except" it is still a fact that – legally – either party can break off negotiations at any time.

Occasionally ships are sold by auction. This particularly occurs where possession of the ship has been taken by an official body due to the financial failure of the Owner. At an auction, the successful Buyer is usually the highest bidder and in such a transaction, Brokers are not usually involved except, often, as advisers before the day of the auction.

Of course an S & P Broker's duty is always that of an adviser to his Principal and it should at all times be his aim to obtain for his principal the best terms and price on any transaction he must always take care not to place his own interests (i.e. his desire to conclude a deal) before those of the Buyer or Seller for whom he acts. In this, flexibility, determination, integrity and hard work are prime requisites for success.

Whatever the variations by which an offer is put forward, the basics of any firm offer remain the same namely:

Name of the ship concerned
Reply time
Price
Place and time of delivery
Conditions of sale (e.g Saleform to be used)

There will be a substantial number of additional requirements depending on individual circumstances and these must be studied and understood. Some of the main ones are set out in the rest of this Chapter.

It is usual to have one Broker acting for the Buyer and one for the Seller. Occasionally, there may be a 'chain' involving two or more Brokers on one side or the other, each requiring a share of the total commission which must be divided.

Very rarely a Broker is the sole intermediary between a Buyer and a Seller when his expertise and impartiality will be fully tested.

4.2 THE STRUCTURE OF AN OFFER

Buyer's Name. When an offer to purchase is received a Seller needs to have some idea with whom he is dealing. If the Buyer's name is well known and of good repute it is usually an assurance that when the time comes there will be no problem of payment. If, however, the Buyer is not widely known or is new to the industry, the Buyer's Broker would be advised to submit as much information as possible even including bank references, in order to ensure that the offer he is putting forward is taken seriously. Reputations also, of course, extend to Brokers and an offer put forward by a first class Broker is expected to be on behalf of a reliable Principal thus a Broker should always acquire as much knowledge as possible of the Principals for whom he or she is working. A reputation can be damaged very easily but repairing it can take a very long time.

Reply Time. All offers must have a time limit. The Broker must therefore make quite sure how long the authority he has been given extends. The limit of this authority must be expressed without ambiguity or possible misinterpretation. Date and time must be clearly expressed. Times differ from continent to continent and there are differing time zones within continents. A Broker must therefore be clear as to when the authority he has been given by his Principal expires and must then put forward the offer he has been given stating the day of the month and the time indicating clearly at what place in the world the actual time of the day is applicable.

For example, a typical offer will be put forward – "Offer firm............for reply here 14.00 hours BST London time Tuesday 25th June 2005". Always use the 24 hour clock in order to avoid confusion between am and pm. Adding BST to London time may seem excessive but it reminds the other party that British Summer Time is in operation. The same would apply anywhere else in the world (e.g. North America) where a daylight saving system operates.

Do not use such loose expressions as "for prompt reply" or "for immediate reply"; they mean different things to different people. One might be quite surprised at just how the law interprets "immediate reply" and it should be avoided at all costs; so establish an exact time.

Price. Obviously the currency to be used for the vessel's purchase must be clearly stated with the actual amount in figures and words. Today the currency adopted is almost always expressed in United States Dollars when ships change hands in the international market. The use of a common currency is useful in making comparisons between similar ships on the same market by obviating the necessity for currency conversion with its attendant fluctuations.

Deposit. It is almost invariable for ten percent (10%) of the agreed purchase price to be lodged by the Buyers in a joint interest bearing account in the names of the Sellers and the Buyers (or their agents) to be released to the Sellers at time of delivery of the ship. Should the Buyers wilfully default on the contract their deposit is forfeit to the Sellers.

Payment. It is usual for payment to be demanded either on delivery or within so many "banking days" (usually three) of delivery. Strict deadlines for payment are essential when such large sums are involved. The ten million dollars used in the example in this and the next Chapter may be considered a relatively modest price. Even so, a day's delay in payment even at moderate rates of interest could mean the loss of over $1200 per day (or almost a dollar a minute!)

Commission. Unless stated otherwise, it is the Seller (i.e. the one who receives the payment) who pays all the Brokers' commissions from the actual sale price. It is customary in second hand ship sales for there to be one percent commission for the Buyer's Broker and one percent for the Seller's. When taking authority to make a firm offer on behalf of the Buyer, his Broker should clearly establish that the price being offered does include 1% commission. Thus an offer of US$10,000,000 is put forward as "Price USD $10,000,000 less one percent total commission".

The Seller's Broker, however, will also require a commission and therefore a further one percent of the sale price is added and the offer put forward to his Principal will be: "Price US $10,000,000 less two percent total commission". So that the Seller would receive a net price for his ship of US $10,000,000 less US $200,000 = US $9,800,000.

Should there be more than two Brokers each Broker will, in turn, add his commission to that put forward to him before passing on the offer to the next Broker or the Seller.

If, for example, there happened to be four Brokers in a deal (an unusual circumstance) the firm offer would reach the Seller with 4% total commission. Occasionally a Seller may try to resist such a "high" amount and try to force the Brokers to share commissions even to the extent of agreeing a total percentage, letting the Brokers "fight it out among themselves"; only the circumstances at the time will dictate what is eventually agreed.

The amount of commission in S & P deals is, in any case, not standard. Much will depend on the circumstances and the price. Very often there is just as much if not more work in concluding a five million dollar deal than one of twenty million plus.

On each deal, therefore, a Broker should consider what is reasonably compatible with the time likely to be involved in reaching a successful conclusion as well as the price involved when adding commission to the price put forward.

For most deals, one percent of the total purchase price for each Broker is considered the norm but Brokers must always be prepared to make a sacrifice, if by so doing, the deal stands a greater chance of success.

On occasions it is the Seller who states his price for a ship "net of commission". Either the Broker must decide to try and arrange with the Seller an agreed fee or a figure must be worked out, mathematically, to ensure what the price of the vessel must be in order to provide the commission(s) required.

For example, if a ship is sold for say, USD $975,000 net of commission, the Broker, in order to earn 1% of the final purchase price, must divide US $975,000 by 99 and add to the net price as follows – US $975,000 ÷ 99 = USD $9,848.48 + USD $975,000 = US $984,848.48. At this price the Seller will receive his US $975,000 net of commission and the Broker will obtain 1% provided Buyers and Sellers agree a contract price of US $984,848.48.

If more than 1% is required, the equation is different. For example, if 2% is required by Brokers where the Seller has specified a final price of US $975,000 net of commission the calculation is as follows:

US $975,000 ÷ 98 = US $9,948.97 x 2 = US $19,897.94 + US $975,000 = US $994,897.94.

Needless to say, if 3% commission is required 97 is divided into the net price and the quotient is multiplied by 3, the product of which is added to US $975,000. If 4% the divisor is 96 and the multiplier 4 and so on.

Fortunately such equations are rarely necessary but it is important to know how to calculate should the occasion arise, as it sometimes does.

Occasionally the Buyer's Broker will find that the principal has already stipulated an **address commission** which is retained by the Buyer. The most common reason for the inclusion of an address commission is to satisfy the Buyer's internal accounting procedures where the address commission becomes the income of the department in the Buyer's company negotiating the sale.

4.3 INSPECTION AND INSPECTION OF RECORDS

Except for demolition, ships are rarely purchased without being inspected by the Buyer's Superintendent Engineer or other qualified Surveyor. It would be like buying a house without even a cursory inspection.

This inspection should not be confused with the inspection carried out by the ship's Classification Society at the time of delivery. That inspection at one time always involved the ship going into drydock but now it may be carried out by specially qualified divers. The full implication of the clause covering this inspection will be covered in the next Chapter.

To clarify the difference between the two types of inspection the one carried out before confirming the purchase is often referred to as **"superficial inspection"**.

Because a ship purchase is a large capital transaction a Buyer will always seek to eliminate margins of error and therefore when inspecting a ship he will wish to see as much as he can, in the time available, in order to be sure that the vessel is in sound working order.

Ideally, for example, it is better to see the holds clean swept but this may not always be possible. All depends upon the movements of the ship and a Seller would be reluctant to hold up his vessel unless he had reasonable assurance that a positive deal was in prospect. Similarly, the same situation applies to the inspection of the tanks in a tanker for which purpose gas freeing would be required.

Occasionally a Buyer may request the opening up of closed areas such as ballast tanks, wing tanks etc. to ensure against deterioration, but this is time consuming and the Seller may resist such delay to his ship. Any desire for opening up must be clearly stated before inspection commences so that there is no misunderstanding when the inspection begins.

Buyers often require for the inspection of log-books while aboard. This is a check on the performance of the vessel so that the Inspector may check if the ship is performing as regards speed and consumption according to how she is described. It is also a check on casualties that may have occurred during recent voyages (e.g. hitting underwater objects or superficial damage) which have not yet been notified to the Classification Society and thus not appear in their records.

The place where it is proposed inspection should take place must be specified and since it is in the interest of Buyers and Sellers to ascertain whether or not the ship is likely to be sold, it is important to state a time within which inspection shall take place and a decision given.

4.3.1 Records Inspection

The inspection of Classification Society records is a part of routine S & P activity. Brokers are not expected to be technical men or marine surveyors therefore they do not inspect records and do not express opinions in the matter. It is part of their job, however, to arrange for inspection of records at the Classification Society and this they will do on behalf of their Principals. The Society will not, of course, permit such an inspection without written authority from the Sellers.

An experienced Marine Superintendent or Surveyor will glean, from an inspection of a ship's records at a Classification Society, a fairly accurate idea of her condition. He will note recurring problems and areas of inherent vice.

Inspection of records usually takes place before ship inspection for the simple reason that when the actual ship inspection takes place, the records will have revealed the parts of the vessel where any trouble has been detected and where examination should be most concentrated.

When arranging records inspection a Broker will first obtain permission from the Sellers of the vessel, either direct or through their Broker. When permission has been granted, he will then arrange with the relevant Classification Society the time and date when it is desired for the records to be inspected and will give the name of the Inspector.

Should an S & P Broker be asked to nominate or recommend a surveyor to inspect a ship or records on behalf of a Buyer great care is essential in case it should be found later that the Inspector was negligent. A Broker should therefore nominate or recommend "without guarantee".

4.3.2 Reply Time for Inspection of Vessel and Records

At one time it was not unusual for S & P negotiations to proceed "subject superficial inspection and inspection of records". This could, therefore, mean that the Buyers and Sellers – and of course their respective Brokers – would devote their time and expertise right up to completing all the details of an intended sale, only to have the whole thing collapse when one or other of the inspections took place. There was no redress; the Buyer would not even be obliged to give reasons for refusing. It was the cause of severe frustration to Brokers at that time.

Fortunately, during recent years, Sellers have been able to refuse to negotiate on a "subject inspection" basis. Thus the intending Buyer must carry out inspection of records and superficial inspection of the ship itself and then make the offer on an outright basis.

Circumstances could change and if ever a pattern of negotiations "subject inspection" were to return it will be vital to ensure that dates and times for the inspections to take place are clearly specified together with a deadline for eventual decision to be declared by the Buyer. It must be appreciated that, if a deal is concluded "subject to inspection of records and ship", the Seller cannot deal with other Buyers in the meantime so that unambiguous time limits are essential.

4.4 DELIVERY – WHERE AND WHEN?

The place and time of delivery must be clearly indicated before agreement can be reached on a ship sale. Obviously Buyers and Sellers will each wish delivery to take place at a port and time most convenient to themselves compatible with the movements of the ship.

Once a deal is agreed, however, both parties will seek to expedite matters to their mutual satisfaction and in any argument which may follow on this particular issue, commonsense will hopefully be the prevailing factor.

It is clearly better for both parties if delivery takes place at a safe place which is accessible for taking off and taking on a ship's crew. A safe berth alongside a quay or jetty is ideal for this purpose and it is usually found more convenient if this can be arranged at the vessel's last port of discharge. If drydocking at delivery port has been agreed, then it must be ascertained in advance that at such a port – or close by – there are drydocking facilities for this purpose. Similarly facilities for diver's inspection must be ascertained if appropriate.

The date of delivery is important for the purpose of signing on a crew by the Buyer and making the necessary arrangements for transfer by the Seller such as arranging (often referred to as "stemming") dry-dock if such is agreed. There are also the numerous other arrangements which must be made in advance which include banking, insurance, documentation, registration and classification amongst others.

Almost invariably the Buyer will have placed a deposit on the vessel he intended to purchase and in the event that the vessel cannot be ready for some reason beyond Seller's control, it is only right that the Buyer should have the option to cancel the deal. Such a contingency might be occasioned by an actual or constructive total loss of the ship, in which case the Buyer will require the return of his deposit, plus accrued interest, and it is for this purpose that a **cancelling date** for completion of the sale should be incorporated. Having inspected and accepted the vessel and placed a deposit with the clear intention of a purchase, the Buyer may not wish to lose the ship, if for example, she was delayed in reaching her port of destination for some reason. The Broker acting on behalf of the Buyer should therefore make it clear that the cancelling date of the contract is "in Buyer's option". This means that should the vessel miss her cancelling date, the sale may still be maintained by the Buyer, if it is in his interests, and if he feels there is a reasonable assurance that delivery can take place without undue further delay. This situation is clearly covered in the Norwegian Saleform 1993 which is dealt with in the next Chapter. The cancelling date is essentially an **option**, the contract is not automatically cancelled if the ship is later than her cancelling date.

4.5 DRY-DOCKING OR DIVER'S INSPECTION

The full implications of the clause covering the inspection at time of delivery will be referred to in the next Chapter. Suffice it to say for the moment that it is an important clause of most S & P contracts, ensuring as it does that the vessel is in full compliance with Classification rules.

The only occasion where such a clause would be omitted would be when a ship is sold "as is, where is" which means in effect "there lies the ship – take her exactly as she is". Also excluded from dry-docking are ships sold for demolition.

The purpose of the dry-docking clause is to enable the parts of the vessel below the water line to be inspected. If such parts are damaged so as to affect the vessel's class, they must be put right by the Seller to the Classification Society's satisfaction. It is quite usual now for the underwater parts to be inspected by the Classification Societies using specially qualified **divers** and this is a method frequently used especially where no dry-docks are available.

The next Chapter will consider, line-by-line, the Norwegian Sale Forms which are the forms most commonly used today. They have been revised many times, the most recent is dated 1993 hence the abbreviation NSF93. Such is the conservatism of Shipowners, its immediate predecessor – NSF87 – is still quite widely used. S & P Brokers therefore need to know about both forms because it may be many years yet before the NSF87 becomes obsolete.

There is no such document as a perfect sale contract. Buyers may well argue that the contract placed before them by the Seller is too much the vendor's favour and *vice versa* but experience has shown that the Norwegian Sale Form is as equitable as can be devised and furthermore, it is known throughout the world which facilitates the drawing up of the final contract for signature once agreement on terms has been reached.

4.6 WHAT IS INCLUDED IN THE PRICE?

Just what is included in the sale price causes possibly more argument than any other item when a ship is delivered. It is therefore of prime importance to define as clearly as possible what are the intentions of Buyers and Sellers in this respect. When a Buyer negotiates a deal he expects everything belonging to the ship to be included in the sale price and will expect all items on board the vessel and also any items ashore or on order if they are the ship's property **except**, that is, for **bunkers** and **lubricating oils** which are dealt with separately. Items involved may include a spare propeller or tail-shaft. During negotiations, the Broker should do the utmost to establish clearly what is the ship's property. It is common for Sellers to exclude from a sale certain items which may be regarded as fleet spares (if there are one or more ships of the same class). Such items as gas bottles, tank cleaning machines as well as things of a personal nature such as a gift from the ship's sponsor when she was launched, pictures which decorate saloons, the ship's bell, crockery and cutlery bearing the Seller's flag or name.

A Broker should anticipate such contingencies and endeavour to clarify what is intended by Sellers, when handing over a vessel, in order to eliminate difficulties. On delivery, a Buyer will expect to have aboard items of equipment which were aboard the vessel when inspected.

If there was, for example, a spare propeller and a spare tail-shaft at the time of inspection, he will naturally expect to see them aboard on delivery. Occasionally however, ships have been known to incur damage to an item of equipment such as a working propeller between the time of inspection and delivery in which event the spare propeller is used while the damaged propeller is taken ashore. A Seller could argue that the spare propeller is aboard the vessel, being used to propel the ship, while the working propeller is ashore and damaged or possibly condemned. It is important therefore to specify that the ship will be delivered with "a spare propeller" rather than "the spare propeller" and such subtleties in negotiation should be noted by aspiring S & P Brokers.

Normally all the vessel's manuals, plans, instruction books etc if not on board should be handed over by the Sellers as soon as possible after delivery and the contract should stipulate a period within which such delivery to be completed.

A list of radio and navigational aids whether on hire or not is also an essential part of the negotiations to be itemised by the Sellers so that the Buyers, on delivery, will be fully aware of what is ship's property and what of the items on hire may be retained under new contracts between the Buyers and the lessors of the equipment. In these days of total dependence on electronics for navigation it is vital for the Buyers to know whether or not the ship can sail as soon as delivered.

4.7 BUNKERS AND LUBRICATING OILS

Ships at the time of delivery will have bunkers and unused lubricating oils and these must be paid for in addition unless otherwise agreed. The exceptions to this may occur when a vessel is sold on an outright basis "as is where is" or when purchased for demolition when bunkers may be more of a liability than an asset.

When taking over bunkers at a port of delivery, there are three possible areas of dispute. The first is the price, the second is the quantity remaining on board and the third is the quality (i.e. whether useable or not).

Bunkers prices vary from port to port and a Buyer will naturally wish to limit as much as possible the amount to be paid for bunkers remaining on board when a ship is delivered. If a ship has taken on board bunkers at a port where they are expensive, it is understandable that the Buyer will object to paying the same price if the delivery port is a place where bunkers are cheap. Agreement must therefore be reached on the basis for determining the cost of bunkers at the time of delivery. Prices of bunkers at any port in the world are readily obtainable through a bunker broker, oil trader, oil company or the Internet and a Broker should always be ready to assist in providing this information if called upon to do so. The current price for bunkers at the port of delivery can therefore be established easily through the same sources as referred above. The cost of lubricating oil can be obtained from any oil company although a ship customarily contracts with only one supplier for lubricating oil and that company's price may differ slightly from another's.

If, at the port of delivery, bunkers are expensive, Buyers may stipulate the maximum quantity to be paid for with a view to having sufficient remaining on board for taking the ship to a port where they are cheaper.

At the time of delivery, the skill of the Brokers in bringing their Principals to an amicable agreement over bunkers can be invaluable. In case of difficulty, an impartial referee in the form of an oil company representative may be sought in order to propose a way to settle the matter. Occasionally, the Buyer may claim that bunkers contain quantities of sludge, in which case the quality will be challenged and again, the decision of an impartial referee should settle the matter to the satisfaction of both parties.

The Broker should, therefore, endeavour to establish which prices should prevail when settlement for bunkers and lubricants is required at the time of delivery. It may seem that this reference to bunker prices is unnecessarily detailed when one considers the cost of bunkers in the context of the price of the ship itself. The fact remains that disputes over bunkers are only too common.

4.8 BUYER'S CREW ON BOARD BEFORE DELIVERY

The time when a ship is to be delivered can be a nerve testing time for all parties involved in the sale, including the Brokers! Buyers are anxious to place their crew aboard as soon as they arrive at the delivery port but experience has shown that it is unwise to allow the Buyer's crew to go aboard before the ship has been paid for and documents exchanged. The essence of any contract, however, should always be goodwill and where possible a compromise should be sought in respect of this difficulty.

The difficulty arises because the Buyers have a natural anxiety to ensure that items of ship's property are not being taken ashore prior to handover while Sellers discourage any interference in the running of the ship while it remains their property. Furthermore, in the event of an accident occurring involving the Buyer's crew, litigation will ensue and the delivery time for the official handing over could be delayed.

During the sale negotiations it is usual for agreement to be reached to allow a limited number of members of the Buyer's crew aboard for the purposes of familiarisation but always at Buyer's risk and expense.

4.9 SAME CONDITION AS WHEN INSPECTED

There are occasions when this stipulation can cause disputes, the difficulty being providing the proof of what was the condition of the vessel when inspected. It could be, for example, that the Buyer's surveyor may not have conducted an exhaustive inspection of the entire ship and as a result may have missed certain items. Such an eventuality must lead to doubt as to whether a particular defect was present on the day when the vessel was inspected.

Obviously a Seller will be anxious to sell his ship and therefore not go out of his way to point out items which are not in perfect repair in which case, the burden of proving that the vessel was in better condition upon inspection will fall upon the Buyer.

The wording "substantially the same condition as when inspected" is a common term and gives the Buyer a degree of assurance that the ship that was inspected will be, except for fair wear and tear, the same ship as when delivered. Furthermore, the Seller is under an obligation to maintain the vessel in the manner of a reasonably prudent Owner between the date of inspection and the date of delivery. It is now not unusual for the Buyer's inspector to take photographs or make a video record so that later arguments are avoided.

Subject Further Details Basis NSF1987 or NSF1993

No two ship sales are the same. Each has its own and often unforeseen complications which test the skill and ingenuity of the Broker whose task it is to bring the two sides together in harmony.

Reference has been made to the Norwegian Sale Forms as being used throughout the world for ship sales and the words "basis NSF1987" (or "NSF1993") mean that the basic form will be used, clause by clause and line by line but with amendments, additions and alterations according to the negotiated ship sale terms agreed at the time of concluding the agreement.

4.10 ENGLISH LAW/ARBITRATION LONDON

Because of its long tradition as a centre of shipping activity, arbitration in London is a most frequently accepted term and since London arbitrators are versed in English law, it follows that these two conditions are complimentary to each other.

When the time comes to study the two forms in the next Chapter it will be seen that the later (1993) form is far more specific about how the arbitration should be carried out.

Brokers must always strive to use their skill in such a way as to ensure disputes which lead to arbitration do not occur. However, where large sums of money are involved and big issues are at stake the final resort of going to law is, at times, inevitable.

4.11 WITH CLASS MAINTAINED FREE OF RECOMMENDATIONS AND FREE OF AVERAGE DAMAGE AFFECTING CLASS

The above condition is commonly used in S & P and it is important to understand its full meaning and implications.

These may be summarised as follows:

1. Nothing relating to surveys should be overdue. All surveys have a date and therefore all must be up to date at the time of delivery.
2. Class surveys may have recommendations, outstandings or subject items of class. This means that the classification surveyor has seen something which must be dealt with by a certain date. If this recommendation is noted, even though it may not be due until after delivery of the vessel, it must be settled at the time of delivery.
3. There are also appendix items which are not given a definite date. Buyers cannot claim an appendix item from Sellers as these do not affect clean class whereas outstandings do affect them.
4. Claims on insurance must be cleared. Average means anything which is to be claimed against insurance underwriters. When the ship is sold, the new Owner cannot claim on the underwriters of the previous owner therefore average items must be cleared before the ship is delivered.

There are differing views on the interpretation and implementation of the conditions imposed above and these will be considered more fully when examining the sale contract in the next Chapter.

4.12 THE OFFER AND COUNTER OFFER

As previously mentioned, there is no standard form for putting forward offers but many Brokers have a check-sheet or pro forma on their desk as an *aide-memoire* in order to ensure that no items are neglected or overlooked.

Let us assume the m.v. *"Georgina"* is for sale and the Seller's Brokers have circularised the vessel with an indicated price of US $10,250,000 with delivery UK/Continent during the following July/August.

An attractive offer might read like this:

---

m.v. ***"Georgina"*** *On behalf of Moya Shipping of New City Court, London (the first offer may omit the intending Buyers name and simply say something like "first class Buyers to be nominated") we are authorised to offer firm for reply Tuesday 10th July 17.00 hours BST London time basis details as set out in your e-mail of 8th July timed 1615 hrs (or state time and date and type of whatever communication was used to give details of the ship):*

1. *Price US $9,750,000 less 2% total commission this end.*
2. *Subject prompt inspection of the vessel with clean swept holds at Southampton within July 2002*
3. *Subject approval of class records after inspection of same.*
4. *Buyers' reply on inspection of vessel and records within 3 working days after completion of vessel inspection.*
5. *Delivery of the vessel, charter free, at a port in Antwerp/Hamburg range at a safe anchorage or berth safely afloat within 30 days after signing of Memorandum of Agreement and deposit lodged with cancelling date in Buyers' option.*
6. *Vessel to be delivered with class maintained, free of recommendations and free of average damage. All safety certificates to be up to date. Vessel to be delivered in substantially the same condition as when inspected.*
7. *Dry-docking as per NSF 1987. (Or could be "divers' inspection as per NSF1993)*
8. *Vessel to be delivered with everything belonging to her on board, ashore and on order including all spare parts and spare equipment including spare propeller and tail-shaft, radio/navaids not on hire (please itemise).*
9. *Purchase price to include bunkers and luboils as on board at time of delivery.*
10. *Vessel to be delivered free of all encumbrances/mortgages/maritime liens/taxes/claims and all debts whatsoever.*
11. *Subject contract details basis NSF (1987 or 1993 as appropriate) – English Law to apply and deposits, payments and arbitration in London.*
12. *Buyer's right to place two men on board at Buyer's risk and expense after contract signed, deposit lodged and Buyer's signed indemnities provided.*
13. *Sellers guarantee the vessel is not black-listed by any Arab country.*

4.12.1 The First Counter Offer

On the assumption that this initial offer is of interest to the Sellers, a counter offer might take the following form:

Behalf Freya Shipping of St. Mary Axe, London, we are authorised to counter offer on the following terms and conditions to your offer of yesterday's date for reply here 15.00 hours BST London time Thursday 12th July.

1. *Price US $10,250,000 less 1½% total commission your end. (Note – the Sellers have maintained their indicated price and only allowed 1½% commission from the purchase price to Buyer's Broker. The fact that there is more than 1% commission at the Buyers' end tends to indicate that either there is another Broker involved in the deal or that the Buyers have included an address commission in their offer).*
2. *Subject superficial inspection only at first port of discharge Antwerp/Hamburg range within July 2005. Buyers will of course have access to holds but as the vessel will be discharging cargo, Owners cannot, in advance, confirm that holds will be clean swept.*
   Vessel's deck and engine logs will be made available to Buyers at time of inspection.
3. *Agreed. (Note – Sellers have agreed inspection of records).*
4. *Agreed except decision of acceptance/rejection of ship and records within 48 hours after ship inspection. (Note – Sellers wish to speed up the decision on whether or not the ship is accepted and have shortened the period for reply. Obviously a Seller must know with minimum delay whether or not he has a deal for the purposes of finding another Buyer or fixing the ship).*
5. *Agreed except delivery during August 2005 with 20th September 2005 cancelling.*
6. *Diver's inspection as per NSF93 (Note dry-docking has been declined and alternative of diver's inspection offered which is now quite common practice).*
7. *Agreed except Sellers will not replace spare propeller or spare tail-shaft if used prior to delivery. Radio/Navaids on hire will be advised soonest. (Note – The Seller is taking the precaution of not being required to replace the spare propeller or spare tail-shaft in the event of the vessel hitting a submerged object prior to delivery, in which case the working propeller and/or tail-shaft might be condemned necessitating the spares to be fitted. Radio and Navaids are listed in the Owner's office and the Broker will obtain details of which are on hire and which are owner's property as soon as the information is forthcoming).*
8. *Remaining bunkers and unused lubricating oils to be paid for extra at current price at port of delivery. (Note – it is normal for Sellers to require Buyers to pay extra for bunkers in ship sales for further trading. As mentioned previously in this Chapter, the Broker can expect some argument regarding prices of bunkers and luboils at the port of delivery, also quantity and quality).*
9. *Agreed. (Note – The Sellers have agreed to clear all debts on the ship prior to delivery. Proof of this must be given at the time of delivery in order to obtain transfer of flag from one registry to another).*
10. *Agreed except after "average damage" add "affecting class". (Note – Sellers have agreed the wording as proposed by Buyers but require the condition that only claims against underwriters which affect the vessel's class will be cleared at the time of delivery).*
11. *Agreed but add words "fair wear and tear excepted" after "the same condition as when inspected". (Note – The addition inserted by Sellers can cause complications because of the difficulty in proving what was the condition of the vessel at the time of inspection. The Seller will be anxious to sell the ship* ***and is under no obligation*** *to point out items which are not in a perfect state of repair and therefore the burden of proving that the vessel was in a better condition upon inspection will fall upon the Buyer).*
12. *Agreed. (Note – Brokers have a key role to play in the avoidance of disputes needing to go to law. Arbitration can of course be convened at any centre of shipping throughout the world which is acceptable to Buyers and Sellers).*
13. *Buyers have the right to place two men on board at Buyer's risk and expense on arrival of vessel at delivery port. (Note – Refer to previous comments regarding Seller's reluctance to have personnel other than ship's crew aboard prior to handing over. The risks are obvious but Buyers also have fears of items which are ship's property being taken ashore. Buyers also have an interest in familiarisation of the vessel by their crew and therefore may wish to have an engineer aboard for the delivery voyage with this in mind).*

14. *Agreed.*
15. *For transfer of flag in Buyer's option, Buyers to state their registration documentation requirements with which Sellers to do their utmost to comply.*

It is emphasised that the above offer and counter offer is an example only of what might happen during a negotiation for a ship purchase. The Brokers will continue their exchanges, clause by clause and line by line until, hopefully, agreement is reached on terms following which it will be their duty to draw up a sale contract for signature.

In the next Chapter, it will be assumed that following offers and counter offers on the above outline basis, agreement has been reached on terms. It will then be the task of the Seller's Broker to draw up a Memorandum of Agreement for signature, carefully observing every item which has been agreed by both parties and recording it in the sale contract.

Whilst all offers and counter offer have to be authorised by the Principal concerned, the process of submitting them in a manner most likely to result in a favourable reply can only be perfected by practice and experience. By this means, the Broker builds up a reserve of confidence essential for his or her ultimate success.

4.13 SELF-ASSESSMENT AND TEST QUESTIONS

Attempt the following and check your answers from the text:

1. When a ship is sold for further trading who normally pays the Brokers' commissions?
2. What is meant by "Free of average damage affecting class"?
3. What is the purpose of the dry-dock or diver's inspection clause in a sale contract?

Having completed Chapter Four attempt the following and submit your essay to your Tutor.

A ship is placed in the open market for further trading.

Discuss and explain the usual procedures for reaching agreement on terms and the various stages to be followed from inspection of records to final delivery of the ship to new Owners.

Chapter 5

THE SHIP SALE (PART 2)

5.1 INTRODUCTION

In the previous Chapter the procedure adopted by Sale and Purchase Brokers, whereby offers and counter offers are exchanged, was examined. During the course of that Chapter, it was pointed out that, when final agreement on terms is reached, it would normally be the duty of the Seller's Broker to draw up a contract – or **Memorandum of Agreement** to use its formal name – for signature by the two principals.

Now the perfect form of sale contract can rarely exist by reason of differing interests between Sellers and Buyers. However, the ultimate desire of both parties, after having reached agreement on terms, is for an efficient and smooth transfer of ownership. To this end the careful preparation of a contract is vital

Experience has shown that the **Norwegian Shipbrokers' Association's Memorandum of Agreement** for sale and purchase of ships is as equitable as can be devised. This document was originally adopted by the Baltic and International Maritime Council (BIMCO) in 1956 and during the past 10 years, it has been revised four times, in 1966, 1983, 1987 and 1993. The Norwegian forms have the advantage of being the most widely known and extensively used of all sale contracts and it is on these forms that this Chapter is based.

Shipping people, no matter how forward looking they may be, when it comes to standard forms tend to be conservative in the extreme. For example, some dry cargo charter parties in current use contain wording that is unchanged from forms devised in the nineteenth century. Thus, although most practitioners in ship sale and purchase will agree that the 1993 form is a marked improvement upon the 1987 version, the 1993 form has not yet entirely replaced the 1987.

In the examinations, as in real life, you will be expected to show a knowledge of where the two forms differ although questions seeking detailed knowledge will usually allow the candidate to choose and declare which form their answer is based upon.

Appendix 10 is a copy of Norwegian Saleform 1987 and **Appendix 11** is a copy of Saleform 1993 by kind permission of the Norwegian Shipbrokers Association both of which should be studied and compared one with the other. During the course of this Chapter students should be prepared to make references to both these appendices as well as to the previous Chapter so that adequate time should be allocated.

5.2 CONCLUDING THE SALE

It is now assumed that the Brokers involved in the offers and counter offers discussed in Chapter Four finally reached agreement on terms.

A telex or e-mail of confirmation of the completion of the sale would be put forward by the Seller's Broker as follows:

On behalf of Freya Shipping of St Mary Axe, London we are pleased to confirm the sale of m.v ***"Georgina"*** *to Moya Shipping of New City Court, London on the following terms and conditions:*

1. *Price US $10,000,000 less 2% total commission your end. Deposit 10% within three banking days of signing contract otherwise terms Saleform clause 2. Payment within three*

banking days of delivery otherwise terms Saleform clause 3. (Note – Sellers agreed to lower their price and have also agreed to allow 2% for the Buyers' Broker, presumably for distribution with others. Brokers usually agree to 1% of the purchase price and so presumably there is either an address commission past the Buyer's Broker or there is another Broker who has to be covered. On commission however there is no hard and fast rule, Brokers having to use their discretion and judgement at all times).

2. *Subject superficial inspection only at Antwerp within July 2005. (Note – Sellers have now nominated the port of inspection following more definite news of the vessel's movements since the initial offer and counter offers were exchanged. Superficial inspection means what it says and excludes opening up of engines but allows the viewing of any part of the vessel within the interpretation of this term).*

3. *The class records have been accepted by Buyers after inspection. (Note – It is usual to inspect class records before inspecting the vessel as they will indicate the vessel's condition, trading history and technical problems under her present ownership and will prove a useful guide as to what areas should be given particular attention when Buyer's inspectors are aboard the vessel at the port of inspection).*

4. *Decision of acceptance after inspection of vessel afloat to be given to Sellers within 48 hours after completion of such afloat inspection. (Note particularly that, depending upon market conditions, Sellers may insist on inspection of the vessel taking place* **before proceeding with negotiations** *in which event Clauses 2,3 & 4 of this offer would be replaced with:*

   The Buyers have approved class records and accepted the vessel following superficial inspection afloat at -----. This sale is definite and outright subject only to the conditions of this offer).

5. *Delivery of the vessel at a safe berth in Antwerp within August 2005 with 10th September 2005 cancelling. (Note that Buyers have succeeded in shortening the cancelling date by ten days. Bear in mind that the cancelling date, is an option which the Buyer may exercise or not as he wishes. This could be catastrophic for the Seller whose ship may simply have been held up through unforeseen delays under a preceding charter. If the market has deteriorated significantly between the time of signing the agreement and the delivery date the Buyer may be very relieved if the ship is a few days late because the clause, without any qualification, legally would allow the Buyer to 'walk away' from the deal without penalty if the ship is so much as a day later than her cancelling date. Prudent Sellers would insert additional wording in the cancelling clause calling upon the Buyer to declare his intentions in advance if it appears that the ship is falling behind schedule. Unforeseen delay can be equally catastrophic for the Buyer who may lose profitable business through the ship being late. Of course if the delay was deliberate then the Buyer would have a remedy in law against the Seller).*

6. *Dry-docking as per NSF 1987.*
   (Note – Inspection of parts below the summer loadline can be carried out by divers specialising in this form of survey where a dry-dock is not available. We shall examine the implications of the dry-dock clause later in this Chapter but it is important to note that the vessel cannot be declined after dry-dock inspection the sale is definite and all that is necessary is for any defective parts below the summer loadline made good to the satisfaction of the Classification Surveyor).

7. *Vessel to be delivered with everything belonging to her on board and ashore and on order including spare propeller and spare tails-haft unless taken out of spare prior to delivery. Buyers to pay extra for remaining bunkers, unused lubricating oils only and pay the current market price at the port of delivery. (Note – What is included in the price of the vessel can be a source of argument and it is important to be as explicit as possible in this matter. Clause 7 of both the NSF 1987 and NSF 1993 is as comprehensive as can be devised in a sale contract but care must be taken over such items as are of individual interest to Sellers such as items bearing a crest or name, a sponsor's gift, etc.*

   Bunkers and the cost of bunkers can always be a source of dispute and this will be examined when the implications of Clause 7 are discussed further).

8. *Vessel to be delivered free of all encumbrances, mortgages, maritime liens, taxes, claims and all debts whatsoever. (Note – This requirement is an essential benefit for Buyers, and is covered adequately in Clause 9 of both Saleforms. The obligation for Sellers to indemnify Buyers should there by any subsequent claims on the vessel after delivery is an essential one. For example, a creditor of the Seller may have obtained a warrant (a writ) to arrest the ship for a debt for which a maritime lien comes into existence. The creditor may not yet have served the writ so that the Seller may be honestly unaware of its existence. The fact is, however, that maritime liens are* ***against the ship*** *regardless of any change of ownership after the issue of the warrant. The creditor is under no obligation to advise the Shipowner that a warrant has been issued so that the first intimation of the writ's existence may be the actual arrest of the ship. Full details of this procedure, known as arrest in rem are discussed in TutorShip's law Chapters).*

9. *Vessel to be delivered with class maintained, free of recommendations, all continuous survey cycles to be passed minimum three months from date of delivery. Free of average damage affecting class and with all class and trading certificates clean and valid. (Note – The meaning of this condition will be explained later in this Chapter when Saleforms are examined line by line).*

10. *Vessel to be delivered in substantially the same condition as when inspected, fair wear and tear excepted. (Note – Buyers have agreed to Seller's stipulation "fair wear and tear excepted". The obvious difficulty here is in proving what was the condition of the vessel at the time of inspection. The Buyer's surveyor may not have carried out an exhaustive survey of the entire ship and there may have been items that are missed. The inclusion of the words "fair wear and tear excepted" does not mean that when the agreement to sell has been reached, the Seller can ignore normal maintenance. He remains under an obligation to maintain the vessel as a responsible and prudent Owner from the date of inspection until the date of delivery).*

11. *Subject contract details basis NSF 1987 (or NSF1993) – English law and arbitration London to apply. (Note – Sellers and Buyers have agreed that the Norwegian Saleform shall be the basis of their contract with additions and/or deletions according to that which has been agreed in this confirmation).*

12. *Buyers have the right to place two men aboard at Buyer's risk and expense at Antwerp immediately after contract signed and confirmation of deposit lodged in accordance with contract and after signing usual indemnities. (Note – Sellers have agreed for representatives to be placed aboard but only after the deposit is lodged. It is natural for Sellers to be assured as much as possible and beyond reasonable doubt that the sale is definite and there can be no better assurance than having a signed contract and a deposit placed by the Buyers.*

    It is usual for the Buyers to obtain P & I cover indemnifying the Sellers for any damage or injury the Buyer's representatives may do to themselves, to the vessel or the Seller's officers crew and servants.

    Unexpected eventualities may always occur but the essence of every contract is good will. It is therefore a reasonable request from Buyers for two representatives to be placed aboard the vessel for obvious reasons. Before official handover, persons, other than Seller's crew are not usually welcome aboard but there has to be some give and take in all transactions and in this instance Sellers have shown their willingness to co-operate).

13. *Sellers guarantee that to the best of their knowledge the vessel is not black-listed by any Arab country. (Note – Some Arab countries still boycott ships which have traded to Israel. Such boycotting is of the ship not the Owner because it would otherwise be so easy for a boycotted ship to be 'sold' to another company, still controlled by the original Owner. Buyers need assurance in writing and in the contract that once the vessel has been taken over there will be no restrictions as regards her trading limits).*

On the assumption that this confirmation (usually referred to as a "recapitulation" or simply "recap") sent by the Seller's Broker to the Buyer or his Broker has been confirmed as a correct record of what was finally agreed between Buyers and Sellers. It will now be the task of the Seller's Broker to draw up a contract or Memorandum of Agreement for signature.

With this in mind **Appendices 10 & 11** will be examined in detail. Saleform 1987 will be used as the basis and **italics** will be used to indicate where the Saleform 1993 is different.

Date. This should be the date on which agreement was reached on terms. That is to say when finally offers and counter offers having been exchanged, all outstanding items were finally confirmed by both parties. The deposit must be lodged within 3 banking days from the date of the agreement being signed by both parties and therefore the Brokers drawing up the contract must be flexible in pursuit of attending to the interests of their Principals and the requirements of the sale in question.

Lines 1,2 & 3, Names of the parties and the ship. These are straightforward containing the full style and addresses of Buyers and Sellers and also the ship's name. *The '93 form more correctly says "agreed to sell" instead of "sold" and "agreed to buy" instead of "bought".*

Lines 4 to 8, Details of the ship. Date of build, classification and name of builders can be obtained from the classification register or from owners. *Classification Society and Class in the '93 form rather than simply "Classification". Events have even overtaken the '93 form because register tonnage is now denoted as GT and NT*

The '93 form then devotes lines 10 to 15 clarifying some words and phrases used in the contract.

NB The ship's call sign can be obtained from the classification register or from Owners. Gross and net tonnage are best obtained from the tonnage certificate in Owners' office.

Clause 1, Price. The price must be expressed stating currency and amount in figures and words.

Clause 2, The deposit. The sale having been confirmed, it is important for the Seller to have some kind of surety of the Buyer's intent. If, for example the ship is deviated from her course and is unfixed in the belief that the ship is sold and there is no serious intention on the part of the Buyer except to have an option on the vessel then the Seller could incur heavy costs. A deposit is therefore a necessity since, with its establishment, the Seller is further assured of the Buyer's seriousness and can make the necessary arrangements for the final handing over of the vessel with despatch. The deposit can be lodged in any Bank but it is usually placed in the Seller's bank so as to facilitate banking arrangements when the ship is delivered although the Seller's Broker's bank is often used.

The deposit is to be lodged within three banking days from the signing of the contract by both parties and any interest on the deposit shall be for Buyer's account. Should there be any fee imposed by the bank for holding the deposit, it shall be borne equally by Buyers and Sellers. *The '93 form goes into a little more detail about the release of the deposit.*

Clause 3, Payment. Obviously the Sellers require to receive the precise amount of purchase money as agreed. Banks charge for their services and therefore Buyers must instruct their Bankers to have the required amount of money available for payment to Seller's account as and when required with any bank charges for the account of the Buyers. This accounts for the wording "free of bank charges". When the vessel is ready for delivery official notice of readiness is given to the Buyers by Sellers. *The '93 form devotes a whole new clause (5) to the question of notices and, incidentally, has already clarified that the word "written" includes any method of transmitting the written word. Note also the '93 form includes the words* **"in every respect physically ready for delivery"** *this is included because the looser wording under the '87 form became the subject of a law case ("Aktion" 1987).* Full payment within three banking days after such notice is generally acceptable but such notice could, of course, be expressed in other forms – for example "within three working days" or "three days, Sundays and Bank Holidays excepted" but the S & P world has almost universally elected to use the expression "banking days" which seldom if ever causes any ambiguity *and "banking days are defined in the '93 form.*

Clause 4, Inspections . As has been mentioned, a ship purchased for further trading is rarely negotiated without inspection of the ship and of her records. A ship purchase is a substantial financial transaction and the future fortune of the Buyer may well depend on its outcome. It is important therefore to eliminate risks and margins of error as far as possible. Classification records can usually give a clear indication of the standard of maintenance, trading history and the general condition of the ship since her maiden voyage up to the last survey. A Buyer will note carefully recurring problems and will pay special attention to these when the physical inspection of the vessel takes place. In the case we are studying – the *"Georgina"*, the Buyers have inspected records and have accepted them. The words in lines 22 and 23 of the '87 form which read "The Buyers shall have the right to inspect the vessel's classification records and declare whether same are accepted or not within" will, therefore, have to be deleted.

Similarly, if the vessel had been accepted after inspection before contract signing we could expect Clause 4 to read – "The Buyers have accepted the vessel's records and also the vessel after inspection and the sale is therefore outright".

Sellers are usually reluctant to allow opening up of the main engine and it is natural that Sellers should require compensation should Buyers hold up the vessel on account of delay in inspection. Log-books for engine and deck are part of the items inspectors will wish to see. In effect, they are the ship's diary and provide information of importance to a Buyer such as speed and consumption and details of any incidents in which the ship has been involved.

It is incumbent on Buyers to inform Sellers whether or not the vessel is accepted within 48 hours after completion of inspection. Thereafter the sale becomes definite, if Buyers have accepted the vessel, subject of course to other conditions of the contract.

Incidentally, there is no debate about the inspection, the Buyer does not have to give his reasons for turning the ship down, he can just walk away from the deal at this stage, and reclaim his deposit; thus there is a risk of a sale collapsing after all the negotiations have been completed. *The '93 form takes note of the growing tendency for negotiations only proceeding once the inspections have taken place and thus provides for this situation in option (a). It even allows for careless preparation of the form by stating that option (a) applies if the Broker forgets to delete option (b).*

Clause 5, Place and Time of delivery. Sellers and Buyers in the *"Georgina"* case having agreed that delivery shall take place at Antwerp within August 2005, it is incumbent on Sellers to keep Buyers posted about the vessel's itinerary and estimated time of dry-docking. The ship will remain Seller's property until paid for and delivery usually takes place immediately after the vessel has been taken out of dry-dock. Obviously, it is more convenient for all concerned in the sale and handover of the ship for delivery to be effected alongside a berth or quay but in a busy port, this may not be possible.

As previously mentioned, it is in the interests of both parties to have a cancelling date in the contract as a precaution lest the vessel, for circumstances beyond the control of Buyers and Sellers, cannot be delivered within the time agreed. Such a circumstance could occur should the vessel be declared a constructive total loss.

If delay in delivery might be occasioned by repairs not anticipated when the vessel entered dry-dock or any other reason for which Sellers were not responsible then the cancelling and delivery date could be re-negotiated, in which case an addendum to the Memorandum of Agreement would be drawn up by the Brokers setting out the terms which had subsequently been agreed.

The Broker's task is to attend always to the interests of his Principals and it is essential that Buyers are kept fully apprised of the vessel's movements, estimated time of dry-docking and delivery.

The '93 form uses clause 5 to go into greater detail about notices and keeping Buyers informed of the vessels itinerary and includes reference to the safety of the place of delivery.

Then there is a long (some Brokers say too long) clause 5(c) which seeks to reduce the fear of the buyer simply "walking away" if the ship misses her cancelling date. There is, however, no obligation upon the buyer to agree a new cancelling date if the ship is delayed so "walking away" is still an option.

Clause 6, the Dry-docking (and diver's inspection) clause. This clause should be studied carefully in order to understand its implications. (In the past it has been a favourite subject for examiners!) The purpose of the clause is to allow inspection of all external parts of the vessel below the water- load-line. *Note that the '93 form refers to "the deepest load-line" in preference to the '87 form's reference to "summer load-line".* The inspector will be the representative of the appropriate Classification Society and he will be accompanied by the representatives of Buyers and Sellers.

Should there be any part of the vessel below the load-line found broken, damaged or defective, so as to affect the vessel's clean certificate of class, it shall be made good by Sellers to the Classification Society's satisfaction. While in dry-dock, Buyers, or the Classification Society's representative, may have the tail-end shaft drawn. Again, should it be found defective or condemned, it shall be made good at the Seller's expense to the Classification Society's satisfaction without qualification.

All expenses incurred during dry-docking shall be for Buyer's account provided no parts of the vessel below the Summer load-line are condemned or found defective as to affect the vessel's clean certificate of class. If such parts are found defective so as to affect the vessel's clean certificate of class then all expenses, including dry-dock dues and the Classification Society's fees shall be for Seller's account.

The expenses for taking the vessel to the dry-dock and from the dry-dock to the place of delivery shall be for Seller's account.

Clause 6 in the '93 form is far more detailed and students should carefully compare the way the two forms deal with this subject. Clause 6(b) covers the option of a diver's inspection in lieu of dry-docking. This is now more frequently adopted and it meant, under the '87 form, that a written clause had to be added.

Clause 7, Spares, bunkers etc. It might seem incredible, when one considers the sale itself involves millions of dollars, that this clause in the Memorandum of Agreement probably causes more controversy than any other. Basically it concerns what is included in the purchase price of the vessel and Brokers should take care when closing a deal to be as precise as possible so as to avoid misunderstandings at a later stage in the transaction.

Obviously a Buyer expects all equipment aboard the vessel at the time of inspection to be available on board at the time of delivery. If the vessel has a spare propeller and spare tail-shaft he will expect these items to be available when he takes possession of the ship and difficulties can be experienced if they are taken out of spare and used prior to delivery. Both Saleforms exonerate Sellers from replacing spare parts including spare tail-end shaft(s) and/or spare propeller(s) which are taken out of spare and used as replacement prior to delivery. It is important for Brokers to establish what navigational equipment is ship's property and what is on hire.

Spares on order are excluded from the sale in the printed wording of the Saleforms but often their inclusion is negotiated by the Buyers. Any equipment belonging to the vessel at the time of inspection that is not on board at the time of delivery, to be forwarded with forwarding charges, if any, for Buyer's account.

Sellers are always reluctant to part with items of particular interest or value, such as sponsor's gifts at the time of launching, works of art, pictures/paintings and any other articles bearing the Seller's name such as crockery, plate, cutlery, linen etc. Should any of the latter be taken ashore because of the reasons stated, Sellers are required to replace them with unmarked items. Personal belongings are obviously excluded and also personal items such as clothing which are part of the slop chest.

Remaining bunkers and unused lubricating oils must be paid for at the current market price at the port of delivery. If there happens to be a large quantity of bunkers aboard at the time of delivery and the price for bunkers at the port of delivery is expensive, Buyers may wish to limit the quantity to be paid for with the intention of taking the vessel to a port where they are cheaper. They may therefore require the wording to limit the quantity to an amount not exceeding a specified number of tonnes but any such limitation should be unambiguously agreed during negotiations.

If the quality is in doubt, a surveyor may be called in from an oil company to act as referee so that Buyers cannot refuse to pay what has been agreed under the terms of the contract by alleging that bunkers are unusable and little more than sludge.

Brokers should try to obtain in advance the approximate amount of bunkers and unused lubricating oils to be paid for and agree the cost with their respective Principals.

Payment under this clause is to be effected at the same time as the purchase money is paid and shall be in the same currency unless otherwise agreed.

Clause 8, Documentation and Clause 9, Encumbrances. A later Chapter of this course will be devoted to documentation on delivery and students will be referred back to the documentation clauses in both Saleforms.

For the time being it should be noted that as the "Georgina" is registered under the Panamanian registry and it is the responsibility of Sellers to provide for the deletion of the vessel from the Panamanian Registry and deliver the certificate to the Buyers.

The Sellers must provide, on delivery, a **Bill of Sale** stating that the vessel is free from all encumbrances and maritime liens and any other debts whatsoever. The Bill of Sale must be **notarially attested** and legalised by the Consul of the country in which the vessel will be registered by the Buyers. Such a document presented in this manner is a surety of authenticity and enables the Buyer to proceed on the oceans of the world in the knowledge that every possible action has been taken to ensure that no debt appertaining to the vessel remain uncleared.

The deposit is released in Seller's favour and the balance of the purchase money paid together with items mentioned in Clause 7 of the contract. Classification certificates, plans which are on board the vessel and other technical documentation are forwarded to Buyers while log books may remain in Seller's possession although Buyers, should they so wish, may take copies of log books.

Clause 10, Taxes etc. Taxes, fees and expenses incurred in registering the vessel under Buyer's flag must, of course, be for Buyer's account while any such expenses incurred by Sellers in closing the vessel from her Panamanian registry must be for Seller's account.

Clause 11, Condition on Delivery. Condition of the vessel at the time of delivery can sometimes cause problems for the reasons already mentioned in this Chapter. It is difficult to prove beyond reasonable doubt that the Buyer's surveyor conducted an exhaustive survey when he surveyed the ship. He may well have missed certain items and a dispute may then arise as to whether a particular matter was present at the time of inspection. The words "fair wear and tear excepted" do, therefore, lend themselves to dispute. ("Fair wear" may be relatively simple to envisage but what about "fair tear"?)

It is important to remember that the Seller is under no obligation to point out items which are not in a perfect state of repair except, of course, damage or defects which affect class. Ship sales are essentially governed by the principle of **caveat emptor** which is the legal phrase which means "let the buyer beware"

Thus the efficiency of the original inspection and the burden of proving any serious differences between condition at time of inspection and condition on delivery fall upon the Buyer

Under the '87 Saleform, when a sale is definite and the ship has been accepted after inspection, the Sellers must notify the Classification Society of **any matter coming to their knowledge**, prior to delivery, which might lead to the withdrawal of her class or to a class recommendation. In other words, the Sellers have an obligation to maintain the vessel in the manner of a reasonably prudent Owner between the time of inspection and delivery. *The '93 form goes further in that it stipulates that the vessel must be "free of average damage affecting class" whether or not the Seller knew about it and reported it to the Classification Society. The term "inspection" is defined in this clause in the '93 form. The different wording of clause 11 in the '93 Saleform is considered by many to be the most significant difference between it and the earlier version.*

Clause 12, Name/markings. On delivery Buyers must change the name of the vessel and also any funnel markings, a fairly obvious obligation.

Clauses 13 and 14, Default by Buyers and/or Sellers. Compensation must be paid to Sellers in the event of a default by Buyers and vice versa. Losses for such defaults can be heavy and compensation must be paid together with interest which, in the '87 form, is stipulated at a rate of 12% per annum but this is often deleted during negotiations, especially at times of worldwide low interest rates *(the '93 form simply states "with interest" without specifying a rate)*. Brokers play an important part in avoiding disputes but however much care may be taken, defaults occur which prove expensive and time consuming for all involved in the transaction. Obviously, the rate of interest will vary according to current rates at the time of the transaction.

The wording under Seller's Default in the '93 form is far more comprehensive including the procedure if the ship should become 'unready' between time of giving notice and Buyers taking delivery.

Clause 15 Buyers representatives. *This clause which is so often the subject of a written clause in the '87 version is self explanatory*,

Clause 15 (Saleform'87) 16 (Saleform'93) Arbitration Brokers must always be on the alert in trying to avoid arbitration or litigation, both of which are unproductive in time and expense. Nevertheless it is necessary in every contract to make provision for any such possibility and Clause 15 of Saleform'87 covers Arbitration in a general way. Because of an ancient maritime tradition, the City of London is widely accepted as a place of arbitration and in accordance with English law. If the parties to the contract cannot agree on a single Arbitrator, three shall be appointed, one by each party to the dispute and the third by the London Maritime Arbitrators' Association. In the Clause, there is provision lest one party to the dispute fails to appoint an Arbitrator or if an Arbitrator, having been appointed, is unable by refusal or other reason to act in the matter. The contract is subject to the law of the country agreed to as a place of arbitration and the award rendered by the Arbitration Court is binding on the parties to the dispute.

The '93 form goes into more detail giving three options, 16(a) sets out the procedure for London arbitration, 16(b) covers the New York arbitration system while 16(c) is available if the parties want arbitration other than in London or New York.

As mentioned previously, it is rare for a printed form to cover all eventualities and the addition of written clauses tends to be the rule rather than the exception.

In the case of the *"Georgina"* sale, item 9 in the telex of confirmation (recap) is extra to the provisions of Saleform'87 and therefore an extra clause is required to the contract. The meaning of this clause (which would be numbered **Clause 16** basis '87 form) can be summarised as follows:

i) Nothing relating to surveys should be overdue. All surveys have a date and therefore all must be up to date at the time of delivery.

ii) Class surveys may have recommendations, outstandings or subject items of class. This means that the classification surveyor has seen something which must be dealt with by a certain date. If this recommendation is noted even though it may not be due until after delivery of the vessel is must be settled at the time of delivery. It may, of course, suit both Buyer and Seller to agree a sum of money in lieu and for the work to be deferred for the Buyer to carry out nearer the specified date.

iii) There are also appendix items which are not given a definite date. Buyers cannot claim an appendix item from Sellers as these do not affect clean class whereas outstandings do affect them.

iv) Claims on insurance must be cleared. Average means anything which is to be claimed against Underwriters. When the ship is sold the new Owner cannot claim on the Underwriter of the old Owner therefore average items must be cleared before the ship is delivered.

Clause 17. In the recap telex it was agreed that Buyers could place two men aboard the vessel with the usual indemnities after the contract signed and deposit has been lodged in accordance with Clause 2 of the Memorandum of Agreement. *A written clause covering this point would not be needed if the '93 had been used as this is covered in Clause 15*

There are conflicting interests in this matter. Sellers are usually reluctant to allow Buyer's crew aboard the vessel before payment in full has been effected. The reasons for reluctance by the Sellers might include the possibility of pilferage, accidental or wanton damage even interference in the running of the ship. More particularly if the '87 form is used, the representatives may spend their time nosing around and bring to the Seller's attention any defects they find which may have been missed at the time of inspection which places the Sellers in the "now you know" position.

From the Buyers point of view, having agreed to purchase the vessel with everything included in accordance with Clause 7 of the Memorandum of Agreement, have a natural desire to ensure as far as is reasonably possible that minor items are not taken ashore by Seller's crew which may be ship's property. A compromise is a reasonable solution to this problem and two men placed aboard as representatives usually suffices. Their presence must be at Buyer's risk and expense and it is understood that they will not interfere with the running or performance of the ship while she remains Sellers' property. Sometimes, Buyers may wish an Engineer to sail with the vessel during her final voyage to the delivery port but this can only be effected with the full permission and approval of the Sellers.

Clause 18. Buyers will wish to ensure that the vessel they are buying is free to trade worldwide – hence the insertion of a "no Arab boycott" clause.

The above notes, combined with those in the previous Chapter, although by no means definitive, provide a useful guide with regard to the business of buying and selling ships.

There is no easy definition as to what it takes to be a successful Sale and Purchase Broker but common sense and an ability to like people and to be liked by people, is an essential attribute for the simple reason that the end result is that there will be more Principals who will rely on his advice and expertise, the more strength to his elbow.

As has been mentioned previously in these notes, few if any ship sales are identical, each one having its own unique requirements which necessitate separate clauses and each one having its own problems and difficulties which need to be surmounted.

5.3 SIGNATURE ON CONTRACTS

Brokers may be called upon to sign contracts on behalf of their Principals in the same way as chartering Brokers sign charter parties. In both cases, the Principles are the same. The Broker must ensure that neither he nor his shipbroking company bear personal responsibility and therefore certain usages must be adhered to. The first is that the parties to the sale are named and described in the contract and are therefore clearly identifiable as Principals. Secondly, Brokers signing sale contracts must always qualify their signature in a way which makes it clear that they are in no way responsible for the execution of the contract. The normal style is therefore as follows:

For and on behalf of ....
(Here spell out the name of Sellers or Buyers, as the case may be)

.... (Name of shipbroker or firm)

signed by ....

As Brokers only

Occasionally the old fashioned wording "as brokers and non-responsible mandataries" may be used. Either way, there is no risk of the Broker being considered a party to the contract.

A further addition to the signature could be the manner in which the authority was given to the Broker by either the Seller or Buyer. This could be expressed after the signature in the following manner:

.... (signature)
As brokers only

By (here state letter, fax or other communication medium)

authority dated .... from ....

The name of whoever granted the authority would be inserted in full in the appropriate place beneath the Broker's signature.

5.4 OTHER SALE CONTRACT FORMS

As was mentioned at the beginning of this Chapter, the perfect sale contract can rarely exist for the reason of the differing interests between Sellers and Buyers. It would be impossible to present numerous sale contracts for study in this course, however **Appendix 12** is a copy of the **"Nipponsale 1999"** published by the Japan Shipping Exchange.

Students should study the Nipponsale and note where its terms differ from the Norwegian forms.

5.5 TO SUM UP

In this Chapter, Three specimen sale forms have been presented for study. The essentials of all such contracts are much the same and must be incorporated in any form of Memorandum of Agreement, viz. time and place of delivery, price, inspection of class records and ship, dry-docking, what is included in the sale and any other conditions mutually agreed.

5.6 BROKERS' COMMISSIONS

The Broker's commission is rarely inserted in a contract. A Broker is responsible for attending to his own commission and must therefore ensure that this is recorded in writing and agreed prior to the conclusion of a sale.

Ideally there should be a separate 'commission letter' signed by the Seller (who technically pays all the commissions) but this is not often done today. However there is no point in being trusting to the point of foolishness because the legitimate earning of commission is why the Broker is there, he or she – like any other labourer – is 'worthy of his hire'. The Brokers should ensure that there is ample written evidence (usually the exchange of telexes) that commission is due. Alternatively FONASBA have devised a formal commission contract which would cover the matter fully.

One may ask why does one not, therefore, include a commission clause on the M.o.A. as is often done in charter parties and the only answer is that it has never been customary to do so. So far as contracts drawn up under English law are concerned. The *Contracts (Rights of Third Parties) Act 1999* allows a Broker to sue in his own name if a brokerage clause is included in a contract between two other parties (e.g. the Owner and the Charterer). Does this mean that the custom will change and brokerage will appear in Sale contracts? Only time will tell!

5.7 SELF-ASSESSMENT AND TEST QUESTIONS

Attempt the following and check your answers from the text:

1. Who, unless otherwise agreed, pays the commission on a ship sale?
2. What is the purpose of the dry-docking clause in Saleform 87 and who pays the dry-docking expenses?
3. A working propeller and existing tail-shaft are condemned after the delivery voyage. Does the Seller of the vessel need to replace them on delivery of the vessel to a Buyer?

Having completed Chapter Five, attempt the following and submit your essay to your Tutor.

Using details of an imaginary ship, draft an opening firm offer on behalf of your Principal, the Buyer, with an explanation of each term forming the offer.

Chapter 6

DEMOLITION

6.1 INTRODUCTION

A merchant ship may stay with one Owner or change ownership several times during its life but that life is finite and at the end, there is only one sale left which is to the ship-breaker.

At one time it was reckoned that a ship's life was 20 years but this varies considerably for a variety of reasons. The state of the chartering market is, of course, a major general influence. Particular factors include the type of trade in which the ship has engaged, the care lavished on the ship by her Owners; even the policy of the owner. To these reasons must now be added the recent IMO convention (MARPOL 13G) on the phasing out of single hulled tankers

One must realise that, when a ship is sold for further trading, she could well commence to trade in direct competition with the Seller. Thus some Owners may insist on selling a ship for scrap even if she has several years of useful trading life left; in this way potential competition is eliminated. The price for scrap will be much less than a price for further trading but the Shipowner's tax accountant can often turn this to their advantage.

The scrap market is quite different from the market for further trading. Different contract conditions, a completely different type of Buyer and quite different pitfalls for the unwary Seller.

When sold for further trading, the ship will probably continue its way of life as before; only the ownership changes. A ship sold for scrap will have been run down to the barest stipulations of seaworthiness and with no concern at all for cargo-worthiness. Seaworthiness in this context means that the ship must still be in good enough condition to retain her Class otherwise, if she became a casualty on the way to the demolition yard, the insurers would not pay out.

There will be cases where a ship has been in a serious accident or has been laid up for so long that her engines no longer work and she is certainly well out of Class. In such a case she would have to be towed to the breaker's yard for which tugs will be hired. Before towage can take place, a '**Towage Certificate**' will have to be obtained from the Classification Society who will demand that the ship be made 'sea safe' which involves all openings – doors, hatches, portholes etc – to be welded shut to make them water-tight. This done, the ship will be able to obtain specific insurance cover for her last voyage.

The actual arrangements for the towage may be made by the Sellers but it is quite common for 'dead' ships to be sold 'as is, where is' leaving the Buyers to make the arrangements which are usually carried out by specialist ship-delivery companies.

This purpose of Chapter is, therefore, to emphasise the specialist skills and knowledge that an S & P Broker trading in the demolition market needs to acquire. The first necessity is to obtain a mental picture of how ship-breaking is carried out.

6.2 THE SHIP-BREAKER'S WORK PLACE

Although most countries with a seaboard carry out ship-breaking to a greater or lesser degree it is in the less developed countries where the major proportion of this industry is based.

In those countries the work is carried out very effectively but in a manner which can, at best, be described as unsophisticated although, in some cases, crude in the extreme may be a better description. Currently the most active ship-breaking areas are the Indian sub-continent, South-East Asia and the Far East.

In many instances the breaker's premises are no more than a stretch of sea-shore with a gently sloping beach. The ship arriving for breaking first anchors off this beach while the transfer of ownership takes place. On completion of these formalities, most of the Seller's crew leave the ship but a few remain because their duties are an essential part of the ultimate delivery of the ship. This ultimate delivery consists of the ship being aimed at a given marker on the shore and then driven – at considerable speed – straight at the beach. The speed is necessary to ensure the ship's hull being firmly stranded because that is where all the work on the ship takes place.

The Buyer then first removes anything which has a second-hand resale value. In addition to items from the engine room such as electric generators, a ship has several objects for which there is a ready second-hand market; visualise the yield from such places as the galley (cookhouse) and crew accommodation.

Before the serious task of demolition can begin some precautions have to be taken. Tankers, of course, have to be gas-freed and sludge removed so that work with cutting torches can be safely carried out. It is a matter for negotiation whether the Seller or the Buyer does this cleaning work. The same applies to fuel tanks on any ship and the question of remaining bunkers is another area for decision during negotiations.

Then the ship is simply taken to pieces with flame-cutters. The ship's own cranes or derricks may be retained as long as possible to handle the sections as they are cut out.

Some of the steel will go to steel-works where it is re-melted; even steel production from raw materials needs a certain amount of scrap to help the molten steel to flow. However, much of the ship's plating only has to be heated sufficiently to re-roll it for its re-use in other ways. The advantage of using scrap steel is that the massive capital investment necessary for making steel from raw materials is avoided. The particular value of steel from ships' plates is that the quality is uniform which cannot be achieved from the use of miscellaneous scrap.

It will be seen that this method of ship-breaking requires very little capital investment in sophisticated equipment and the fact that it is labour-intensive is an attraction in the countries concerned. This in itself is beginning to give cause for concern because the minimum technical skill required of the workers means that casualties are not uncommon. Furthermore the health hazards for the workers themselves and the environment in general is exciting reaction from such organisations as Greenpeace who are especially concerned about the dangers from such things as oil residues and more especially the presence of asbestos in many ships where it has been used for insulation of such items as steam pipes.

With the world becoming increasingly environment-conscious, the long-term future of current methods of ship-breaking is not easy to predict but for the immediately foreseeable future that is the main buying end of the demolition market.

6.3 THE BASIC PRINCIPLES OF A DEMOLITION CONTRACT

Before studying any contract in detail some fundamentals from the **Buyer's** viewpoint need to be considered.

It is estimated that the average ship, in scrap terms, is comprised of the following:

86% scrap steel
7% cast iron
1% non-ferrous metals (e.g. brass, copper, bronze)
6% non-metallic materials (e.g. timber, plastics)

Ships are traded in the demolition market according to their actual weight of metal and it will be recalled from Chapter One that this is referred to as the **Light Displacement** which is the weight of the hull completely equipped plus the weight of her machinery, boilers, water in the boilers and spare parts but excludes cargo, bunkers, provisions stores and other water.

Prices are quoted in US$ per light displacement ton (often shortened to "lightweight" or LDT). Care must always be taken to check whether it is the ton of 2240 pounds, or the metric tonne of 1000 kilograms. (The American "short ton" of 2000 pounds is seldom if ever used in this context). Although the LDT is the way prices are quoted, the eventual contract of sale usually quotes an agreed total (lumpsum) price as well as a price per light displacement ton.

Prudent Buyers will insist on some independent confirmation of the ship's light displacement which can be checked from the original builder's plans or a letter from the builders. The same information may also be gained from the ship's deadweight scale or trim stability booklet. Enquiries should also be made to check from the ship's records whether any modifications have been made which might affect her lightweight. Some ships have permanent ballast, the weight of which should be deducted from the lightweight when calculating price.

As with any ship sale, confirming what is included in the sale is important. For example the steel in a spare tail-shaft is of particularly good quality also one should check what material any spare propeller is made of. The spare propeller is usually of cast iron but if, like the working propeller, it is made of bronze this is a bonus because scrap bronze commands a very high price. The nature and weight of any other spares, such as an anchor, need to be checked.

6.4 SELECTING THE RIGHT BUYER.

A primary concern from the **Seller's** point of view is the identity of the Buyer. In a recent listing of ship-breakers there were over 100 names in India alone and it stands to reason that there will be a wide variety of financial stability when such a large number is involved.

At the beginning of this Chapter the point was made that a ship is allowed to run down once it has been decided to place her on the scrap market. Conversely a ship being sold for further trading is usually in a reasonably seaworthy and cargo-worthy condition. In the unlikely event of a sale for further trading collapsing at the last minute, due to default by the Buyer, the Seller can continue to trade his ship until a new sale can be arranged. True, the Seller will have incurred losses which may or may not be recompensed from the deposit or from legal action against the defaulting Buyer.

Consider, however, the plight of a Seller of a ship for scrap, perhaps anchored off a remote beach somewhere in Asia and the Buyer decides he has changed his mind. Such a Seller would be very vulnerable to having to renegotiate the sale at a much lower price. That situation was not unknown in the days before the demolition market became properly organised.

To defeat such a predicament it will be seen, when a demolition sale contract is examined, that much of the clausing is concerned with making payment of the agreed price at the agreed time as foolproof as possible.

The principle device in this context is the way that payment has to be arranged via a **Letter of Credit**. The Buyer is obliged to open a Letter of Credit in a bank convenient to the Seller. The two parties agree as to the documents which the Seller has to present to the bank at the time of delivery of the ship in order to release the money. The Letter of Credit has to be **irrevocable.** The only item over which the Seller has no control is that the cash is not released until the Seller's bank receives confirmation from the Buyer's bank that delivery has taken place although some contracts seek to overcome this problem. Unless the Letter of Credit is established and the agreed deposit made within three banking days of the signing of the contract, the Seller has the option to cancel the deal.

One hundred percent certainty is seldom achievable so that the reputation of the Buyer and the Buyer's Broker is important. Even more vital is the task of the Broker representing the Buyer to be sure of his Principal; it has already been stated that a reputation is easily damaged but difficult to repair. In a busy market, top class Buyers will tend to have little difficulty in filling their demolition berths and so have to retreat from the market for a time. Sellers will then have to look to the less well-known Buyers and so the Seller and the Seller's Broker have to ensure that the eventual contract contains no loopholes.

6.5 THE SALE CONTRACT

The **Baltic and International Maritime Council (BIMCO)** have produced a standard sale contract for demolition with the codename **"SALESCRAP 87"** a copy of this will be found in **Appendix 13** which will be studied clause by clause.

Most of the major areas where there are a large number of ship-breakers have devised their own standard form and as BIMCO is an international shipowners' association, one can expect some clauses to be more favourable to the Shipowner (the Seller). Nevertheless the SALESCRAP 87 form provides an excellent example for studying the structure of a sale form for demolition as it covers all the main features clearly and in detail.

It will be seen that, in common with many BIMCO forms, the first part is in a "box" layout containing all the facts relevant to the ship and the terms agreed, while Part II embodies the clauses which govern the contract.

Study first, page one of the contract **(Appendix 13)** where it will be seen that boxes 1 to 15 identify the parties to the contract, the name of the ship being sold and some detail about its main engine, the generators, spare propellers and spare tail shaft.

Box 18 is the all-important item, the price and the currency in which it is to be paid. The rest of the boxes on that page deal with the deposit and the basic details about the Letter of Credit with references to the clauses involved.

Page 2 of the contract **(Appendix 13)** Clauses 21-25 deal with the position of the ship and her delivery including the all-important place of delivery with expected readiness and the cancelling date. The remaining clauses cover documentation required, rates of interest in the case of default by either party, arbitration and, of course, the signatures of the parties.

Refer now to page 3 **(Appendix 13)** where the first clause allows for more details of the ship, if they are required, to be set out on the last page which also has space for listing any items <u>not</u> included in the sale in addition to those mentioned in Clause 2.5.

Note especially (Clause 2.1) that unlike sales for further trading, it is not usual for the ship to be inspected either at the time of negotiation or at time of delivery.

Again unlike sales for further trading where bunkers remaining on board tend to take on a disproportionate amount of concern, bunkers become the Buyer's property. For the Buyer they may be a useful source of fuel for the dismantling operation but they may also be something of a nuisance.

Clause 2 also covers the removal of Seller's property bearing the Seller's flag or name as in a sale for further trading. Unlike a sale for further trading, if, for example, the spare tail shaft had to be installed between signing and delivery, the condemned shaft must remain on board. It may be no further use for driving the ship but it is still a useful piece of high grade steel to the breaker.

Clause 3 simply states how the light displacement has to be verified. Note that if the proof of the lightweight differs from the originally agreed figure, the lumpsum price (Clause 3) shall be adjusted accordingly. This explains why on page 1 of the contract both the agreed lumpsum and the price per lightweight are stated in box 8.

The deposit clause (No.5) is substantially the same as such a clause in a sale for further trading.

Study Clause 6 carefully. It deals with the mechanics of the **Letter of Credit,** the all-important system of endeavouring to achieve a foolproof method of payment which seeks to be as fair to the Seller as to the Buyer.

Full details of the way a Letter of Credit (often referred to as a **Documentary Credit**) are dealt with in TutorShip's course for Shipping Business but the basics are that the Buyer gives detailed instructions to his bank as to how payment shall be made. In Letter of Credit (L/C) parlance this bank is called the **Opening Bank** and it will be seen from line 57 that this has to be a "first class bank".

The opening bank then makes contact with a bank in the Seller's country which becomes known as the **Advising Bank**. Line 59 states that this bank is to be "nominated by the Sellers" but there is usually some mutual agreement between the parties because the opening bank will prefer wherever possible to deal with its own branch office or its corresponding bank in the Seller's country.

The instructions given by the Buyers to the opening bank which will, in turn be passed to the advising bank will detail the documents which the Sellers have to present to the advising bank in order to receive payment; these are set out in Clause 13.

It will be seen that safeguards for both parties are built into this system.

a) The opening bank will not accept instructions from the Buyers unless there are adequate funds to make the payment.

b) The advising bank will not accept instructions unless satisfied that the opening bank is indeed first class.

c) The Sellers cannot collect the money until all the required documents are presented and the ship has in fact reached the Buyers.

d) The Buyers cannot withhold payment if all the requirements of the L/C have been satisfied.

Note particularly that the clause calls for a **Confirmed Irrevocable Letter of Credit**. "Confirmed" means that the advising bank undertakes (confirms) to pay the full amount when all the requirements of the L/C are satisfied *even if the advising bank has not received the funds from the opening bank.*

"Irrevocable" means just what it says, the Buyers cannot change (revoke) the L/C in any way once it has been opened except with the agreement of the Sellers.

Line 71 provides for an expiry date for the L/C which will be the subject of negotiation between the parties as the Seller will wish to ensure that if the ship is delayed and a new cancelling date is agreed, the money will still be paid. The Buyer will try to keep this date a tight as possible to reinforce the cancelling date and to ensure that the Buyer's funds are not "tied up" any longer than necessary.

Clauses 7 & 8 deal with where the ship physically is at time of signing the contract and how she intends to reach the place of delivery, and Clause 9 covers the actual delivery. Note that if the actual breaking berth (the stretch of beach in many cases) is not immediately available, delivery as near as possible shall be considered as fulfilment of the contract. Study 9.2 carefully as it goes into detail on this point even to the extent of what happens if the Buyer fails to nominate a waiting place.

The cancelling date procedure set out in Clause 10, whilst still allowing the Buyer to cancel if the ship is delayed, imposes the obligation upon the Buyer to declare that option as soon as notification of delay is given or, in the alternative, to agree a new cancelling date. This treatment of the cancelling date can be seen as being sympathetic towards the fact that a ship run down preparatory to scrapping would be in dire straits if the Buyer was able to defer cancelling until the last minute.

Clauses 11 & 12 deal with keeping the Buyers informed of the vessel's progress and with actual notice of readiness to deliver which is tendered to the Sellers and to the Buyer's bank (the Opening Bank). Take note that, in this sale form, a tanker would not be accepted as ready until she is able to present a certificate from an independent competent authority stating that her tanks are gas and sludge free so that men can safely work inside the tanks with flame-cutting gear.

The documents required to release, to the Seller, the funds held by the Advising Bank in the Letter of Credit are detailed in Clause 13. This particular saleform (Clause 13.2) ensures that the Seller can demand payment even if the Buyer's bank (Opening Bank) fails to confirm receipt of the notice of readiness.

Clause 14 endeavours to ensure that once the ship has been accepted by the Buyer, there should be no argument about the ship's condition. A clause like Number 15 would be important in a sale for further trading but it seems almost superfluous when one assumes that the first thing to be cut down will be the funnel!

The procedure regarding encumbrances, taxes, dues and charges (Clauses 16 & 17) are similar to those found in any saleform. What is worthy of note is that whilst a ship-breaker is not concerned with the ship having valid safety certificates (e.g. safety radio, safety equipment etc.) a valid Deratisation Certificate (Clause 18) is demanded. The risk of disease which rats can carry is of particular concern to people in the tropics where so much ship-breaking is carried out.

As with a sale for further trading, the Buyers wish to have the option to place their representatives on board. They will be concerned with monitoring what is removed under Clause 2.5, they will also start planning the work schedule so that no time is ever lost between delivery and commencing work.

In some cases such representatives carry out another, quite unusual, function. Sailing a ship at speed straight for the beach is a manoeuvre totally alien to the normal ship's officer's way of life and some firm encouragement at the crucial time can be very helpful.

Clause 20 is most important because there have been cases in the past when a Buyer has bought a ship ostensibly for scrap only to resell it for further trading. Mention was made earlier in this Chapter that some Owners sell for scrap as a policy to avoid creating competition. Thus a clause committing the Buyer to scrapping the ship provides some protection.

It would be very difficult and time-consuming to argue what damages the Seller has suffered through the Buyer trading rather than scrapping the ship which is why this saleform spells out the amount (liquidated damages) that the Buyer would have to pay.

Clauses 21, 22 & 23 are routine but should nonetheless be studied carefully. Clause 24 Deals with arbitration and the law to be applied with various alternatives for the parties to select the one mutually acceptable.

6.6 OTHER SALE FORMS FOR DEMOLITION

Earlier it was mentioned that the BIMCO standard form is by no means universally used and that different buying areas have their own favoured forms. The basic principles are the same, the differences tend to be only in detail.

For example, in the form used by ship breakers in **Pakistan** there is a clause reading:

> VENDOR'S CREW to leave the vessel after physical delivery with the exception of seven crew members who are to remain on board for a maximum of seven days after delivery

> to assist the Purchaser's beaching operation at Gadani Beach. However, if the Buyers require their services for any further time then all expenses, wages, victualling from then onwards will be for Buyer's account. The beaching at Gadani Beach will be at the Purchaser's sole risk and responsibility.

Most demolition contracts make provision for an alternative place for delivery should the breaker's berth be inaccessible. This is covered in Clause 9.2/9.3 in the BIMCO form. The **Taiwan** contract treats this situation in a slightly different – and slightly less easily understood – way:

> If the vessel on its arrival at the entrance to Kaoshiung Harbor should not be immediately furnished a safe berth by Buyer, the Buyer shall pay to the Seller demurrage at the rate of $—— per day or pro rata commencing 3 business days after Notice of Readiness is given to Buyer as provided in paragraph 5 herein. Should the Buyer fail to provide a safe berth for the vessel inside Kaoshiung Harbor within 3 business days after the aforesaid Notice of Readiness is given, the Seller shall have the right to deliver the vessel to Buyer at the entrance to Kaoshiung Harbor or inside Kaoshiung Harbor at Master's discretion. Buyer must make full payment of the presented demurrage invoice through Seller's agent in Kaoshiung to a bank account in Taiwan designated by the Seller's agent prior to physical delivery of the vessel.

The **Korean** demolition contract requires that the ship's maximum height shall not exceed 45 metres from sea level and one assumes that anything protruding higher than that has to be lopped off by the Sellers before arrival. The main ship breaking ports in South Korea both have draft restrictions, at Inchon it is 4.5 metres and at Ulsan 6.0 metres.

6.7 THE DEMOLITION MARKET

The extracts from other sale forms for demolition are simply given as examples. Not only will different ship breaking areas tend to favour certain forms but individual breakers may wish to include special clauses to suit their own circumstances.

The demolition market is a specialised one and in many respects quite different from the second-hand market for further trading. A major difference is that ship-breakers are demolishing ships all the time. They do not want their berths to be idle, so they will wish to arrange their purchases in such a way that as soon as one ship is completely demolished there is another ready to occupy the berth. Once a breaker has arranged purchases for a reasonable period into the future, he will temporarily drop out of the market (unless an irresistible bargain is on offer) but after a few weeks he will be back again. One could almost say that ship breakers are in the market all the time – which is seldom if ever the case for Buyers for further trading.

The prices breakers will offer will not only be affected by the freight market which influences the number of ships available for scrapping but will also react to the price the breaker can obtain locally for the scrap steel he is producing. This internal market for scrap steel can vary from area to area so that an S & P Broker specialising in the demolition market will be expected to know which breakers are paying the best prices at any one time.

As with most activities in shipbroking, sales of ships are reported in the shipping press and **Appendix 14** is a page from an old copy of the weekly magazine "Fairplay". As was mentioned early in this Chapter, the activity in the demolition market is strongly influenced by the strength of the chartering market. If rates are high, an Owner will trade his ships as long as possible but in a weak chartering market, not only is the income low but Charterers will tend to prefer more modern ships than those nearing the end of their working life. Thus the number of sales for scrap will vary as the market fluctuates.

Appendix 15 is a sale report from Lloyds List which, although not recent, raises an interesting point. Take special note of the sale of the *"FAST ALEXANDRIA"* which is referred to as a sale "as is". The main thrust of this Chapter, so far, has assumed that the Seller will deliver the ship to the Buyer's place of work. Very occasionally the task of delivering the ship to where it will be broken is undertaken by the Buyer; who may employ a delivery crew for the final voyage.

It will be seen that the price paid for "as is" is much lower than the rest of the sales. This is understandable because apart from bearing the cost of the last voyage the transfer of ownership is complicated by the fact that the Buyer has to "trade" the ship for that last voyage and so has to register it, insure it and become in every way the same as a trading Owner for just that last trip.

Alternatively the Buyer can arrange, as in the case of the **"EGE K"**, for the ship to be towed to her final destination but this is a costly business and, as mentioned in the introduction to this Chapter, has its own complications. In the report in question the actual price paid was not reported but again it would have been much lower than for ships delivered to the breaker's berth.

6.8 SELF-ASSESSMENT AND TEST QUESTIONS

Attempt the following and check your answers from the text.

1. What is the light displacement of a vessel and how is it expressed?
2. What comprises the scrap content of a vessel?
3. The purchase price of a vessel sold for demolition is expressed in the Memorandum of Agreement by a lump sum. On what basis is this calculated?
4. What does the expression "confirmed irrevocable" mean in connection with a Letter of Credit?
5. Why does a sale contract for demolition usually include both a lump sum price and a price per light displacement ton?
6. Which of a ship's normal safety certificates is the only one that ship-breakers normally insist upon?
7. To whom was the *"Mentese"* sold and for what price?
8. What type of ship was the *"Rastina"* and where are the Sellers domiciled?
9. BP-Amoco sold one of their tankers, what was its name and who bought it?

Having completed Chapter Six, attempt the following and submit your essay to your Tutor:

Assume you are the Broker for a ship breaker for whom you have received an indication of a ship which the Owner wishes to sell for scrap. The ship in question is a motor tanker of 7,500 tonnes light displacement which has a bronze working propeller and a spare cast iron propeller. The ship is able to proceed to your Principal's demolition yard under her own power.

Compose a firm offer, giving a brief explanation for each of the terms of the offer.

Chapter 7

FINANCE, NEWBUILDINGS AND INSURANCE

7.1 INTRODUCTION

The purchase of a ship is a major capital transaction and although it is quite rare for S & P Brokers to become directly involved in arranging the finance, it is important to understand how their principals arrange the necessary finance.

In essence the Buyer either uses his own money or uses someone else's – or a mixture of the two. To express that in more formal terms, a ship is purchased either from the Buyer's own resources or the Buyer seeks a source of external finance.

7.2 FUNDING THE PURCHASE FROM OWN RESOURCES

It is rare for a ship of any reasonable size to be bought entirely from the Buyer's own resources. Some **ship breakers** may be the exception because once they have become established, their sale of the scrap metal can generate the **cash flow** necessary to purchase the next ship for breaking and so on.

Another exception would be where the Buyer has sold a sufficient number of older ships in his fleet or other assets to provide enough cash for the new acquisition.

One may argue that a big corporation would have no difficulty in buying ships from its **own resources** but this would seldom be strictly true. Students will recall from *Introduction to Shipping* that a commercial company needs **capital** in order to operate. In the case of a limited liability company this capital would come from the sale of **shares** in the company. Thus, when a limited company uses its own funds to purchase a ship, it is actually using its shareholder's money.

There may be cases where a company will arrange for additional shares to be created and placed on the stock market in order to increase the company's capital base to enable the fleet to be expanded.

However, for all practical purposes, a company using its capital raised from shares is better looked upon as using its own financial resources because even for major companies this source of funding is often the exception than the rule.

7.3 BORROWED MONEY

The fact is, the majority of ships, whether newly built or second hand, are purchased with loans specifically arranged for that purpose. The provision of those funds is a specialised sector of the financial market.

The principle providers of loans for ship purchases are, of course the **commercial banks** – those which do day-to-day business with the general public. Such banks often have specific departments for maritime business.

Other types of bank providing ship finance are **merchant banks** which do not carry out ordinary banking but concentrate entirely on providing funds for business enterprises. Slightly different but only in detail are the **finance houses** which tend to specialise in providing money for purchasing goods ranging from a hire-purchase agreement for buying a car to more major items such as ships. There are some such lenders which deal exclusively in ship financing.

Whichever source is used, the procedure is similar. The first thing the lender will do is to check the borrower's financial status. There are many and varied ways of doing this, all quite legitimate. They include such things as studying the borrower's published accounts, consulting with experts on the stock market, checking with credit reference agencies and generally listening to informed market information. Specifically the lender will want to see the borrower's **cash flow forecast** sometimes referred to as a **business plan.** This will go into general detail about the borrower's working, earnings from other sources and financial commitments then, particularly, it will look at the anticipated earnings of the ship in question over the period of the loan.

The lender, as will be explained later, will also demand some form of **collateral** (security for payment) as protection should the loan not be repaid but the principle comfort the lender seeks is the reassurance of the borrower's ability to repay the loan. The lender will usually also require that a percentage of the purchase price will be paid from the borrower's own resources.

In some cases especially when the future market prospects do not engender optimism, the granting of a loan may be conditional upon a long-term charter being arranged which makes for complex negotiations. The loan is offered subject to the charter, while the charter has to be negotiated subject to concluding the purchase of the ship and the S & P negotiations have to be subject to the charter and subject to the loan. In extreme cases the lender may demand a proportion of the freight being directly assigned so that loan repayments are more certain. Arrangements like these were rife around the middle of the twentieth century often with unhappy results because the market weakened severely and the Owners were left with inadequate cash flow to operate efficiently.

At the other end of the scale when banks have a surplus of funds and are, therefore, anxious to make loans, lenders will be sympathetic to the borrowers' problems in the early stages of operating a newly acquired ship, and may grant a "period of grace" which can mean, for example, no repayments having to be made during the first year.

The security for the loan is almost always a **mortgage** on the ship being purchased although the lender may require mortgage(s) on other unencumbered units in the borrower's fleet. A mortgage is a legal document the full title of which is the **mortgage deed** which serves two purposes. The first is the borrower's undertaking to repay the capital sum and agreed interest, the second gives the lender the right to take possession of the ship if the borrower fails to comply with this undertaking. Usually the actual **loan agreement** is a separate document which details the amount of each repayment **instalment**, the frequency of repayments and the way in which the **interest** on the loan is to be calculated. Some loans are agreed with a fixed rate of interest but most lenders endeavour to arrange for the interest to move with the market. This can be done because there are several officially published lending rates such as the **LIBOR** which is the London Inter-Bank Offered Rate. The agreement could, therefore, stipulate that the rate of interest on the sum outstanding shall be "2% over LIBOR".

In other countries, loan agreements arranged with a variable rate of interest may use different bases for establishing the rate. Almost all industrialised nations have a Central Bank which publishes changes in that country's official base interest rate.

It is important to have the terminology of mortgages clear in one's mind. The borrower *gives* the mortgage and is called the **mortgagor** and thus the lender is the **mortgagee** being the one who *receives* the mortgage. The act by the lender in taking possession of the ship in the case of the borrower "going under" is referred to a **foreclosing**.

Interest is not the only cost incurred by the borrower because the lender will require a **commitment fee** which is a single payment and is intended to cover all the preparatory work the lender has to carry leading up to granting the loan and preparing the documents. Then there is a **management fee** which is an annual charge intended to cover the lender's work supervising the loan throughout its life. This fee would be particularly important if the amount of the loan is so large that no single lender is happy about covering the whole amount. In such a case one lender will lead a **syndicate** of a group of lenders. The leader will have additional work keeping the other members informed (and happy!).

One can easily see that much skill is needed on both sides in order to get the best out of a ship loan agreement. The borrower must obviously make a convincing case as to the ability to repay the loan in order to persuade the lender. Compiling a realistic forecast is just as important for the borrower' own purposes because there is no point in borrowing money to buy a ship if the income will be insufficient to provide enough gross profit to run the ship, fulfil the loan obligations and still leave a net amount to make the venture worthwhile.

The lender must also be shrewd because a fixed interest rate at a foolishly low level could prove costly. Even more dangerous would be an unquestioning acceptance of the borrower's cash flow forecast. Gullibility at that stage could, within a few years, leave the lender with no other recourse but to foreclose on the mortgage. Having this right is vital to prevent total disaster for the lender but banks are in business to "sell money" not to operate ships.

The pitfalls for both borrower and lender are manifold. Shipowners are incurable optimists and historically, when the freight markets were buoyant, the desire to commit themselves to new purchases seemed irresistible. Similarly, in the past, banks have had surpluses of funds and have been rather more willing than was wise in believing cash flow forecasts. No one can be sure that history will not repeat itself

The problems that have overtaken such over-confidence include the obvious one of a severe recession in the freight market. Even a modest down-turn in freights, if accompanied by a world-wide increase in interest rates, could mean the owner's cash flow no longer being viable. A third difficulty can arise when there is a severe distortion in exchange rates where the loan has to be repaid in one currency with income being generated in another which undergoes devaluation.

It has been argued that the considerable increase in the number of independent ship-management companies during the penultimate decade of the twentieth century was due to so many ships being **repossessed** by banks. Apparently banks had been over-enthusiastic in their lending only to be faced with borrowers unable to repay. The S & P market was then in such a depressed state that the value of the repossessed ships was well below the sums outstanding at the time the mortgages were foreclosed; such a situation was responsible for many people learning the meaning of the expression "**negative equity**" (the value of the asset being less than the loan outstanding). Some banks, therefore, decided to trade the ships until the market improved, using ship managers to provide the commercial and operational expertise, this being a better option than selling the repossessed ships at an enormous loss.

In all cases, lenders are naturally reluctant to foreclose and will far rather look into **rescheduling** the loan agreement if that offers a serious hope of the rescuing the situation. Usually this simply means spreading the loan over a longer period so that the repayment instalments are lower.

A mortgage is not the only security that lenders will require because the right to foreclose is worthless if the ship becomes a serious casualty. Thus the lender will demand that every risk, which could diminish the value of the ship, is covered by **insurance** and that the insurance policies name the lender as the beneficiary. Such policies include, hull and machinery, war risk, loss of freight/hire and cover with a Protection and Indemnity Association (P & I Club) to cover claims from third parties. The lender will take care to check that the Owner renews these insurances at the due dates and that the value declared in the policies keeps pace with any increased value that a market upswing might bring about.

7.4 INCENTIVES TO BORROWERS AND LENDERS

7.4.1 Shipbuilding

Has been a staple heavy industry in many countries. During the first half of the twentieth century, the United Kingdom was among the world leaders in shipbuilding but only a few British shipyards now remain. As industrialisation has developed throughout the world, those countries with a lower cost of living have so successfully competed in ship building that countries such as South Korea now probably produce more newbuilding tonnage than any European country achieved at its best time.

As the forces of competition began to move against a 'traditional' shipbuilding country there was a tendency for its government to try to find ways of subsidising shipbuilding. The simple economic factor being that subsidising the wages of shipbuilding workers costs the government less (both in terms of money and votes) than having a vast army of unemployed. Furthermore, there is the added advantage of having ships to sell to the benefit of a healthy trade balance.

Different schemes have been tried, the simplest being state ownership of shipbuilding with selling prices being dictated by what the market will bear with no thought to the actual cost of production.

More subtle means to attract foreign buyers when interest rates were high was the provision of "soft" loans. At one time these were offered through the shipbuilders themselves which received recompense directly or indirectly from the country's central bank. Competition in this area became so intense that in the 1960s it was possible to obtain 100% finance with about 80% of this at interest rates which bore no resemblance to the money market at the time; such schemes often included a lengthy grace period before the first repayment fell due.

Some regulation was brought to bear through the efforts of the **Organisation for Economic Cooperation and Development (OECD)** which succeeded in getting a degree of international agreement as to the maximum proportion of the purchase price to be lent (80% at that time) with a maximum period (8½ years) and a minimum rate of interest (8%).

With the competition and anti-dumping laws within the European Union, more stringent safeguards against unfair subsidisation have been introduced.

To encourage **shipowning** there have been various schemes at a less frenetic level. These have usually been achieved through tax incentives the simplest of these has been the **tonnage tax** which was introduced in Greece (1990), The Netherlands (January 1996), Norway (July 1996), Germany (January 1999). The United Kingdom committed itself to such a tax in its 1999 budget and the system is now operative; tonnage tax is under active consideration in other European countries. In essence this system allows Shipowners based in the countries concerned to enjoy a lower and more clearly forecastable amount of tax than other sectors of industry. The UK tonnage tax scheme differs from many others in that an Owner declaring for this form of taxation also has to undertake to train a minimum number of seafarers each year.

Many other schemes have been tried in the past, for example Germany and Norway particularly targeted self-employed professional individuals by agreeing to a very much lower taxation upon funds invested in ships under the national flag. Known as "K/S" schemes it has resulted in many ships in those countries being owned by groups of doctors and dentists. These schemes were withdrawn in 1998 but they had resulted in a dramatic growth in the ownership of small to medium size vessels in Germany during the 1980s and early 1990s.

There are also incentives to lenders whose main worry is the borrower becoming unable (or deciding to be unwilling) to continue repaying the loan. This worry would be more intense should the S & P market be in a depressed state so that repossessing the ship would fail to yield enough to cover the outstanding debt.

In the case of inability to pay it is fairly certain that the shortage of cash would have resulted in the maintenance of the ship being neglected which would further reduce its resale value.

More serious still would be the case where the borrower's country is unstable politically and a sudden possibly violent change in government could make repayment of the loan impossible; the deposed government might even have been the Owner of the ship. In such a case, not only is the loan not going to be repaid but repossessing the ship is impossible.

Fortunately it is possible for lenders to insure against such an eventuality and those offering such cover are often government agencies or are private insurers underwritten by the government. In the United Kingdom, this is a function of the Export Credits Guarantee Department.

Many such incentive schemes have passed into history as a result of the general lowering of interest rates in most developed countries but the world of finance tends to work in unpredictable cycles and the future could well see a resurgence of incentives or subsidies.

7.4.2 Leasing

Although leasing is not much in demand by entrepreneurial Shipowners who always like to have an asset to sell if the market makes that an attractive option. Some corporate Shipowners, however, including even major container operators, prefer not to raise the capital at all and leave this to a finance house. There are tax advantages to be gained by the financiers, details of which are beyond the scope of this course. The advantage to the operator is that vast amounts of capital do not have to be raised and serviced and the fleet is paid for out of revenue. This system requires a bareboat charter to be drawn up and under such charters the name and even the flag of the ship may be changed so that an operator is not bound to lease from a financier in his own country.

Such transactions are almost invariably in the newbuilding market and the S & P Brokers who become involved in them tend to be specialists. The principal terms of a bareboat charter tend to follow the impression given by its name; the Owner (financier) simply provides the ship; the Charterer (operator) provides everything else including the crew and behaves in every way as if it is the actual Owner. The agreement would contain clauses to protect the Owner, such as making certain that all insurances are kept up to date and at adequate levels.

What happens at the end of the contract period varies and in some cases the ship becomes the property of the Charterer on paying a final amount so that one occasionally hears reference to "lease purchase" which involves a contract with remarkable similarities to a domestic hire-purchase agreement.

7.4.3 Other Methods of Finance

Less traditional ways of raising finance but becoming increasingly popular need a knowledge of high finance which is beyond the scope of this course but students should be aware of their existence, they include:

Bond issues, often favoured by shipyards usually secured against the yard's receivables and paying quite a high percentage above LIBOR

Securitisation which is the use of a stream of income and/or a portfolio of assets to back the issue of securities.

Mezzanine Finance, which is usually provided by specialist ship finance houses and is defined as "unsecured, higher yielding loans that are subordinate to bank and secured loans but rank above equity"

7.5 NEWBUILDINGS

The contract for the purchase of a new ship is quite different from that which has been discussed in earlier Chapters which dealt with second hand ships. One particular difference is that with a second hand purchase there is a significant element of *caveat emptor* – let the Buyer beware. With a new sale there are far fewer imponderables because integral parts of a newbuilding sale contract are the detailed plans and specifications.

Another clear difference is concerned with the payment. When a second-hand sale is involved the actual payment is quite straightforward, a deposit (usually ten percent) is placed in a joint account at the time of signing the contract. Upon delivery the deposit is released and the remaining 90% plus agreed amounts for bunkers etc. is paid over. With new ships being purchased from the builder the payment schedule is quite different as will be seen later in this Chapter.

7.5.1 The Sale Contract

The first part of the contract, as with any agreement, identifies the parties being the builder and the Buyer. It then identifies what is being purchased which is in fairly brief terms because later in the contract it stipulates that plans and specifications have to be mutually agreed and signed.

The ship has no name at this stage and so is identified by a **builder's hull number**. This section then usually goes on to set out the basic dimensions, the main machinery, the speed and the fuel consumption. Then there is a clause stipulating which Classification Society's rules will be followed in the construction and it is also customary to mention at this stage under which flag the ship will be registered on completion.

Then comes the all-important clause covering the price to be paid, the currency in which payment is to be made and here is where the greatest difference arises between second hand sales and new sales, the contract lists the **instalments** which have to be paid and when they become due.

Whilst this is a matter for negotiation a typical pattern would be a deposit on **signing the contract** of sale, a second payment when building starts – when the **keel is laid** is the term usually used. Then a third payment when the ship is **launched**, remember there is still a lot of work to do fitting the ship out after launching. The final instalment is made upon **delivery.**

This is by no means the end of clauses dealing with payment. With a ship being specially built to the buyer's specifications, it would hardly make sense to have a simple cancelling clause as there is with a second hand sale. Instead it is usual to agree a delivery date and then to have a **penalty clause** which details price reductions if delivery is later than this date. This is normally on a per-day basis and it is quite usual to have a table whereby the daily rate increases as the delay goes on.

Lawyers refer to such a scheme as "liquidated damages" in the same way as one has demurrage in a charter party. The scheme takes the similarity to charters further as there can be a clause stipulating price increases if the ship is delivered earlier than the proposed delivery date.

No matter how skilled the naval architects and ship designers might be, unless the ship is a standard design – identical to others – the eventual **performance,** the ship's speed and fuel consumption, can only be estimates. For this reason it is usual to have clauses covering **penalties** if the performance is poorer than stated in the contract and additional payments if the performance is better. Such clauses deal with speed differences in tenths of a knot and fuel consumption in percentage points.

Even the **deadweight** – the crucial earning capacity of the ship – can vary from the agreed specification and so a table of penalties and bonuses is normally agreed to cover any variations.

The tables of penalties have to have a cut-off point and it is usual for the Buyer to have the **option to cancel** the contract if delivery is delayed by more than six months or if other specifications are widely awry. The clause covering this option can be complex because the builder clearly does not want to be left with a ship designed especially for a particular Buyer which may have characteristics that no other Buyer wants.

It will be recalled that there tends to be reluctance on the part of Sellers to allow Buyer's representatives on board prior to the delivery of a second hand ship but with newbuildings, it is the rule rather than the exception for a **Buyer's representative** to be present in the builder's yard from the moment building starts until final delivery. The yard has to provide this person with suitable office space for the representative plus an assistant and the representative usually has written authority from the Buyer to agree any adjustments and/or modifications, including any price changes these may cause. The representative ideally is a senior member of the Buyer's technical staff but occasionally an independent marine surveyor will be employed for this particular task.

There are, of course, clauses dealing with **modifications** which may be agreed during construction. These can be modifications in the construction specification; the Buyer may have second thoughts Modifications suggested or requested by the builders; certain items of equipment may no longer be obtainable. Modifications may be imposed by changes in the Classification Society's rules. There may also be modifications in the terms of the contract such as a revised delivery date. All such modifications have to be mutually agreed and an addendum to the contract duly signed.

Extensive clauses may be involved in setting out the manner of the sea trials and eventual delivery. There is rather more to such a handover process than the equivalent to a half-hour test drive of an automobile. Such clauses set out the process of the trials as well as listing the documents which must be handed over at time of delivery. One of these documents is, of course the **warranty** because, unlike the finality of taking over a second hand ship, the Buyer of a new ship has to be protected against faults which do not become apparent until the ship has been in service. This one-year warranty is surprisingly similar to that which one receives when buying a new automobile with one particular difference; it is quite usual for the builders to provide a "**Guarantee Engineer**" to serve with the ship for an agreed period; his function is to assist the officers and crew in operating their new acquisition and to liaise with the builders about any suspected faults .

7.6 INSURANCE

The large sums involved in sale and purchase deals demand utmost vigilance about insurance. Whilst the S & P Broker is unlikely to be directly involved in the Principal's insurance it is important, from the point of view of understanding the Principal's problems and even the possibility of feeling the need to offer a discreet reminder, that a knowledge of the insurance involved in the purchase of a ship work is essential for the S & P broker

First of all the Buyer of a second hand ship has to make arrangements well in advance of delivery so that, at the precise moment when the ship becomes the Buyer's property, the insurance cover comes into effect. The basic cover is for **hull and machinery** which, as the name implies, covers risks to the ship itself. In addition, a wise Buyer will have business lined up as soon as possible after taking delivery and so will need also to have cover for **freight** (the policy would also include hire if the ship is going on time charter).

Students will know from their *Introduction to Shipping* and *Shipping Business* studies, that this form of insurance will be placed, through an insurance broker, either with **Lloyds** or with an Insurance Company specialising in marine insurance.

The Buyer will also need **third party** insurance, which is usually covered through a **Protection and Indemnity Association** more colloquially known as a **P & I Club**. Such associations are unlike Lloyds or Insurance companies in that they are non-profit making mutual associations run by and for their members. They cover all forms of third party risks including *inter alia* claims by merchants for loss or damage to cargo, claims by parties whose property has been damaged such as port authorities and claims for death or injury to members of the crew.

Specific to ship purchase is the **Mortgagee's Interest Insurance** which a lender may insist upon as part of the terms and conditions of the loan. This would be in addition to the normal insurance. One would have expected that the normal insurance policies, suitably claused to include the mortgagees as joint beneficiaries, would have been sufficient but there are, of course, cases where the insurers may refuse to pay the Shipowner. Payment could be refused if, for example, the Owner had failed to comply with expressed or implied warranties written in the main policy. Similarly, if the Owner failed to maintain the ship's Class the policy would be void and in such cases there would be no pay-out in the event of a total loss leaving the lender with no payments from the Owner and no ship upon which to foreclose. The Owner takes out the policy and pays the premium because the level of premium will be assessed by the underwriters on the Owner's (not the lender's) reputation. The policy is, however, drawn up with the lender as the beneficiary and is held by them as security.

Where a newbuilding is involved it is usual for there to be a **Building Risk Insurance Policy**. In this case the builder takes out the insurance and pays the premium (as it is their record upon which the premium will be based) but the Buyers will be shown as the beneficiary with the finance house lending the money wanting their name included also. Such a policy covers loss or damage to the ship during its period of construction, fitting out and sea trials and covers the Buyer for the loss of progress payments (instalments) already made to the builder as well as consequential losses such as loss of earnings, and extra costs arranging for the building of a replacement ship.

There is also a special policy available to Owners to cover a ship on its final voyage to the breaker's yard called a **Breaking-up Conditions Policy.** Such a policy recognises that the ship is in a run-down state although still in Class to sail under her own power. It covers any repairs to, say, the main engine in order to ensure that the ship does reach its final destination.

7.7 INSURANCE FOR THE S & P BROKER

No matter how painstaking a Broker may be, accidents can happen it is, therefore, prudent for a Broker to seek insurance cover. As has been mentioned several times in this Chapter, the sums involved in S & P are often enormous and it follows that quite a small error could result in a hefty claim. Even a completely unjustified claim (the mis-directed arrow), once entered into the legal arena, has to be fought and fighting legal battles is a very costly business.

One can find **Errors and Omissions Insurance** from several sources although taking such cover through a **P & I Club** specialising in Brokers' problems can bring greater benefits including friendly advice such as a suitable course of action to avoid a claim arising. Such a club, as well as providing legal defence against claims and eventual payment if negligence is proved also offers a service to assist in extracting legally due commissions from reluctant Principals.

7.8 SELF-ASSESSMENT AND TEST QUESTIONS

Attempt the following and check your answers from the text:

1. What is meant by the acronym "LIBOR"?
2. Define the following:
   a) Mortgagor
   b) Mortgagee
   c) Commitment Fee
   d) Management Fee
   e) Negative Equity
3. What are the main methods of raising the capital to purchase a ship?
4. What are the advantages to leasing rather than buying outright?
5. What type of operator is unlikely to prefer leasing and why?
6. What is the purpose of "tonnage tax" to a government?
7. What is the most significant difference between a sale of a second hand ship and a newbuilding?
8. What happens if the performance of the ship is not exactly as set out in the contract?
9. At what stages do the instalments of the purchase price have to be paid?
10. How long is the usual warranty period for a new ship?

Having completed Chapter Seven, attempt the following and submit your essay to your Tutor:

1. Discuss the different ways a Buyer can finance the acquisition of a ship and explain the documentation which may be involved.
2. Analyse the risks Buyers and Sellers face around the time of a sale taking place and the types of insurance necessary.

Chapter 8

LEGAL ASPECTS OF SHIP SALE AND PURCHASE

8.1 INTRODUCTION

This Chapter deals with the law from two points of view. First, the legal framework within which S & P negotiations take place and secondly, a brief consideration of the types of disputes that may arise and the methods used for their resolution.

A general approach to the law will be covered by readers in their reading of the *Legal Principles in Shipping Business*; this Chapter concentrates on S & P matters.

8.2 THE SHIP SALE AND PURCHASE BROKER

Broker, in this context, is another name for **Agent** and all the law relating to agency apply. In particular, the S & P Broker when involved in negotiations may only make offers on the Principal's behalf, strictly in accordance with the authority received from the Principal. Unlike port agents and liner agents who often have to act on the basis of **implied authority**, the S & P Broker almost invariably acts on **express authority**.

S & P Brokers and their Principals have the right to assume that, when receiving a firm offer, the Broker making it has authority to do so – that is **warrants** that he/she has that authority. If, deliberately or accidentally, the offer being passed is not exactly in accordance with the Principal's authority then the Broker is in **breach of warranty of authority**. In the situation described the breach would be considered as "with negligence" and any financial loss suffered by either or both the Principals would result in a claim for damages being made against the Broker who made the incorrect offer and there would be little chance of any defence against such a claim.

There are rare occasions when more than two Brokers are involved and if an error is made by the Broker for the Principal to the intermediate Broker it is still the latter against whom the claim will be made. This is described as **breach of warranty *without* negligence**. This may seem unfair to the defendant Broker who, after all, passed the offer forward in good faith but the law says that the injured Principal was certainly blameless and should proceed against the Broker with whom there is direct contact; the injured Principal has no contact with the errant Broker. It is up to the defendant Broker to proceed against the negligent Broker in due course, regardless of the success or failure of the outcome.

Another area where a Broker can be in trouble is in the **failure of duty of care**. For example, in his or her enthusiasm to bring about a successful sale, a Broker may give an over-optimistic opinion of the financial integrity of one of the Principals. If, later on, this is proved to be false and financial loss is suffered by the other Principal, there would be a case against the errant Broker.

A seller's Broker can be inadvertently guilty of **misrepresentation** if false information about the ship is passed on. Even innocent misrepresentation can leave the Broker open to a claim to indemnify the victim for any actual expenses unnecessarily incurred. This is why all lists of particulars circulated on the market by whatever means should include the words **"believed to be correct but not guaranteed".**

If the misrepresentation is not inadvertent (innocent misrepresentation is how lawyers describe it) and if a party is induced into concluding a contract based upon deliberately false information it goes beyond the *tort* of a failure of a duty of care and becomes **fraud**. This, as the

Americans put it, becomes "a whole new ball game". The damages that the injured party can claim are far greater and there is the added risk of criminal action also being taken.

As a passing note in the law of agency, although it is common in tanker chartering, it is very rare for there to be only one Broker involved in ship sale and purchase negotiations. Nevertheless it does happen occasionally and in such a case the situation is rather different in that the Broker is not the Agent for either Principal except for the purpose of receiving and transmitting offers. But the penalties for errors are much the same.

8.3 THE BROKER'S COMMISSION

A Broker who brings about a successful sale or purchase has a right to be paid a commission. As mentioned in earlier Chapters, this is customarily 1% of the purchase price to each of the Brokers involved although this may vary as a result of negotiation. Although it is normal for one Broker to represent the Buyer and the other to represent the Seller, it is the Principal who receives the money – the Seller – who pays both (or all, if there are more than two) Brokers involved.

In a charter party, there is usually a commission (brokerage) clause and now, even under English law, since the introduction of the *Contracts (Rights of Third Parties) Act 1999*, the Brokers have enough legal power to enable them to sue for their commission if it is not forthcoming. It would be very rare indeed, however, for a commission clause to appear in a contract of sale of a ship so that S & P Brokers may have no protection under the 1999 Act. In some countries, the many references to commission in the negotiations would be sufficient evidence of an obligation to pay the Brokers their due but there is still a hang-up under English law that the Brokers do not have "privity" to the sale contract and so cannot sue under that document. Thus it would always be wise for the Brokers, once the deposit has been paid, to write to the Seller confirming their position and the brokerage agreed as being due to them when the sale is finalised. Most jurisdictions would accept such a letter plus the supporting evidence of the negotiation messages as enough to give judgement in the Brokers' favour. The Brokers' letters may not necessarily have to be acknowledged as the law in many jurisdictions recognises "silence means assent" but of course, there has to be proof that what was sent by the Brokers was received by the Seller.

With second hand sales and sales for demolition, special care is needed in those cases where the Seller is a one-ship company; once that one ship has been sold the company can become a mere shell in a matter of minutes; in lawyers slang they have become "men of straw" or "are not worth powder and shot".

In such cases, however, the S & P Broker should be sufficiently expert to know who the Seller really is and should make appropriate arrangements – S & P commissions are too hard to come by to leave anything to chance.

There have been unpleasant cases in the newbuilding market. Because so much of the negotiations for a new ship are tied up in the technical specification, it is not unusual for the Buyers to talk directly with the builders. Such discussions can take a very long time and when the deal is finally agreed, the Broker may be left out in the cold. If such a sale was genuinely initiated through the introductions made by the Broker, a clear understanding about commission should be reached at the outset; courts will demand a great deal of proof after the event.

Another commission situation which arises more often in newbuilding contracts than with second hand or demolition sales, is when the Brokers fulfil all their tasks during negotiations culminating in the production of the appropriate saleform, which is duly signed by both Principals. Then, at a later date, usually well before building has actually commenced, the two Principals decide to cancel the contract. The Brokers feel that as they have fulfilled all they were expected to do, at some significant expense in cash as well as time, that they deserve payment. At this point the Sellers point out that commissions are payable on payments received by them for the ships but as there were no ships there will be no payment. Brokers have fought cases like this in the courts and lost.

Thus when compiling their commission letters at the completion of negotiations, Brokers would be well advised to include a clause protecting them against their Principals cancelling the contract.

8.4 THE LAW AND THE SALEFORM

If legal problems arise in a ship sale, they will almost always be between Buyer and Seller. It is, however, in the S & P Brokers' own interests first, to endeavour to ensure that the sale contract is as watertight as possible so that disputes do not occur. Secondly, if trouble does arise, the Brokers need to be ready to supply any help or advice with a view to reaching a solution. Thirdly, if the dispute becomes insoluble without recourse to arbitration or the law, the Broker will almost certainly be called as a witness and his files and any contemporaneous notes may be subpoenaed.

A note of caution here. S & P Brokers should not give up their files at the first request especially if that request is made by the lawyers representing "the other side". If in any doubt, the Broker should seek the guidance of his/hers firm's own legal adviser.

8.4.1 When Does a Binding Contract Exist?

It should be noted that the title printed at the top of the Norwegian Saleforms is **"Memorandum of Agreement"** which mean what it literally states that an agreement has already been made and this document merely sets the details down on paper. The agreement becomes binding when everything has been agreed between the parties and any "subjects" have been lifted. The messages exchanged between the Brokers and between the Brokers and their Principals provide adequate evidence of what has been agreed.

The one exception to this rule relates to the inspections referred to in Clause 4 of the Saleform. It will be recalled from an earlier Chapter that it is now rare for a sale to be agreed and an agreement signed without the inspection of the ship's records and superficial of the ship itself having taken place and approval given. The form does, however, allow for agreement to be reached with either or both of these inspections still to be undertaken and in the unlikely event of this being so, it is important to remember that the buyer can "walk away" from the deal after the inspection without giving any reason. The agreement is binding insofar as the seller is bound to provide the opportunity for buyers to inspect.

It will be recalled from Chapter 5 that the Norwegian Saleform 1987 uses the expressions "sold" and "bought" whilst the 1993 form more correctly states "agreed to sell" and "agreed to buy" as the ship is not finally sold until it physically changes hands

Even as relatively recently as 1990, a court held that the contract of sale was definite when negotiations were concluded and it was not conditional upon signatures on a formal document. Conversely, if a sale is concluded "subject details" it would be very rare, in most jurisdictions, for it to be considered a binding agreement until the details had all been agreed; the American courts have been known to rule otherwise.

8.4.2 Identifying the Parties

Normally, the **Sellers** are the Owners of the ship although, in the case of one-ship companies, the negotiations are conducted on behalf of the real Owners who sit behind the shell company registered as the Owners. From both the Buyer's and the Brokers' points of view it is vital to establish who the Seller really is and is in a position to sell the ship.

There can be an exception to this rule if the ship being sold is the subject of the sort of bareboat charter which allows the Charterer the option to buy the ship outright at the end of the term on payment of a final sum. The market could favour taking up this option and then selling the ship as soon as it becomes the Charterer's property. In such a case the negotiations may be taking place during the closing weeks of the bareboat contract. This should be clearly understood during negotiations and protective steps taken to cover any unforeseen snags.

It is equally important to identify the **Buyers** because it is not unusual, especially if the beneficial owner places each of his ships under separate companies, for the intended owning company not to be incorporated at the beginning of negotiations. It is vital to realise that any agreement finalised with a company that does not legally exist is null and void.

8.4.3 The Price and Payment

In Chapter Five it was stressed that there are certain items included in the sale but not included in the price. Agreement has to reached concerning the amount to be paid for bunkers, lubricants, stores and provisions on board at time of delivery. S & P Brokers would be well to remember that time spent achieving watertight agreement on these items during the course of negotiations will save far more time on disputes at time of delivery which are out of all proportion to the amounts involved.

The Saleform is very strict regarding the deposit which has to be paid and how soon after the date of the agreement payment must be made. Modern parlance now uses the expression "banking days" when referring to time, which is thankfully clearer than such expressions as "working days" when talking about payment. The form allows the seller to cancel the contract if the deposit is not made within the time agreed. This is not an easy way for the Buyer to get out of the contract if he has changed his mind because a contract has been made and if it collapses due to failure to provide the deposit, the Seller can claim compensation for his expenses and losses.

The terms relating to final payment are even stricter and it is important for the S & P Broker to establish just what method will be employed because the Broker is often called upon to "stage manage" the actual handover which will include, among several other items, ensuring that the payment takes place. So often the Buyer, the Seller and the place of delivery are in three separate locations so that getting bankers in line at the crucial moment needs careful planning.

8.4.4 Inspections

Superficial inspection was dealt with earlier in this Chapter, but before leaving the subject it is worthy of note that so far as inspection of Classification Society records is concerned there is no contractual relationship between the Society and the intending Buyer. This means that if there is something amiss with the records and the Buyer considers he has suffered as a result, his only recourse against the Society would be in *tort*, on the basis that the Society had failed in its duty of care. The courts are, however quite cautious as to how strictly to apply this duty of care towards a Buyer and in any case, damages under *tort* do not include pure economic loss.

The other inspection is the dry-docking clause, (clause 6 in the Saleform). Not strictly dry-docking now that qualified divers can be employed to carry out inspection below the waterline. Students should study the dry-dock clause to the point of learning it by heart because although it appears complex, it is really a masterpiece of fairness. However, its very apparent complexity makes it a favoured question by examiners.

A vital point to remember is that whilst the intended Buyer can walk away from the deal at the time of superficial inspection (clause 4) all the remedies are covered in the dry dock clause (clause 6) and there is no walking away from the deal at this stage unless there has been flagrant misrepresentation.

8.4.5 Cancelling Date

All sale contracts will include a cancelling date. It is important to bear in mind that if the ship is late, cancellation is not automatic. The cancelling date clause essentially provides the Buyer with an option to cancel. Almost invariably the "sudden death" aspect of a cancelling is modified. It would be rare indeed for a contract to allow a situation to arise where the Seller presents the ship just an hour late only to have the Buyer walk away demanding his deposit back. It is more normal for a clause to be agreed which allows for the Seller, as soon as it becomes apparent that the ship is falling behind schedule, to advise the Buyer. The Buyer then has to say whether he intends to cancel, if so, contract is cancelled there and then. If the Buyer wishes to maintain the contract parties agree a new cancelling date.

The S & P Broker (in his or her own interest) will keep careful watch on the ship's position and must be prepared to remind the Seller if the need arises. Furthermore, the S & P Broker may become involved in passing on such information and it is vital that this and any notices of readiness are transmitted meticulously. Failure in this respect could result in one or other Principal suffering financial loss and will then have a claim against the errant Broker.

8.5 SPARES, BUNKERS ETC.

Enough has probably been said about how disputes can arise in this area and Brokers can do much to ensure that the clauses covering these items are crystal clear. If the Broker needs more incentive, remember there is no commission payable on the money paid for these items so that unnecessary work in this area is totally unproductive.

8.6 MARITIME LIENS AND ENCUMBRANCES

Debts incurred by a Shipowner or claims made which have not been settled can result in the plaintiff obtaining a writ to enforce the claim. Some such claims are such that they are considered to be against the ship itself and thus remain in force even if the ship changes hands. This is referred to as a **maritime lien** and to enforce it the ship can be arrested. The new Owner cannot lift the arrest by arguing that he was not involved and so may be in the unenviable position of having to pay – perhaps a large sum – to settle the previous Owner's debt.

Under the heading of "encumbrance" the outstanding claim could be for repayments under the previous Owner's mortgage. Note that there could be more than one mortgage. A vessel can well become worth substantially more than is left to be repaid upon the original mortgage, either through the passage of time allowing much of the debt to have been repaid, or through the market being in a far more buoyant state than when the ship was bought. In such cases an Owner could take out a **second mortgage** to raise capital for another venture. There is, in fact, no limit to the number of mortgages that can be taken out on a vessel beyond the fact that the lenders will make sure that there is enough value un-mortgaged to justify another one. In the event of a foreclosure when there is more than one mortgage, the priorities are taken in the order in which they were entered into, so second mortgages may turn out to be worthless if things turn bad.

Thus, Saleforms include a clause confirming that the ship is free of any such liens or encumbrances and goes on to require that the Seller indemnifies the Buyer against any claim that may come to light.

The Seller may state that there are no outstandings in good faith because he may be unaware of the existence of a writ. The creditor is under no obligation to advise the Owner that a writ has been obtained, he may simply be waiting for the ship to arrive at a place where the arrest laws are least complex.

There is no guaranteed way of ensuring a ship really is free of any claims but in, theory at least, some checks can be made. For example, in many countries the Owner is obliged to declare to the ships registrar if there is a mortgage outstanding. Similarly in some countries the statutory accounts, which are lodged with the registrar of companies, may disclose any mortgages. Even a study of the ship's logbooks will indicate if any incident had occurred (such as damage to port property) which might be the subject of a claim. A Buyer may seek the Broker's assistance in appointing someone to check some of these details.

There is one circumstance where there is an "encumbrance" about which all parties are fully aware. This is when the Seller seeks to dispose of his ship while it is still **under charter.** This is, of course, only likely to arise if the ship is on a long term time charter or consecutive voyage contract but it is by no means an uncommon occurrence.

Unless the charter party covered such a situation in advance, the Charterer is not automatically obliged to agree to the change of ownership. The Buyer, in the Charterer's view, might be considered less reliable than the Owner with whom the charter party was originally agreed. The Buyer might wish to change the ship's flag which could cause problems for the Charterer. In fact there are several possible snags so nothing may be taken for granted.

It is vital, therefore, that the S & P Brokers ensure that someone is keeping the Charterer fully informed and that he is not finding any part of the intended outcome repugnant. Even so, the sale negotiations must be conducted "subject charterers approval" and when all the sale terms have been agreed, a **tripartite agreement** has to be signed by the Buyer, the Seller and the Charterer which will form an addendum to the charter party.

8.6.1 At Place of Delivery

Law books have more cases about disputes relating circumstances at time of delivery than any other part of the Saleform. Many of these concern arguments about the ship's condition being in a worse state than at the time of the superficial inspection. There is little the S & P Broker can do if such disputes arise as they are almost always concerned with the physical state of the ship rather than any ambiguity in the wording of the contract.

Among the areas of dispute at the time of delivery is that phrase which is included in all negotiations but is often misinterpreted. The ship is to be delivered **"free of average damage affecting class".** The key word here is "average" because the words do not refer to *any* condition which might affect class but only that type of damage which has been occasioned by a peril of the sea and can be insured against. This problem can be circumvented only if the clause is modified to read "free of average damage *or defects* affecting class".

Of course the delivery clause does place an obligation upon the seller to report any other defects '*coming to their knowledge*' which could result in class being withdrawn or a recommendation being made by the society. The Seller could not fail to be aware of any accidental ("average") damage but could be genuinely unaware of a condition brought about by fair wear and tear which could affect class. Thus if, shortly after taking delivery, the Buyer discovers the need for some repairs without which class could be in peril it would be necessary to prove that the Seller was aware of this problem but failed to report it which is not an easy thing to prove as evidence would be hard to find.

One may see that, in this vexed area of condition at time of delivery, there is another reason for Sellers to be anxious to avoid Buyer's representatives being allowed on board prior to delivery as they could spend their time rooting around looking for defects which should be reported to the classification society.

An area of dispute peculiar to sales for **demolition** is over the ship's light displacement. As was mentioned in an earlier Chapter, the light displacement of a ship is the actual weight of potential scrap for which the Buyer is paying. The saleform allows for the lumpsum and the price per light displacement tonne to be shown and there have been cases where time and money have been wasted through the Buyer (often quite correctly) challenging the light displacement.

If such a dispute arises, it could well be appropriate to blame it upon sloppy broking. Any Broker working in the demolition market is fully aware of the importance of the light displacement and if either Broker had the faintest hint that the light displacement might be other than as stated in the exchanges of offers, then a brief investigation at that time might save a great deal of time being wasted later on. Principals are always ready to blame Brokers if things do not go smoothly so that reputations as well as time may be saved by careful checking.

8.6.2 Default by Either of the Parties

If either the Buyer refuses to accept the ship, or the Seller refuse to hand it over there is certain to be either an arbitration or a court case. In either instance, the Brokers will almost certainly be involved as witnesses. In the worst situation they may be joined in the action if some negligence on their part was in any way a contributory factor. At the first hint of the Broker being involved is the moment to seek professional advice.

8.7 DISPUTE RESOLUTION

In earlier part of the text reference is made of "arbitration or court action" but most Saleforms specify arbitration as the method of dealing with disputes. In most jurisdictions the courts will refuse to hear a case if the contract has a clear arbitration clause as is found in the Norwegian Saleforms.

There are several centres of arbitration with London and New York having rival claims as to being the pre-eminent. London can claim to have been in existence longest and it will be noted that in the 1987 form, London is the automatic centre if the parties do not state otherwise. The 1993 form goes more fully into the matter having three options, London, New York or a different centre agreed by the parties.

In the case of London being chosen, it is common for the parties to specify "subject to London Maritime Arbitrators Association Terms". Brokers should have no hesitation in recommending this to their Principals because it ensures that the parties know where they stand as to procedure. Were the parties simply to state "arbitration London" it would not even guarantee that the arbitrators would be expert in S & P law.

Incidentally, unless otherwise stated, arbitration in London will be according to English law and arbitration in New York according to United States law. It is theoretically possible for arbitration in one place to be decided according to the law of another, for example arbitration in London according to Republic of South African law. It is important, if option C in the Saleform93 is used, that the legal code to be employed is clearly stated.

As it is highly probable that the Broker(s) will be involved to a greater or lesser extent in any arbitration, some knowledge of the procedure is important.

Under the Saleform 1993, as soon as one or other party has decided that arbitration is necessary, he will appoint an arbitrator and inform the other Principal who has to appoint his own arbitrator within 14 days. If this is not done, then the first party can insist on his appointed arbitrator being the sole arbitrator.

It is possible that the two arbitrators will be unable to agree; in such a case, they have to appoint a third arbitrator, referred to as an umpire.

The procedure as printed in the 1987 Saleform is rather different. It begins by saying that the dispute should be referred to a single arbitrator but if the parties cannot agree to a single arbitrator then three arbitrators are to be appointed one by each of the parties and the third to be appointed by – and here a blank space is left but a footnote makes provision for the President of the LMAA to appoint the third.

Serious and/or complex arbitrations will probably require **oral hearings** at which the parties present their respective cases and produce their evidence; witnesses may be called. including expert witnesses if appropriate. It is becoming the rule rather than the exception for solicitors and barristers (attorneys and advocates) to become involved which makes the whole procedure very expensive and time-consuming. Many feel this destroys the spirit of arbitrations but the whole world seems to be becoming more litigious so this practice is to be expected.

Arbitrations for relatively simple disputes are often settled on **documents only** which is obviously going to be cheaper and quicker. For this procedure, if agreed by the parties, the party initiating the dispute presents his case in writing with supporting evidence to both the other party and the arbitrators. The respondent then presents his submissions, with any counterclaim if appropriate. Both parties may give seven days notice of their intention to present further submission(s) after which the arbitrators consider the case and make their award.

Most other centres have their own arbitration associations, typical is the Society of Maritime Arbitrators Inc based in New York and their terms are largely similar to those of the LMAA. One notable difference is that New York arbitrations are published in the same way as the result of court hearings whilst in London, the outcome of an arbitration is considered to be confidential to the parties involved. Either way, unlike courts decisions, the decision of one arbitration cannot be cited as a precedent when hearing a subsequent case.

The original idea behind opting for arbitration rather than going to court was that the dispute should be decided by fellow practitioners in the business who would seek a commercial solution to the problem. Thus arbitration was indeed quicker and cheaper than taking the dispute to court. There are some, however, that feel that things have changed for the worse and that the greater involvement of lawyers, whose instinct inevitably is to seek a purely legal solution, has resulted in there now being little to choose between arbitration and a court hearing.

To circumvent this difficulty, there have been several innovations introduced on both sides of the Atlantic most are geared towards relatively small claims where the cost of a full arbitration could exceed the amounts involved. These schemes endeavour to bring the non-court way of dealing with disputes back to the original spirit of arbitration. They tend to be referred to under the heading of ADR – Alternative Dispute Resolution and these can include Mediation, Conciliation, Fast and Low Cost Arbitration.

Sometimes a party to a dispute can become emotional about the "injustice" of other party's behaviour but a trusted S & P Broker can often help to guide the Principal to a simpler and cheaper form of resolution of the dispute rather than rushing headlong into full arbitration or – worse still – a court action

English law recognises that the courts have more than enough to occupy them and legislators constantly seek ways to make arbitration as swift and clean as possible. Thus, under the most recent *Arbitration Act (1996)*, an appeal against an arbitration award is only possible where the arbitrator was obviously wrong, especially on a point of law or in the case of considerable general importance.

8.8 THE S & P BROKER'S ROLE WHEN PRINCIPALS ARE IN DISPUTE

As has been mentioned earlier, the Brokers involved in a transaction about which a dispute has arisen are very likely to be called as witnesses which is never a pleasant experience. Even less pleasant if there is any hint that the Broker's negligence may have been a contributory cause. It was also mentioned earlier that if in any doubt, the Broker should seek the guidance of his or her own legal advisor.

Any testimony the Broker gives will invariably involve referring to records of events at the material time. In the pre-electronic era, such records would be found in the Broker's day-book in which, hopefully, a note of every conversation would appear and there is nothing that lawyers arbitrators and judges like better than contemporaneous notes.

Today, much of the interchange between Broker and Principal and between Broker and Broker will be via a computer screen. It is vital, therefore, that all these exchanges are able to be recovered which demands a foolproof method of keeping archives and this must be part of the Broker's system in much the same way as the Broker half a century ago could produce old notebooks out of a convenient cupboard.

8.9 ETHICS AMONG S & P BROKERS?

In the days when the most advanced electronic aid was the telex machine and lists of particulars were distributed by Sellers' Brokers via the postal services, life proceeded at a more leisurely pace. At that time there was an unwritten rule among Brokers and their Principals of a "first come first served" principle; one dealt through the one who first mentioned the business to you. In this far faster electronic age where nowhere in the world is further away than the screen of one's computer, there seems no room left for such niceties. The task now is to consolidate one's reputation and rapport with one's Principal so firmly that if a distant Broker, on learning of a ship for sale from you, goes direct to your Principal, that Principal will still continue to work through you.

8.10 SELF-ASSESSMENT AND TEST QUESTIONS

Attempt the following and check your answers from the text:

1. What is the difference between express authority and implied authority?
2. How can breach of warranty of authority without negligence occur?
3. Who pays Brokers' commissions?
4. Where does the clause about S & P Brokers' commissions appear?
5. What are maritime liens and encumbrances?
6. What expression do the Saleforms use to describe days?
7. How can there be a maritime lien without the Seller knowing about it?
8. When does a binding contract exist?
9. What words should always accompany the description of a ship which is in the market to be sold?

Having completed Chapter Eight, attempt the following and submit your essay to your Tutor.

1. As the Buyer's Broker, you have successfully concluded the sale for further trading of a second hand ship and the Saleform has been signed by both parties. Draft a letter to be despatched to the Seller, securing your position as to payment of your 1% commission.
2 The Principals in your current ship sale negotiations do not want either London or New York arbitration, preferring it to take place in Ruritania. Draft a clause suitable for option C in the Saleform 1993.

Chapter 9

THE MARKETS AND THE PARTIES INVOLVED

9.1 INTRODUCTION

This Chapter will discuss the practitioners in the S & P world, their location and the national, international and geographical factors that influence this most capital intensive of all the shipbroking markets.

9.2 SHIPOWNER PERSONALITIES

In the days when a large majority of the world's broking was carried out on the floor of the Baltic Exchange in London, a senior member of one of the broking firms attended the Exchange as a visitor. He was not a Broker himself; he was an economist. His discussion revolved around his trying to relate – without much success – what was going on around him to what he had studied for his economics degree. In exasperation, a seasoned Baltic Exchange Broker told him to forget about his economics degree because, in that centre of shipbroking, a degree in psychology would be far more use.

The days of face-to-face, pocket notebook broking have long gone but in the S & P markets the influence of psychology rather than economics can still be encountered in some quarters.

Containers. In an earlier Chapter, mention was made of the "entrepreneurial Shipowner" versus the "corporate Shipowner" which is a fair division of the two basic types. Taking the **corporate** category first, the best examples are to be found among European and Japanese **container operators** in the general cargo world..

They would claim that very little psychology affects their decision-making. They argue that no decision is taken until all the economic factors have been assessed in the most scientific manner possible. Certainly, in Japan, there is a tradition of reaching decisions via a consensus in a committee; individual personalities are seldom overtly apparent. In Europe, however, the top man is usually well known and will tend to have considerable influence over the basic philosophy of the company. Nevertheless, the final decisions tend to be made by committees which do not reach conclusions until reports from economists, market researchers, naval architects and other experts have produced their reports. This description is probably epitomised by P&O/Nedlloyd but in the same league of major container operators there is the Maersk organisation, which can still be described as a family company and no doubt there is a high degree of individual decision making involved.

In the case of **major container operators** such as these, the main influence will be economies of scale and market share. This does not automatically mean ever-larger ships because three major limiting factors will influence their decision-making.

First, the physical accommodation of the ports and their approaches. Assuming that, for some trades the restriction of Panamax has been circumvented resulting in the largest ships today gaining the title of Post-Panamax, depth of water is still an obvious constraint, not only at the berths themselves but already some sea areas such as the English Channel, and the Malacca Straits are reaching the limit of their capacity in draft terms. The shore cranes also have reached the limit of their reach and extensive new equipment will be needed if ships become larger.

Secondly, these ships depend mainly upon manufactured goods to fill their containers and there is a limit to how much the producers can turn out and the consumers can absorb in any given time. There is no point in having the world's biggest container ships if one cannot generate enough cargo per voyage. In any case shippers prefer more ships rather than bigger ships in order to provide them with the sort of frequency of sailings that permits both exporter and importer to maintain the lowest possible inventory such as is the essence of the "just in time" system.

The third limiting factor to size increases is the technical one. Naval architects are of the view that ships of around 8000 teus are the largest that can be propelled with a single screw and single engine. The increase in capital cost to install two engines would demand such a huge increase in carrying capacity that the other two factors mentioned above would come into play even more forcibly.

It is interesting to note, as was mentioned in Chapter One that some transatlantic container operators are thinking smaller rather than larger but with a much higher speed. A 40 knotter can cross the Atlantic in seven days and it will be interesting to see how attractive this fast transit time will prove to the merchants. One of the principle attractions that speed offers is the fact that working capital is tied up for a shorter period but that appeal only becomes really pressing when interest rates are high.

As container operators move to ever-larger ships, so they reduce the number of ports at which they call. This is both for reasons of voyage economy and the fact that the larger the ship the fewer the ports big enough to accommodate them. These are referred to as "hub" ports and a classic example would be Singapore. Singapore has a relatively small amount of traffic for its own purposes but acts as a base for transhipment to places all around south-east Asia, even as far afield as Australia.

Larger ocean carriers means fewer "hub" ports able to accommodate them thus more **feeder ships** will be required and this is where the entrepreneurial Shipowners come into their own. There is a flourishing charter market in small to medium container ships many of them "self sustaining" (with their own cargo gear) to serve the unsophisticated ports which have no shore cranes. Just as there is a busy chartering market coping with the fluctuating demand for feeder vessels, so there is in ship sales. Shipowners in this speciality keep a constant watch on trends in container cargo movements and seek to own those ships which are most sought after by the major operators. S & P Brokers need to be just as knowledgeable about the container feeder business and the salient features of the types of ships in greatest demand if they are going to impress Principals.

There are no dominant geographical locations for Owners of container feeders. Those ships serving the 'hubs' in northern Europe and Atlantic North America will be owned under a variety of flags. Hong Kong and Japanese Owners will be prominent among those concerned with hub ports either side of the Pacific. In south and south-east Asia, especially, the Owners of ships trading to the least sophisticated ports, one will find local Owners predominant.

9.3 DRY BULK CARRIERS

Market research and route planning are not such pressing problems for the owners of **large bulk carriers** in the dry cargo market. In the case of the two main commodities, coal and iron ore, the market research is the affair of the consumers of the raw material who decide what level of manufacturing the market demands. The routes will be dictated by the price of the raw materials; distance has rather less influence than it did when a large ship was measured in tens rather than hundreds of tonnes.

A significant proportion of the supplies of dry bulk materials tend to be contracted on a long term basis; many of the ships being specifically built to the specifications demanded by the Charterers. However, being prudent Charterers they avoid becoming overstocked with material. This means that for most of the time there is a thriving voyage charter market in which ships required to fill gaps in the Charterers' programmes are taken on; once again this type of market is a magnet for the more speculative Shipowners.

This is probably a suitable place to refer to the most notable of the entrepreneurs in the shipowning world – the Greeks. They have been making highly individual decisions since the first half of the last century and certainly prior to the Second World War there was a community of "London Greeks" regularly attending the Baltic Exchange. Immediately post-war this community grew with the availability of a large number of redundant, mass-produced ten thousand tonners, the so-called Liberty Ships. Towards the end of the war. these were being built at the rate of about three ships a day in North America to replace losses caused by submarine attacks. Liberties became available at knockdown prices just as the freight markets started to soar with the demand for grain and coal, especially in war-torn north-west Europe. It was said that some of these ships covered their purchase cost in their first voyage under their new private ownership. Liberty ships lasted far longer than was originally predicted – they were designed to be "expendable". They were followed by various attempts at "Liberty-replacements" which tended to be 14000 tonner tweendeckers. One of the most famous was the UK-built the SD14 (Standard Design 14,000/14 knots) and a few of these may still be afloat today. There was a lot of over-ordering of these ships at the time and several Owners (and several finance companies) suffered when the market inevitably slumped.

Such calamities in no way daunted the shipowning Greek families and it is the sons and grandsons of those 1940's risk-takers who provide much of the tonnage that fulfils the chartering requirements of the dry-bulk merchants and provide a significant proportion of the second hand purchases and sales of this class of ship. Nor are the Greeks confined to London, there is a similar community in the New York area and, of course, many of them now operate out of their own country since the Greek government adopted a more pragmatic taxation approach to the people who specialise in the industry at which Greeks excel – shipowning.

Grain Charterers are also big players in the dry-bulk markets and they tend to depend more upon single voyage or short-term charter because although the basic demand is highly predictable, the merchants constantly seek the lowest grain prices which affects the favoured loading area. Thus the individualistic Shipowners tend to dominate this market.

Tankers. Chapter one explained how many different types of ship fall under this heading, from Ultra-Large Crude Carriers (ULCCs) to small highly specialised chemical tankers

The **crude oil** market is, of course, dominated by the oil companies. The "oil majors" including, for example, such multinationals as Exxon, Shell, BP etc. all have considerable fleets of tankers themselves. In the period in the mid-twentieth century their tendency was to own or have on long-term time charter, large enough fleets to cover their average requirements and so they seldom had recourse to the "spot" market. More recently, their tendency has been to slim down the balance sheets of their ship owning divisions by actually owning barely enough to cover their minimum requirements. This has resulted in an active chartering market with very many of the ships being owned by entrepreneurial Shipowners. So extensive has the community of independent tanker Owners become that they have their own international association INTERTANKO which is so well established that it produces its own standard form of charter party. Incidentally, entrepreneurism is by no means confined to the shipowning side because **oil traders** are a significant element among Charterers of crude carriers.

The next type of tanker in size terms is the **product carrier**. You will have read in your *Shipping Business* text how, since shortly after World War Two, the oil companies have operated on the basis of establishing their oil refineries close to the points of consumption rather than close to the points of crude oil production. Once the crude oil has been broken down into its many different parts in the refinery, those products which are not distributed by pipeline or land transport, become available for transport in ships of many sizes depending upon the product and the consumer.

As with crude oil, the oil companies have their own fleets to cover the movement of products within their own organizations but there is a wide variety of buyers of refined petroleum products as indeed there are several different grades of product. These range from the heaviest of fuel oils such as is used in ships bunkers and oil-fired power stations referred to as "dirty" cargoes. Those coming under the heading of "clean" cargoes range from the lighter burning oils such as may be used in domestic heating appliances and vast quantities of diesel oil for road and rail vehicles. Then, as the grades get 'lighter' one encounters the special kerosene used to fuel jet aircraft and at the lightest end there is, of course, gasoline (petrol) for use in automobiles. Some products are not destined to be burnt but are the feedstock – the raw material – for the production of such things as plastics.

The oil companies sell much of their product on a CIF basis so they are constantly in the chartering market but a fair proportion of the output from an oil refinery is sold on an FOB basis so the consumer has control of the shipping.

All this chartering activity demands a wide variety of Shipowners ranging from the arch-entrepreneurs to the more staid traditional Shipowners who tend to build their fleets of tankers with particular types of clients in view.

Some of the most valuable products from oil refining are far removed from the simple process of being burnt; these fall under the heading of **chemicals**. Whilst the names and nature of these commodities are outside the scope of this course, the ships themselves are very much more sophisticated than those used for products intended for combustion. Many chemicals are either capable of eroding steel or will be contaminated by contact with steel. This demands that the tanks have to be coated with a chemical resistant material and these vary according to the types of cargo intended to be carried.

The Owners of these highly specialised ships are themselves specialists and any S & P Brokers contemplating becoming involved in this market will have to be just as specialised. Most of the more sophisticated chemical carriers are built to the operators' own stringent specifications so that any S & P activity is likely to be concentrated in the newbuilding markets.

9.4 GENERAL PURPOSE SHIPS

There are no defined areas in the market for what are still the genuine "tramps" of the shipping world. Most Owners in this market are relatively small as compared with the multinationals in the specialised markets and many of the potential Buyers and Sellers have their decision-taking under the control of an individual. It is this market where one also finds most of the trade in ships that have had several Owners and the next stop is likely to be the breaker's yard. For sheer interest and variety rather than the high stress of the high reward markets, this is the one to be in. It has its characters and, not to put too fine a point on it, it has more than its fair share of rogues but sorting the sheep from the goats must always be part of the S & P Broker's expertise.

9.5 SMALL SHIPS

The so-called small ship market has changed a great deal over the years. At one time a 2500 coaster after its life carrying coal round the British coast would find a ready market among those Owners trading within the Mediterranean. Now the small ship market is probably dominated by ships used in the container feeder trade.

Some of the traditional markets for small ships remain virtually unchanged, in particular those serving the vast amount of inter-island traffic in south and south-east Asia.

'Small' also includes such craft as fishing vessels, barges, tugs and other specialised vessels. The word 'specialised' is the operative one because it stands to reason that a small ship equals a (relatively) small price which equals a small commission. One should not, therefore, 'play' at it. For a Broker who is normally seeking to sell or buy bulk-carriers or even general purpose tramps, to break off and become involved in negotiations for the sale of a ship in the low thousands of tonnes is a waste of the most valuable resource – time.

Having said that, there are several Brokers who do specialise in the small end of the market. They simply work on the basis that their throughput of sales has to be much higher to earn the same income. This is helped by the fact that sales of small ships tend to take a far shorter time in the negotiation and because their voyages are far shorter, the time between signing the saleform and delivery is proportionately less.

9.6 PASSENGER SHIPS AND FERRIES

Large passenger liners designed to carry people from one place to another across oceans have long since given way to the air lines but their place has been taken by cruise ships. Cruising started its present boom during the last quarter of the twentieth century and the major operators (rather like their counterparts in the container world) are constantly seeking to build bigger and better cruise ships. These are brought into service long before the ships they are replacing have ended their useful life which has created a thriving S & P market in second-hand passenger ships.

A similar situation is seen in the passenger ferry market. As more people take their vacations in other countries and wish to take their automobiles with them so the major ferry operators are encouraged to acquire larger, more sophisticated ships. The same trend can be seen among vehicle ferries with the steady increase in the use of road transport for smaller consignments of cargo. Redundant ferries from north-west Europe can usually find a ready market among the operators of inter-island services in South and South-East Asia.

Brokers dealing in passenger carriers need extra skills in dealing not so much in deadweight tonnes or teus but in passenger accommodation. Not just in numbers of berths but in description of the cabins; what passes for first class in one Owner's mind may be considered steerage in another's – and *vice versa*.

9.7 OBSOLETE TONNAGE

By the way, avoid a frequently encountered mistake. 'Obsolete' means no longer in service whilst 'obsolescent' means old and out of date but still in service. But obsolete is usually the term used to describe ships intended for the demolition market.

In Chapter Six you learnt how ship-breaking is a somewhat crude industry and tends to flourish in those areas where the cost of living is low so that wages are commensurately low. Thus many buyers of ships for demolition will be found in parts of the Indian sub-continent, south-east Asia and the Far East with China a major player.

In addition to the factors influencing the demolition market which were referred to in Chapter Six, S & P Brokers need to keep a watch on external influences. The governments of both India and Pakistan want their share of the demolition market and so impose import duties on ships bought by their ship breakers. The level of this tax changes from time to time and will inevitably have an effect on prices being offered.

Another external influence comes from the environmentalist lobbies, particularly Greenpeace who are a highly laudable body but occasionally become over-enthusiastic. They have been known to use the laws in Europe, which ban the export of toxic waste, to declare a ship with asbestos lagging round its steam pipes to be in this category and prevent its sale to an Indian ship breaker.

9.8 WHO SHOULD AN S & P BROKER KNOW?

First, obviously, the Broker's own **Principals**. This is not so easy as in, say, a chartering context where one's Principal tends to have a repetitive need to be in the market; a Shipowner needs a constant supply of cargoes and a charterer a constant supply of ships. Most Buyers and Sellers of ships acquire ships in order to operate them and only dispose of them when circumstances make it necessary to do so.

Lucky indeed is the S & P Broker who acts for a Principal who looks upon ships themselves as the trading commodity and only seeks employment for them in order to have them profitably engaged whilst waiting for the right market conditions to enable them to be sold at a profit.

As well as knowing the Principals, it is necessary to know how each **Buyer** operates; one needs to identify the DMU – the decision-making unit. If dealing with an entrepreneur, then it is likely that the decision-maker will be the direct link but if the Principal is a large limited company, contact is likely to be with a subordinate and the larger the organisation, the greater number of people between the contact point and the final decision. This chain of executives between Broker and decision will be even longer if the Principal is a member of a **shipping pool** where other pool members may have to be consulted before negotiations start in earnest. The same problem arises if the buying Principal is a **finance house** which buys for bare-boat charter to the actual user of the ship.

Similar constraints will apply if the Principal is the **Seller** where the entrepreneur will possibly give a response right there on the 'phone but the big company man will need to consult colleagues before providing a response. Further complications arise if the ship is to be sold with an existing **chartering commitment** because the Charterer will have to be a signatory to a tripartite agreement and will, therefore have to be consulted.

Another important difference among Principals is the attitude to Brokers. Some will lean heavily on the Broker's advice as to terms to be agreed or to be amended during negotiations and will also expect guidance from the Broker as to what is or is not a fair price. At the other end of the scale are Principals who will require no more from the Broker than that of a dealer, transmitting their instructions and reporting back the replies. And, of course, various shades between these two extremes.

Almost as important as knowing one's potential Principals one needs to know **other S & P Brokers**. With the possible exception of sectors of the newbuilding market, it is the rule rather than the exception for there to be a Seller's Broker and a Buyers Broker, and occasionally intermediate Brokers.

By 'know' in this context one means knowing what type of buyer/seller/ship type that Broker specialises in as well as knowing the reputation of those Principals and – by extension – the reputation of the Broker. The reputation of the Broker is especially important when dealing in ships for demolition because it is difficult for a Seller's Broker to recognise and know the standing of the very many ship breakers. The same safeguard applies when the buyer is a small enterprise in a remote part of the world.

S & P work, like so many branches of shipping business, depends so heavily on person-to-person contact so that 'knowing' is important in the usual sense of having friendly personal links with fellow Brokers.

Then during the course of negotiations, especially towards the end, there are a host of people to which the S & P Broker may have to refer in some haste. Documents may need to be notarised, that is by an independent professional person whose signature and seal confirms the validity of a signed document. Such a person specialising in this work in many countries is called a **notary public** whilst in others, this duty is performed by a lawyer.

Knowing how to reach the **consulate** of any country and the representative of its shipping **registrar** as well as the local office of every **Classification Society** is an essential part of the S & P Broker's armoury of contacts. The role these officials play will be covered in the next Chapter.

9.9 WHAT SHOULD AN S & P BROKER KNOW?

An S & P Broker is only as good as the data in the office which is instantly available. Some of this has to be in the Broker's head so that a knowledgeable response can be given to the first approach by a potential Principal. Very shortly after that response the Broker must be able to provide details of suitable ships within the range of interest of the Buyer and whether the Principal is Buyer or seller, the Broker must have at his finger ends, the sort of prices being paid for such ships as are the subject of discussion.

It goes without saying that an S & P Broker's office needs a remarkably comprehensive store of easily accessible data for which the computer is ideally suited. However, a computer is only as good as the data fed into it – remember the watchword GIGO – garbage in, garbage out – so a staff dedicated to keeping that data right up to date is indispensable.

Finally the Broker must know the market, the price of ships depends of course upon supply and demand; it is, however, vital to know what circumstances affect that demand. These range from the immediate factors such as the current prices being paid for second hand ships all the way up to the view expressed by (believable) economists as to the state of the world economy in the more distant future.

Maintaining a watch on the chartering markets is almost as important as the S & P market itself because signs of firmness or weakness of a general nature as opposed to temporary blips will inevitably influence the views of Buyers and Sellers of ships.

Unusual events particularly wars (if these can be termed 'unusual' today) can radically affect demand for ships, often on a regional basis. Political unrest short of actual conflict can be a factor. Similarly a sudden shift in demand, such as the discovery of oil reserves can trigger a demand which may be local or widespread depending upon the magnitude of the discovery.

All these factors may have to be drawn upon from time to time if one's Principals expect written market reports to be prepared. Skill in reading and understanding reports made by others, especially statistical summaries prepared by official bodies, is a necessary quality.

Finally, reverting to the anecdote at the beginning of this Chapter, knowing the *psychology* of one's Principals is probably the most important skill of all.

9.10 TEST QUESTIONS

Having completed Chapter Nine, attempt the following and submit your essays to your Tutor.

1. One of your Principals, who owns a fairly small fleet of general-purpose tweendeckers, now feels he would like to be part of the container shipping world. Within his fleet are two elderly 14,000 tonners he could dispose of. Using a country of domicile and nationality of your choice for your 'Principal', draft a letter to him with your suggestions as to how he might proceed.

2. Draft an internal memo to a new subordinate detailing what you expect to be able to obtain quickly from the computer system he is devising for you.

Chapter 10

DOCUMENTATION AND SHIP VALUATION

10.1 PART ONE – DOCUMENTS AND PROCEDURES ON DELIVERY

The transfer of a ship from one Owner to another is often a time of tension for the S & P Broker. This is not a simple matter such as buying a car where the buyer hands over cash or a certified cheque and the seller gives in exchange a couple of documents and the keys of the new acquisition; all taking place in one location without a lawyer in sight.

With the transfer of a ship from Seller to Buyer there are many more documents involved, the several parties concerned may be in different parts of the world, many miles and possibly several time zones apart and finally the amount of money involved is considerable. Add to this the fact that lawyers will probably be involved and their role is to ensure that the exchange of the money and the ship is simultaneous; they are paid to work on the unhappy Principle than no one can be trusted.

Apart from the legal, financial and bureaucratic elements concerned, the very human element, namely the old and the new crews must not be overlooked. The Brokers may well be obliged to play a part in ensuring there is no problem in the changeover although one hopes that much of this work will fall to a port agent.

A well-rehearsed drill is vital for this procedure and it is a matter in which the S & P Broker should be prepared to play an active part when called upon to do so. It must be remembered that much of the work will be the responsibility of Lawyers acting on behalf of Buyers and Sellers together with Notaries Public but the S & Purchase Broker must understand the procedure and protocol for delivery because the Broker may well be the one to ensure that everyone concerned and every piece of paper is in the right place at the right time.

Having a check sheet for handovers is a useful tool in any S & P Broker's office. Incidentally, outmoded though it now is for most broking work, the telex is still considered by some to be valuable at the time of a handover because of the security the answerback code provides

Have **Appendix 11** to hand and refer to its Clause 8 which deals with documentation. There are several documents that are peculiar to the hand over process, these include:

Bill of Sale This is the document of title to the ship. Once executed – notarially attested and legalised by the appropriate Consul when necessary – it is the document that hands the ship over from the Seller to the Buyer. In order to register the ship, the new owner has to produce evidence of title, thus the Bill of Sale is probably the most important document at time of hand over.

An example of a Bill of Sale will be found in **Appendix 16**

Deletion Certificate If, as is often the case, the Buyer will be registering the ship under a different flag from the seller's, a certificate confirming that the ship has been deleted from the seller's flag has to be presented to the registrar of the Buyer's flag. On occasions the actual Deletion Certificate is not actually available at the time of hand over. In such a case the sellers have to produce a signed undertaking to present it as soon as possible; such an undertaking will probably also have to be notarially attested and legalised by the Consul.

Board Resolution Readers will recall reference being made in their law studies to 'ostensible authority' when it was pointed out that, even within a company, different levels of management have different degrees of responsibility and authority. The Buyers obviously want to be sure that the person in the seller's office has authority to sell such a large capital item and this is achieved by the production of a certified copy of a Board of Directors Resolution confirming the decision to sell the ship concerned. This certificate is usually signed by the Company Secretary (or his/her equivalent) then notarially attested and legalised.

Just the same type of certificate must be prepared by the Buyers showing authority to purchase the ship

In addition to these certificates it is customary for the persons authorised to sign the various documents on both side, at the completion site and on board the ship itself,

To have their companies' **Powers of Attorney** which again have to be notarised and legalised by the appropriate Consul.

Protocol of Delivery and Acceptance This is a very simple but vital document showing the seller's name followed by the words:

> "hereby deliver on (day, month, year) at (hours) the ship described below"

This is followed by the identity of the ship namely name, flag, call sign and official number. Then the Buyer's name is spelled out, followed by a statement reading:

> "pursuant to the Memorandum of Agreement dated (*day month year)* made between Sellers and Buyers and Buyers hereby accept delivery of the ship described above"

Then both representatives sign the document which is the moment that ownership transfers.

At the time of handover

Let us assume the following:

1. A ship has been sold with delivery in Nagasaki on the 10th April 2005
2. Payment for the vessel where the hand over officially takes place will be in New York.
3. The sellers's office is in Lausanne, Switzerland.
4. The ship under her new Owners will fly the Greek flag.
5. The ship shall be delivered mortgage free but the Buyers will register a mortgage on delivery.

The broker's check sheet could look something like this (each party's telephone fax and telex numbers would be noted against the names):

DATE OF CLOSING Estimated for the 10th April 2005

PLACES AND TIMES OF CLOSING

1.	New York	at Greek Consulate	9.30 am local time
2.	Lausanne –	Sellers at office of Swiss Maritime (sellers)	3.30 pm local time
3.	Nagasaki –	Seller's broker at Matsumoto & Co	11.30 pm local time

ATTENDING THE CLOSING

Telephone numbers are those where representatives can be reached before closing date:

1. IN NEW YORK

For Swiss Maritime (Sellers)	Mr A Schmidt
For Posidonia Maritime (Buyers)	Mr A Pericles
For Hellenic Trustee Bank (Buyer's banker)	Mr P Guy

2. IN LAUSANNE

Swiss Maritime (Sellers)	Mr P Favre

3. NAGASAKI

Swiss Maritime (Sellers)	Mr A Georges
Posidonia Maritime (Buyers)	Mr D Dimitria

Then the **closing procedure** would be arranged as follows:

At the time of closing two lines will be open. One between New York and Lausanne and the other between New York and Nagasaki so that exchange of documents, payments, registrations, etc. will be effected simultaneously.

Alternatively if Sellers agree only one telephone link between New York – Nagasaki may be opened and as soon as closing is completed then advice shall be given to Sellers in Lausanne in this regard.

With the vessel being ready for hand over and with the telephone link between New York and Nagasaki open, the Seller's and Buyer's representatives in New York will receive confirmation from their counterparts in Nagasaki that the vessel is ready for delivery and that they have checked all the necessary documents are on board. These will include vital items such her Tonnage Certificate, Plans, Suez and Panama Certificates plus a host of **trading certificates** which include:

> International Load Line Certificate, Cargo Ship Safety Construction Certificate, Cargo Ship Safety Equipment Certificate, De-Ratisation Exemption Certificate, Life Raft Inspection Certificate, Cargo Record Book, Cargo Gear (derricks/cranes) Inspection Certificate, Radio Licence, International Oil Pollution Prevention Certificate, Minimum Mandatory Safe Manning Certificate, Stability Information.

If the ship were a tanker there would have to be pipe-line layouts, pumping rates, and the gas-free certificate. If a dry-cargo ship then the grain and bale cubic capacity records. Also copies of the log books and certificates covering the various surveys the ships has to undergo

The **Sellers** will have provided the certificate of no mortgages or other encumbrances as well as the deletion certificate from the Swiss registry. They will also have provided a proof from the Classification Society confirming that the ship is in class and noting any recommendations (these will already have been disclosed during negotiations)

The **Buyers** will have to obtain and provide to the Greek registrar the appropriate class certificates.

The **Buyer's bank** in New York will hand over a draft for the full purchase price less the ten percent deposit (and less address commission if any). The **Buyers** will provide a letter to the bank in which the deposit is lodged releasing the deposit to the Sellers less any bankers charges and plus any accrued interest

When all is agreed as being in order, the Buyer's and Seller's representatives in Nagasaki will be authorised to sign the protocol of delivery and acceptance.

Variations

The forgoing was simply an example because circumstances will vary and procedures will differ according to flag and nationality of Buyers and Sellers.

Whilst not necessary in the example above where the deal was between a Greek Buyer and a Swiss Seller some countries may demand that the Seller obtains an Export licence before a ship may be sold; in some rare cases there may be a prohibition on sales to certain other countries.

Similarly some countries insist upon ships bought by their nationals for registration under the country's flag that an **Import licence** is obtained. The S & P Brokers will have established whether these are necessary at time of negotiations but the certificates themselves have to be presented for scrutiny by the parties or their lawyers at time of delivery.

On occasions the Bill of Sale has to be executed in two originals, the second one marked "second original",

It may be necessary to provide a commercial invoice stipulating the sale price of the vessel. This document must state that it is a commercial invoice and include name of Buyers and Sellers together with purchase price and date.

Bunkers on delivery

In a previous Chapter the matter of bunkers and lubricating oils on delivery has been discussed. Unless otherwise agreed, these must be paid for by Buyers after quality and quantity have been agreed. They must be paid for at the current market price at the port of delivery. Payment must be made at the same time and place, and in the same currency as the purchase price.

10.2 PART TWO – SHIP VALUATIONS

Introduction

It is part of an S & P Broker's daily function to estimate the value of any ships in which he or she becomes involved; that is all part of "knowing one's market". Some Brokers undertake to provide valuations on an official basis.

Who needs an official valuation?

No one is prohibited from seeking a formal valuation of a ship providing they are willing and able to pay the appropriate fee. Among those who are likely to seek valuations include:

Lawyers and **arbitrators** are probably the most frequent users of ship valuers' services because the market value of a particular ship at a particular time may be essential evidence in a dispute.

An independent valuation of a ship (or several ships) may be needed during **company takeover** negotiations.

The Inland Revenue Service may need to have a ship valued if it was substantially owned by an individual who has died and the amount of **Inheritance Tax** has to be calculated

Banks and **auditors** may need an up-to-date valuation in order to re-assess the asset value of a company.

Average adjusters need an accurate value of a ship at the time that the General Average sacrifice took place.

Those involved in a **Salvage Arbitration** have to know the value of a salvaged ship before calculating the amount to be paid to the salvors.

Perhaps the most delicate situation is when a **Government department** seeks a valuation because of an allegation having been made of illicit dealing being involved in the sale or purchase of a ship.

The basis of valuations

It is important at the outset to stress that ship valuers are seldom, if ever, also ship surveyors. Thus a valuation is invariably made with no inspection of the ship itself or its records. It is based entirely on the premise that the vessel is in sound condition, charter-free and that it is based upon a willing Buyer and a willing Seller.

Although ship valuation can never be a precise art because of the many variables, the valuer must provide a figure that would stand up to examination in a court of law as a ship valuer can be – and often is – *subpoenaed* to give evidence before a court or an arbitration.

There are several ways of valuing ships and no two Brokers will use the same methods but the following guidelines should be common to all, if not in detail then in principle.

A ship is worth what she can earn on the oceans of the world and therefore ship values vary according to the vagaries of the freight market and the availability of certain types of tonnage, able to take advantage of the prevailing market at any given time.

The first task of the valuer is therefore to establish the value of the vessel per deadweight ton which should offer no problems because keeping records of ship sales is an essential part of the S & P Broker's armoury.

Let us assume he has been asked to value, as of a given date, a bulk carrier of 35,000 tons deadweight built in Japan in 1985. The valuer must first of all look at other similar type vessels sold or currently offering for sale at about the time in question. In this case, let us assume there was a similar bulk carrier sold for US $8,750,000 which was built in Japan in 1983 and which had a deadweight of 32,409 tonnes. One can thus calculate that the sold vessel obtained US $270 per deadweight ton (US $8,750,000 ÷ 32,409). If one then multiplies the deadweight of the ship to be valued (35,000 tons) by US $270 one obtains a value of US $9,450,000.

To that initial figure one can/would add or deduct any features which might favour one ship to the detriment of the other. For example, differences in age, type of gear, make, type and size of engine, place of build etc. In the case in point, the ship to be valued was two years younger therefore on the "5% per annum rule" one could would add 10% to US $9,450 and obtain a figure of US $10,395,000.

The 5% per annum rule, applied for differences in age, is based on the assumption that the life of the average ship is 20 years. This is a very rough guide because different types of ships and different states of the market may dictate a much shorter life-span for certain types of ship which would produce a proportionately higher annual depreciation rate.

The important rule is, of course, always to compare like with like i.e. tankers with tankers, dry cargo tween-deckers with dry cargo tween deckers, bulkers with bulkers and so on.

Brokers and owners have preferences for shipyards and countries of build. Some would consider that a ship built in a north European yard would be preferable to a ship built in a Far East yard and would make an allowance accordingly. Type of gear is an important consideration and in comparing one bulk carrier with another bulk carrier, it is essential to establish the type of bulk carriers which are being compared, whether geared or gearless and the type and quality of gear i.e. derricks or cranes.

Size of engine is important and also type of engine. Here again, individual preferences and perhaps prejudices may influence a valuer's judgement but it is important to compare like with like. For example a valuation comparing a vessel with a turbine engine cannot be compared exactly with a ship having diesel propulsion.

Valuers will allow a differential when comparing the speed of ships. Thus, a vessel having a service speed of 14 knots would have an advantage on the overall price when compared with a ship having a service speed of 13 knots. Applying such a differential becomes more relevant and important in the case of fast vessels such as container ships and reefers.

Whilst, when presenting a valuation the only information given is the estimate of value, the valuer must always keep in mind that when giving a valuation, that it could be challenged in a court of law when the valuer will be interrogated by learned counsel who will endeavour to find flaws in the arguments. A valuation should, therefore, never be given until the valuer is satisfied that he or she has a logical and well marshalled argument with all the facts available to back his case.

A valuer presents himself as an expert thus an allegation of a false or misleading valuation, although probably falling under the legal heading of "innocent misrepresentation", could have most unfortunate consequences. A valuation by one of the leading S & P Brokers was challenged a few years ago and the plaintiffs succeeded in their claim that the valuation was totally incorrect with most unfortunate consequences.

It is vital that the written valuation presented to the client clearly identifies the ship in question and the period for which the valuation is valid. It should then include all the necessary *caveats* regarding no physical inspection of either the ship itself or the classification society records and that it is an opinion of the market for the period stated and should not be taken to apply to any other date. For good measure it should conclude with the warning that anyone intending to rely on the valuation should satisfy himself about the physical condition of the ship.

Except perhaps in the case of valuations for a loyal Principal, valuers will, of course, charge a fee for their services, the fee depending on the amount of work involved. In most countries the competition laws prohibit the publishing of any form of scale of charges. However, valuers are first and foremost Brokers and "knowing one's market" is the essential quality of any Broker worthy of the title.

10.3 SELF-ASSESSMENT AND TEST QUESTIONS

Attempt the following and check your answers from the text:

1. Who signs the Protocol of Delivery and Acceptance?
2. Why are Board Resolutions considered necessary?
3. What role does a Notary Public play?
4. Who gets the interest on the ten percent deposit?
5. What is the reasoning behind the "5% per annum rule"?
6. What types of clients seek the services of a ship valuer?
7. Why might the Inland Revenue Service seek a ship valuation?

Having completed Chapter Ten, attempt the following and submit your essay to your Tutor.

1. A Panamanian ship is being sold by a United States domiciled owner to a Greek Buyer with delivery in Piraeus and payment in London. Discuss the arrangements necessary for payment and transfer of ownership.
2. You have to give a valuation on a 1988 Korean built 100,000 tonne British owned tanker and the only similar sale around the period in question was a 1990 Japanese built 150,000 tonne Greek owned tanker. What factors will you take into consideration when making your valuation?

CONTENTS

Appendix 1	Ship Profiles	105
Appendix 2	General Arrangement Plan	126
Appendix 3	British Registration Certificate	127
Appendix 4	History of Flags of Convenience	129
Appendix 5	Lloyd's Register Abbreviations	130
Appendix 6	Lloyd's Register Column Headings	132
Appendix 7	Copy of a Lloyd's Register Page	134
Appendix 8	Copy of a Germanischer Lloyd Page	135
Appendix 9	Copy of a Bureau Veritas Page	136
Appendix 10	Norwegian Saleform 1987	137
Appendix 11	Norwegian Saleform 1993	142
Appendix 12	Nipponsale 1999	148
Appendix 13	BIMCO "Salescrap"	151
Appendix 14	"Fairplay" Market Report	156
Appendix 15	Lloyd's List Market Report	157
Appendix 16	Bill of Sale	158

APPENDIX 1

Ship Profiles

Tanker

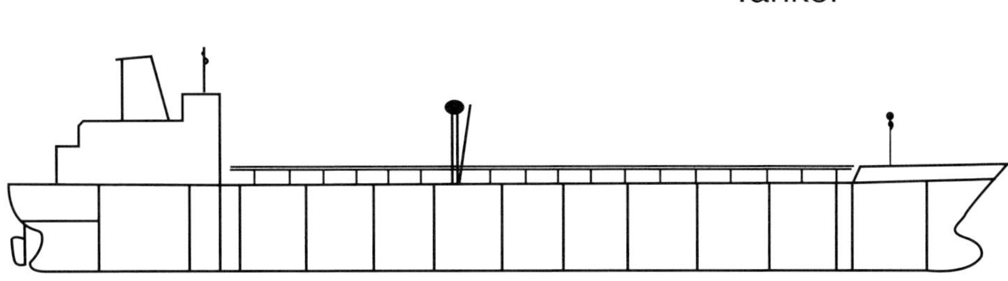

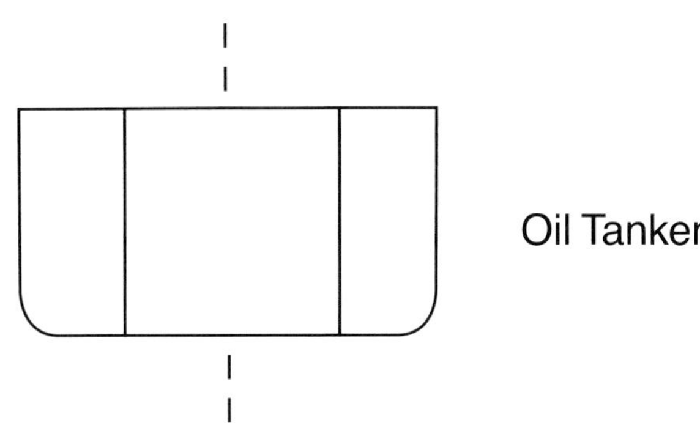

Oil Tanker

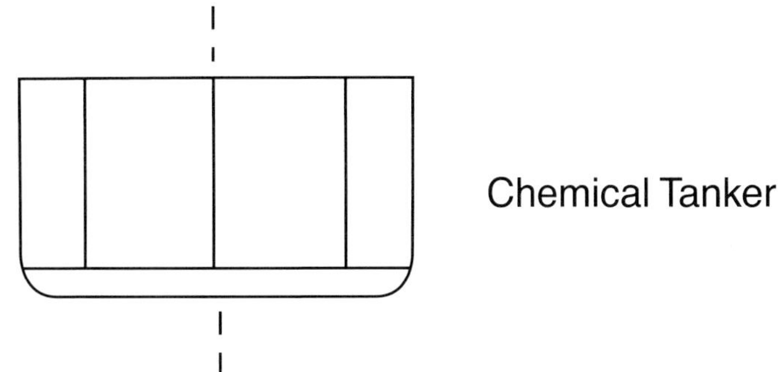

Chemical Tanker

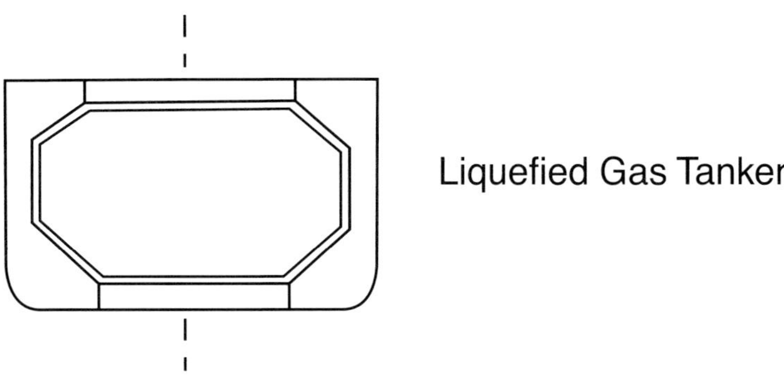

Liquefied Gas Tanker

APPENDIX 1

Ship Profiles (Continued)

Liquefied Gas Carrier

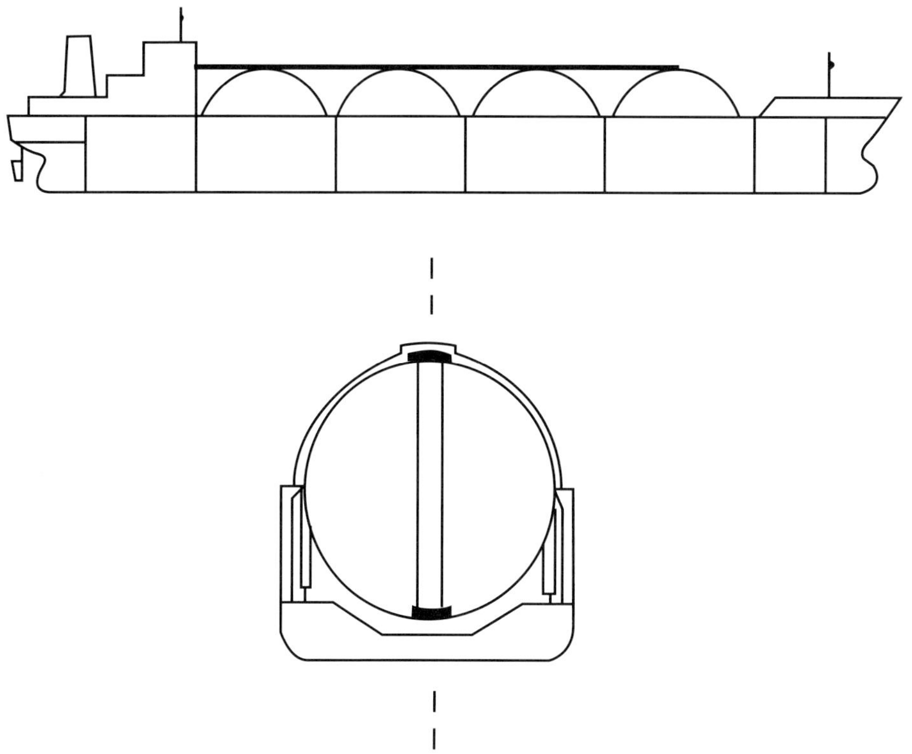

Fruit Juice Carrier

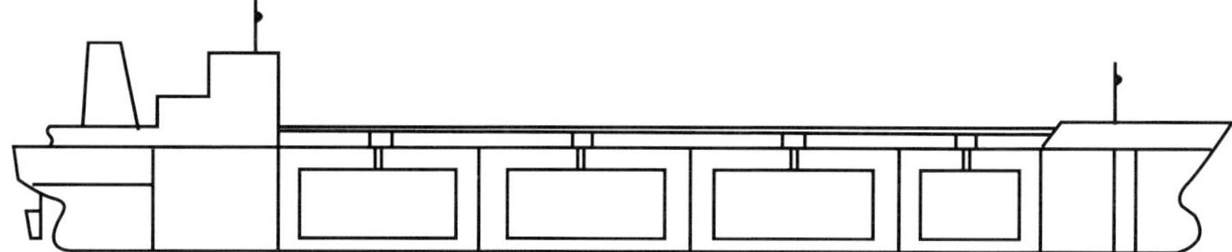

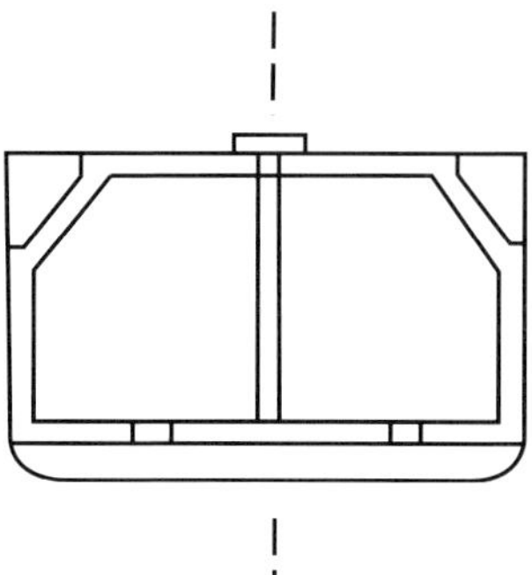

APPENDIX 1

Ship Profiles (Continued)

Bulk Carrier

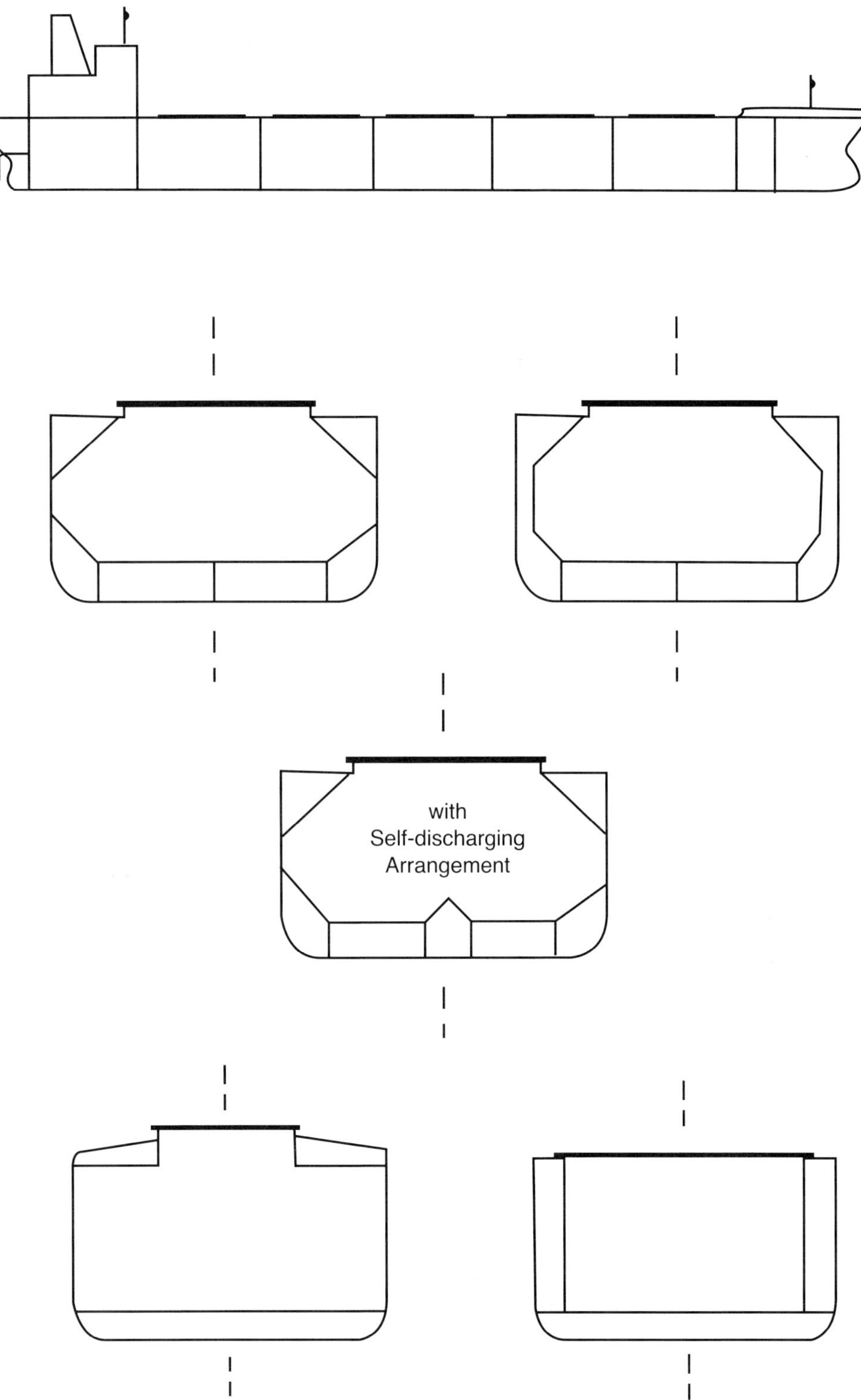

APPENDIX 1

Ship Profiles (Continued)

Ore/Bulk/Oil Carrier

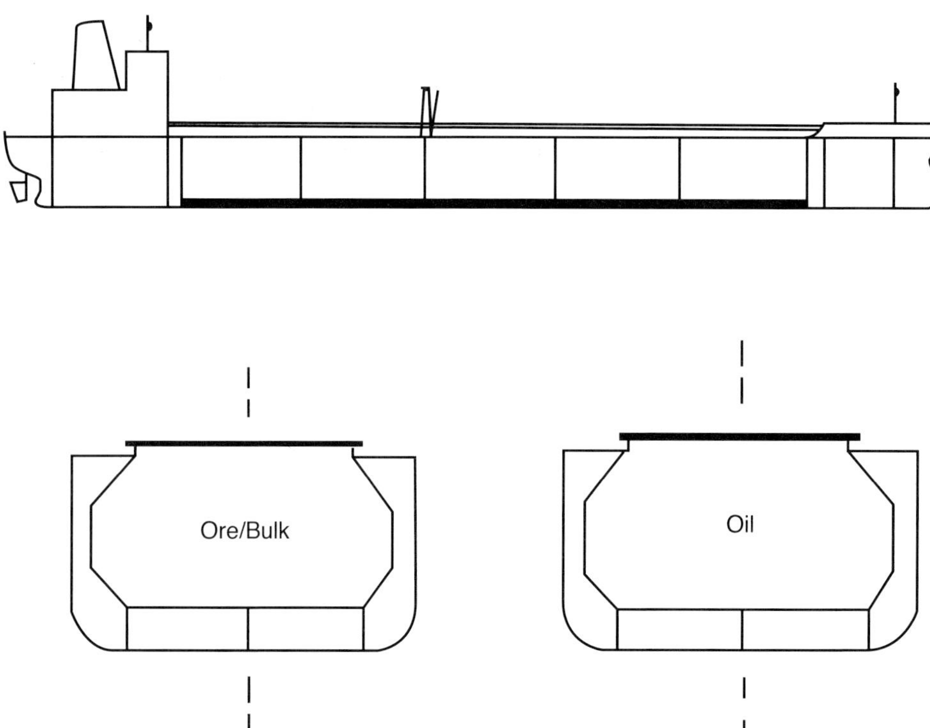

APPENDIX 1

Ship Profiles (Continued)

Ore Carrier

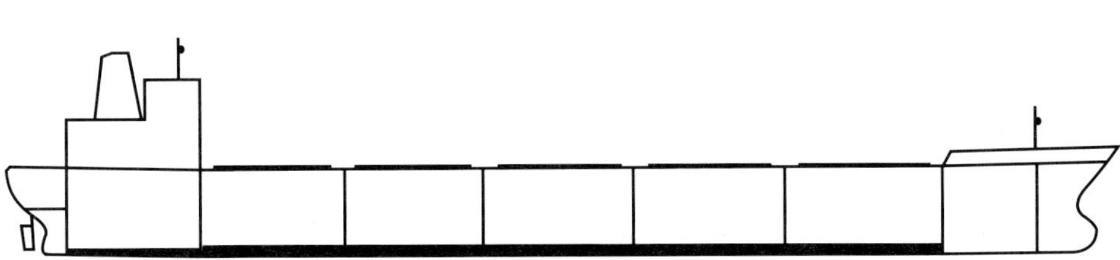

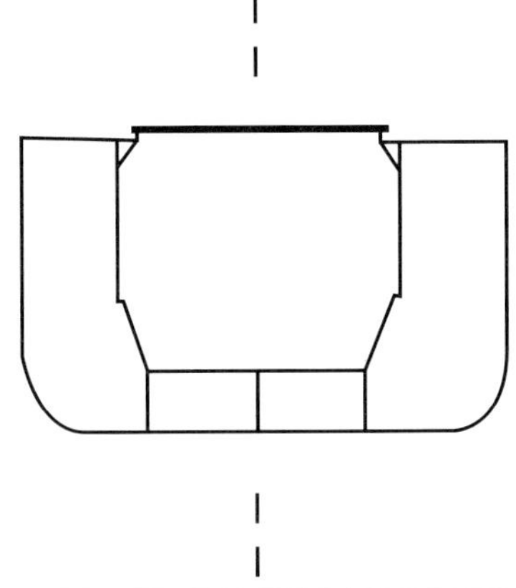

Ore/Oil Carrier

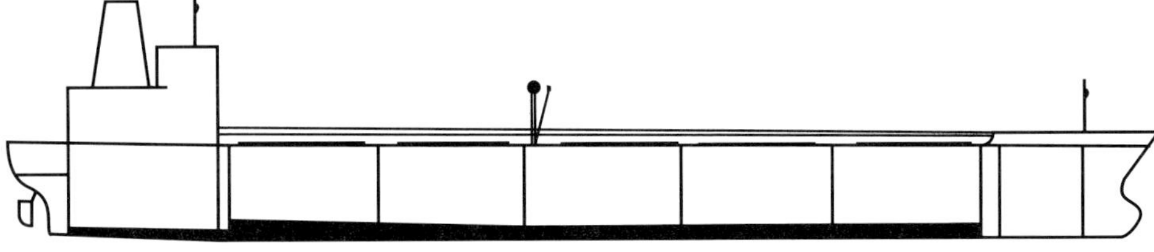

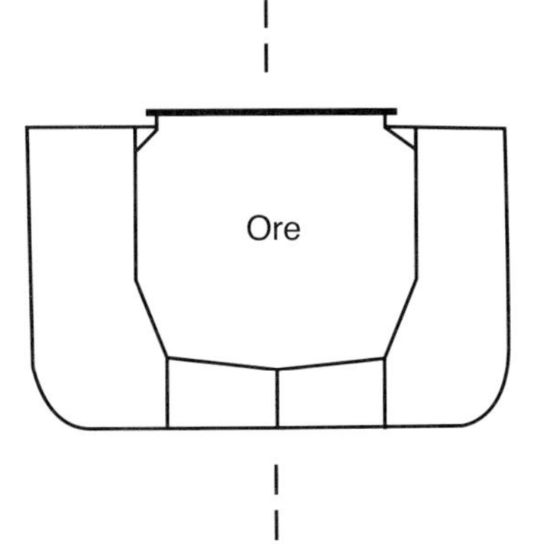

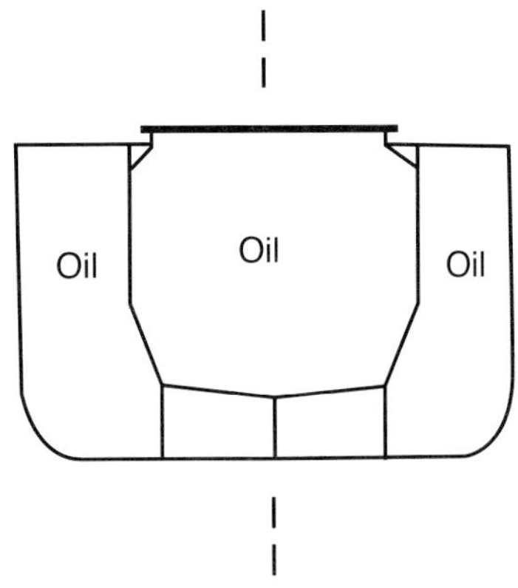

APPENDIX 1

Ship Profiles (Continued)

General Cargo Ship

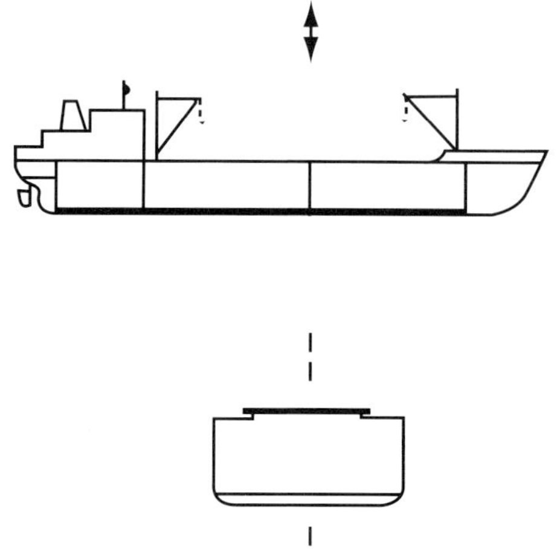

General Cargo Ship

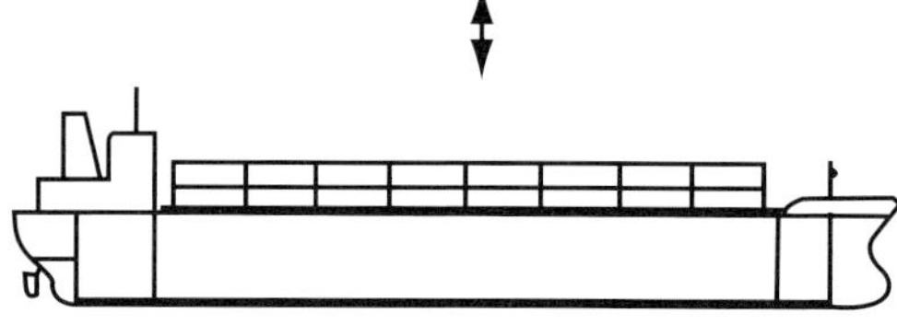

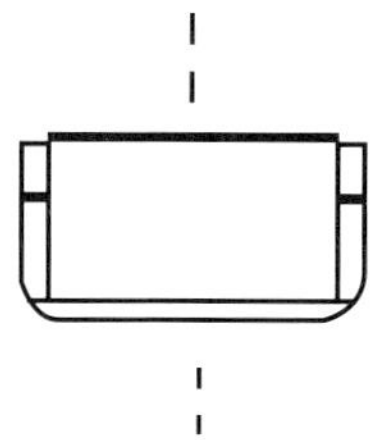

General Cargo Ship

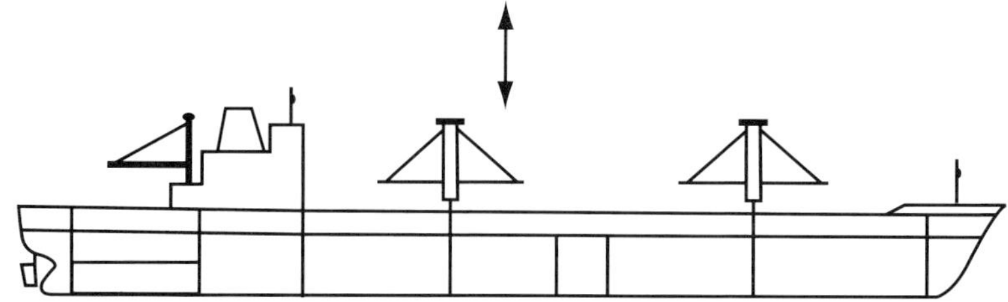

APPENDIX 1

Ship Profiles (Continued)

General Cargo Ship

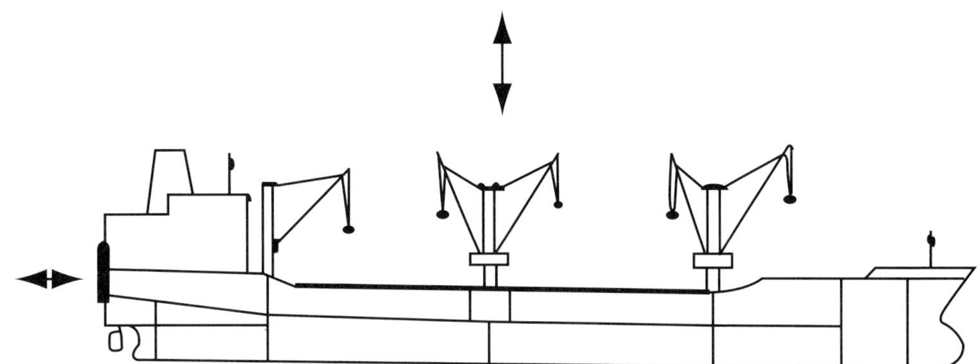

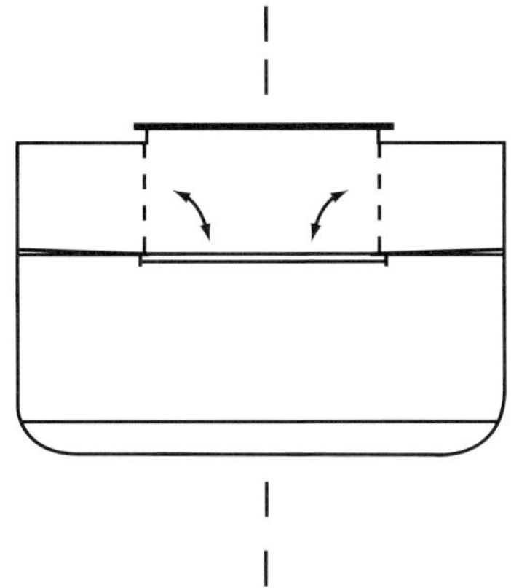

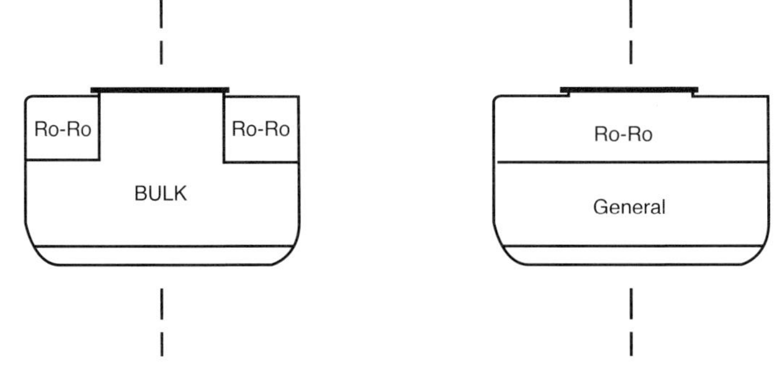

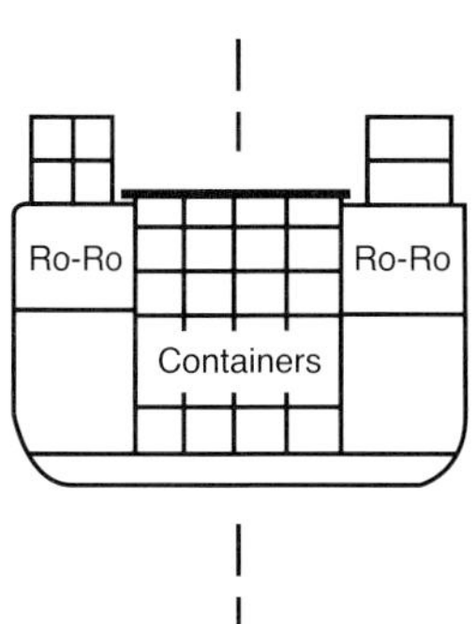

APPENDIX 1

Ship Profiles (Continued)

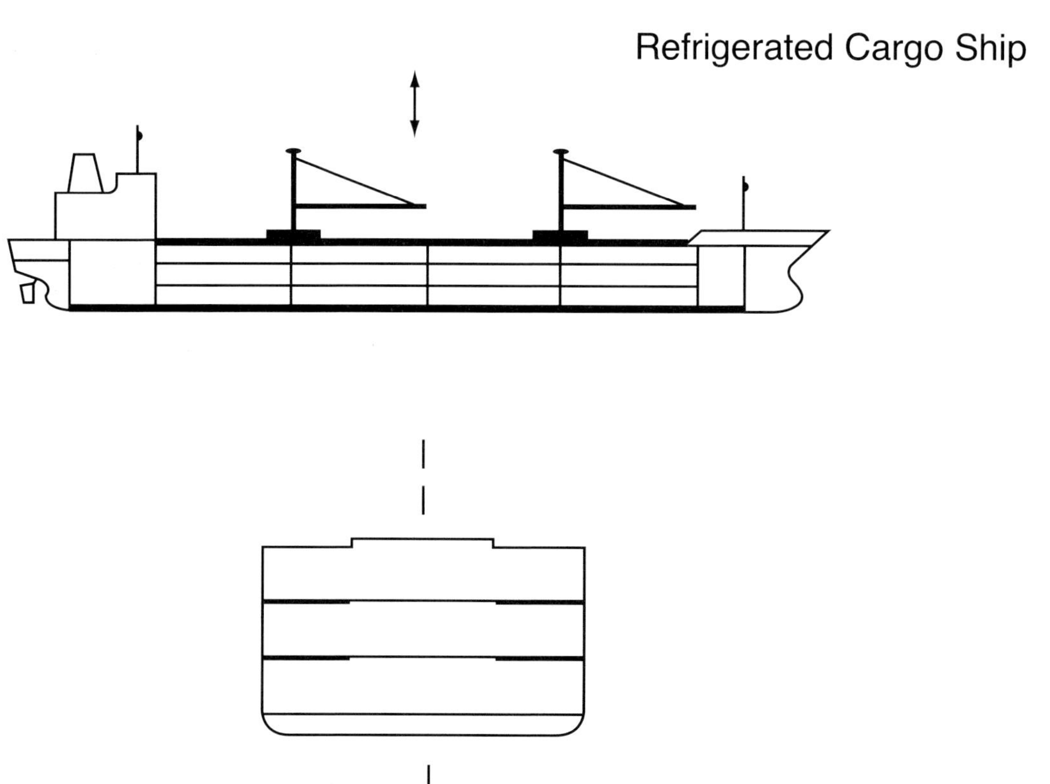

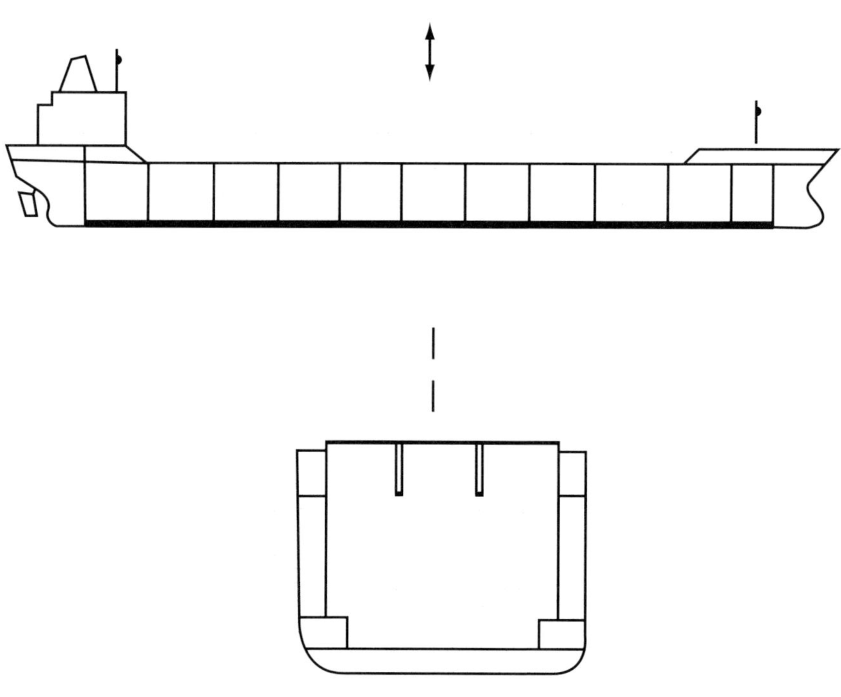

APPENDIX 1

Ship Profiles (Continued)

Ro-Ro Cargo Ship

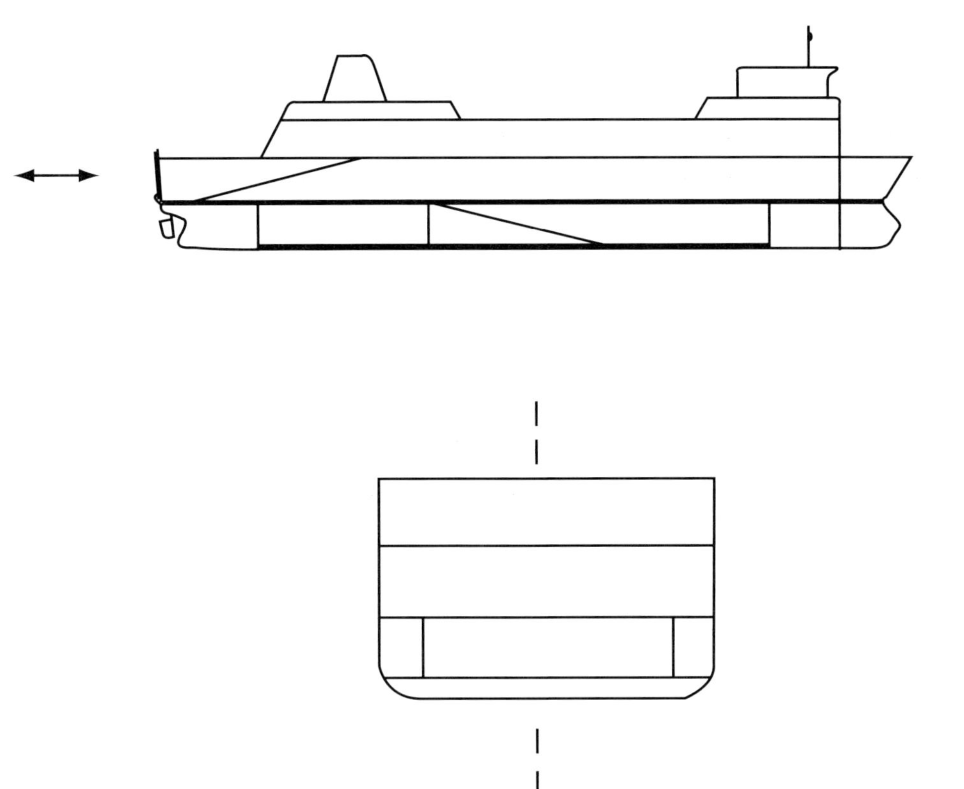

Ro-Ro Cargo Ship

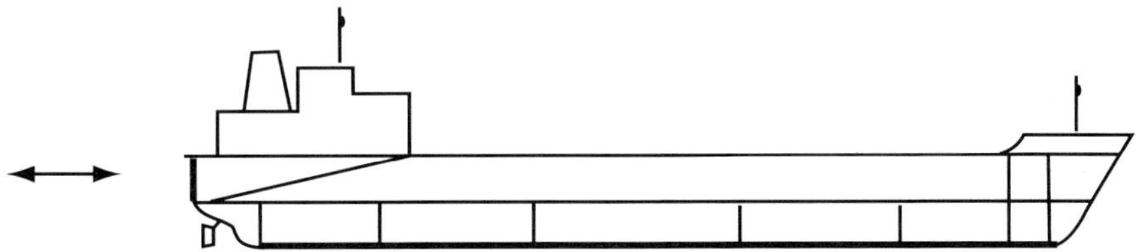

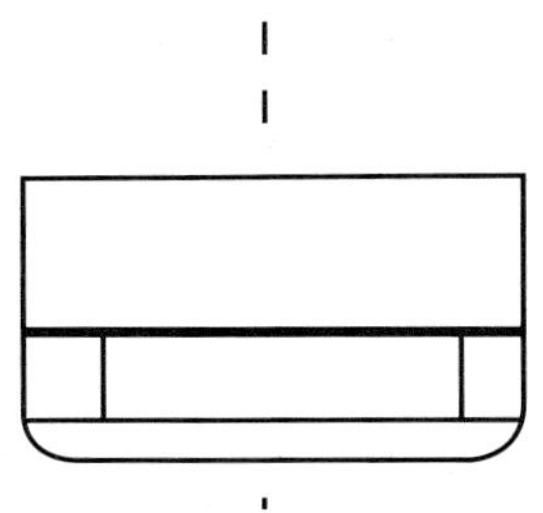

APPENDIX 1

Ship Profiles (Continued)

Ro-Ro Cargo Ship

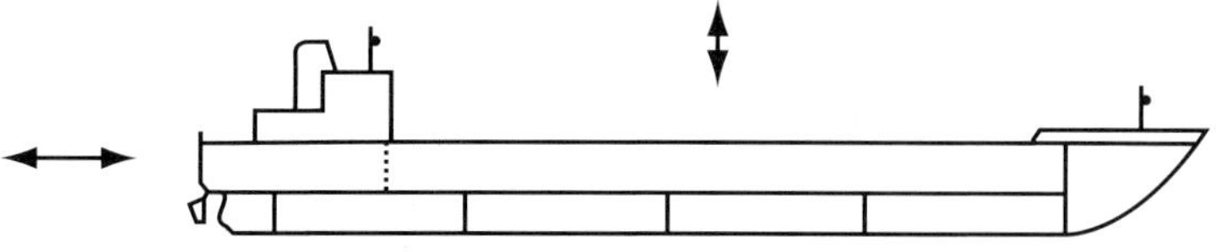

Ro-Ro Cargo Ship

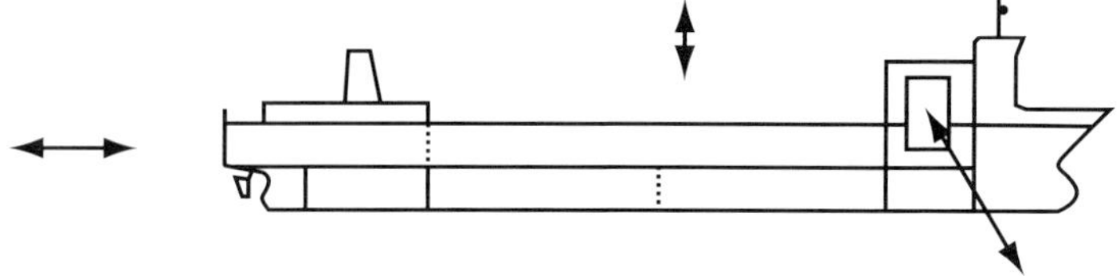

Train Ship

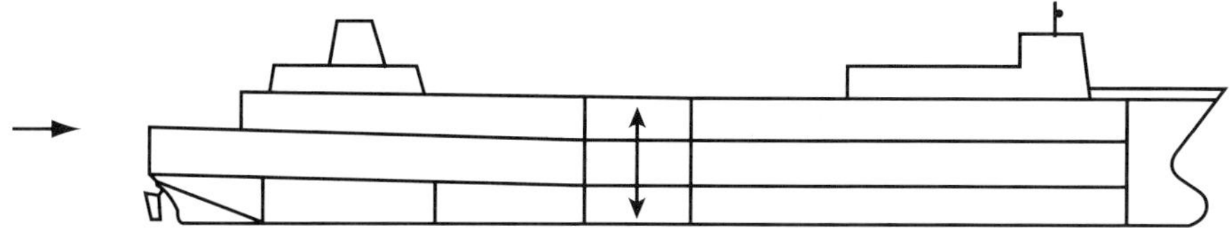

APPENDIX 1

Ship Profiles (Continued)

General Cargo/Passenger Ferry

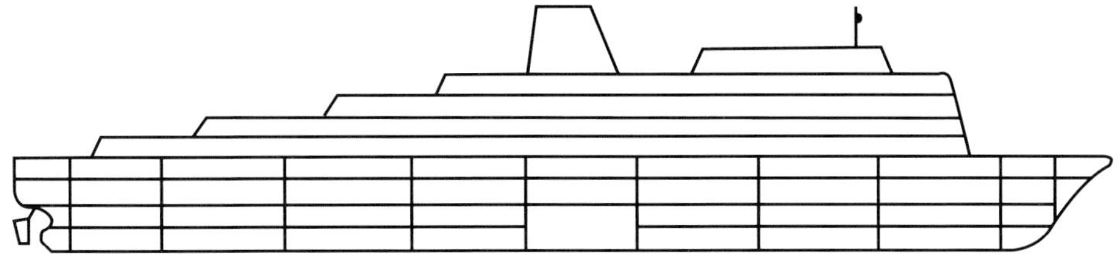

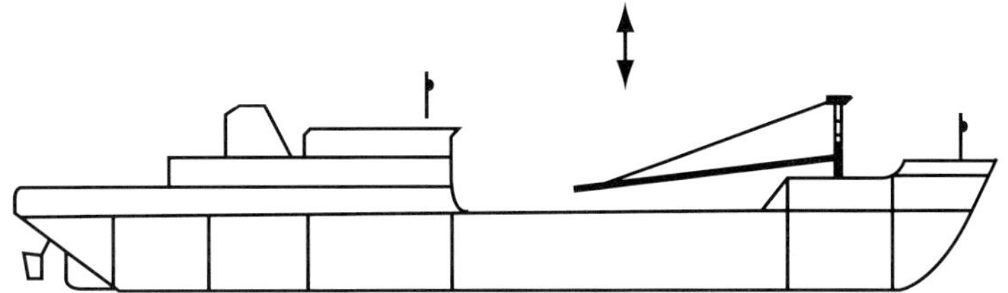

Vehicle Passenger Ferry

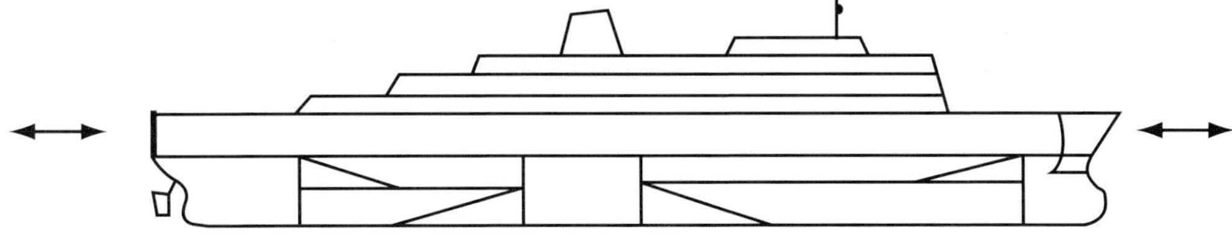

APPENDIX 1

Ship Profiles (Continued)

New Vehicles Carrier

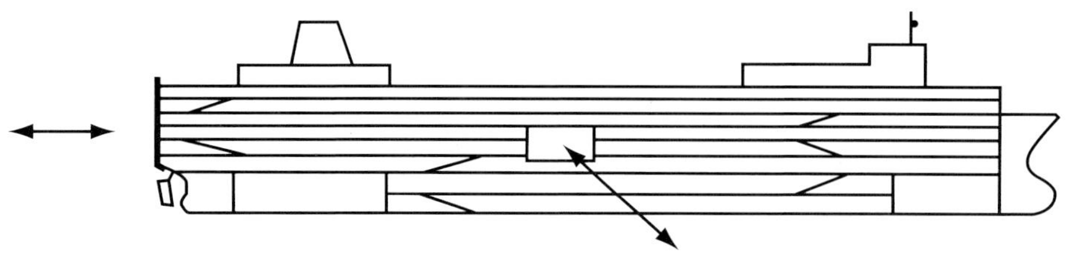

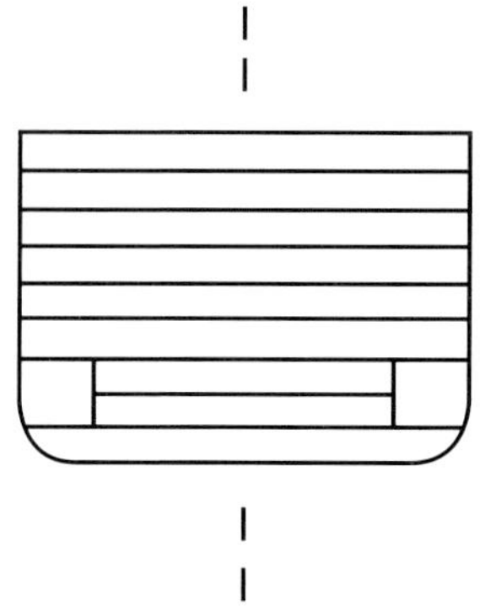

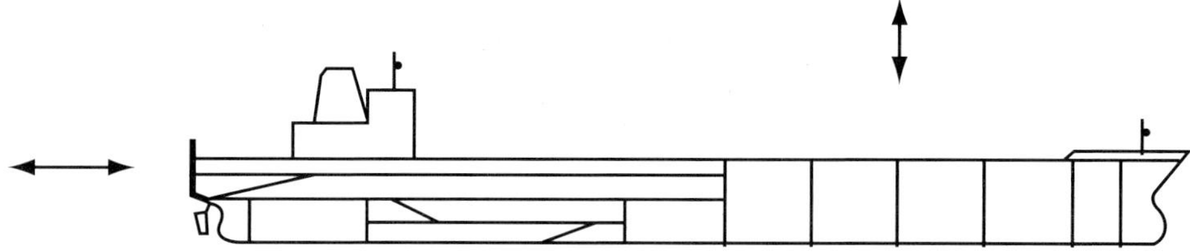

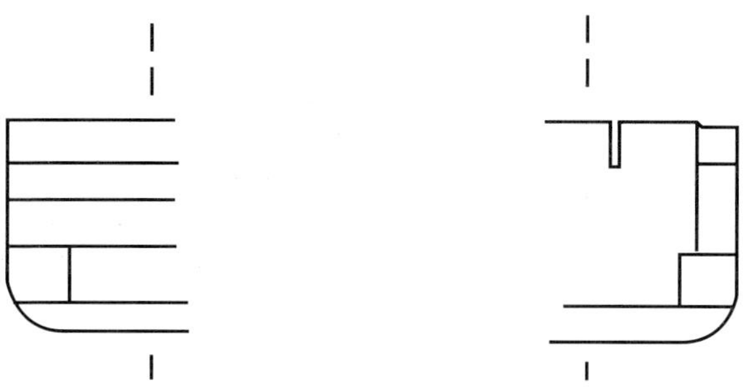

APPENDIX 1

Ship Profiles (Continued)

Nuclear Fuel Carrier

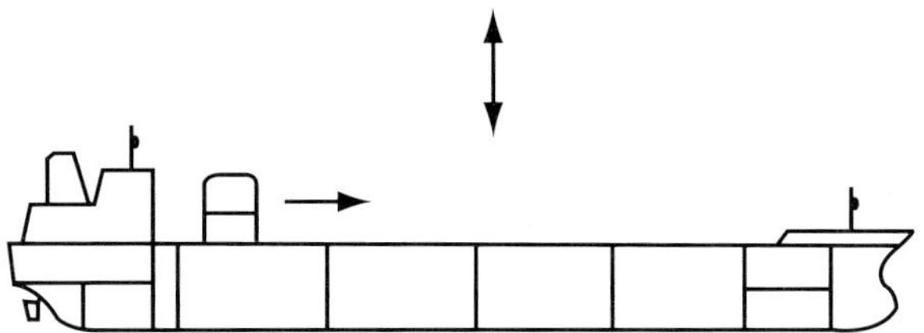

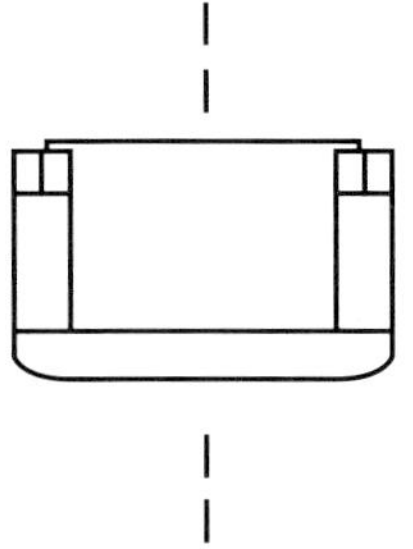

Livestock Carrier

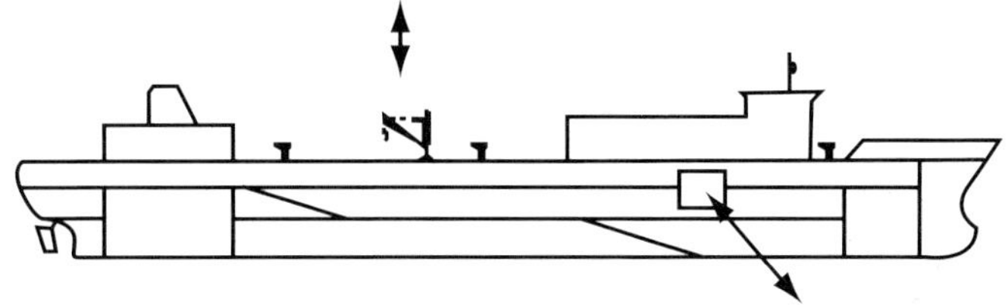

Livestock Carrier

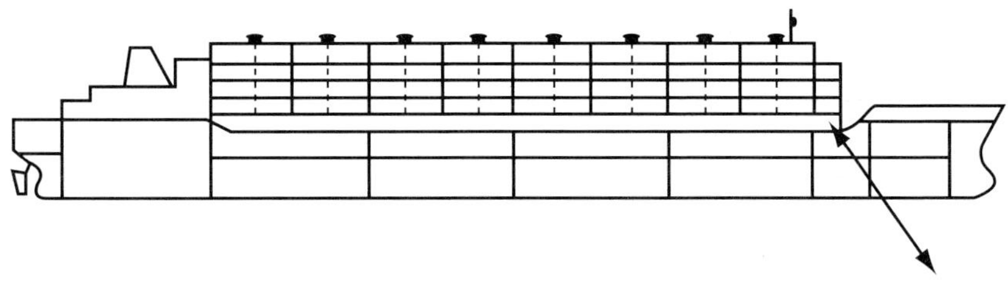

APPENDIX 1

Ship Profiles (Continued)

Fishing Vessel

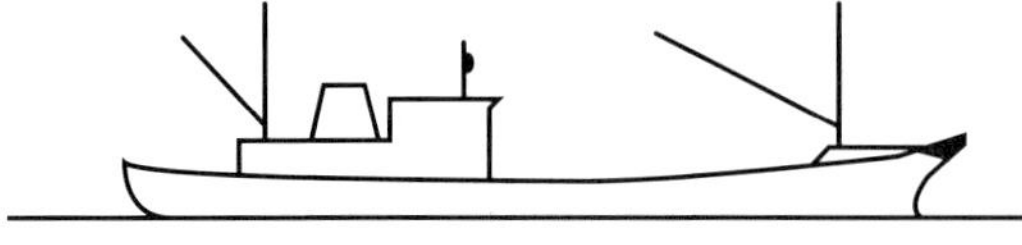

Trawler

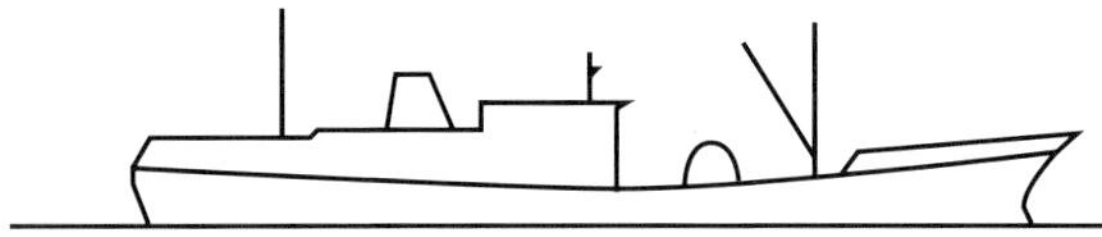

Stern Trawler

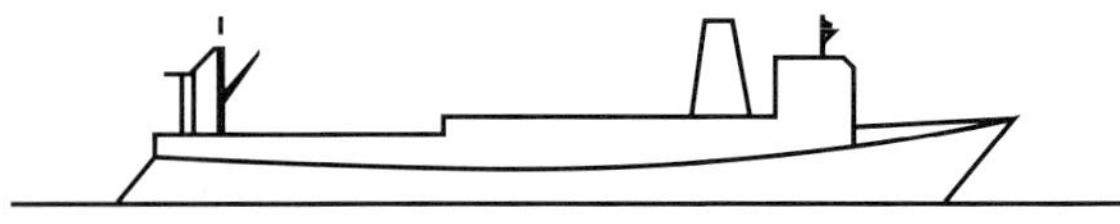

Fish Factory Ship

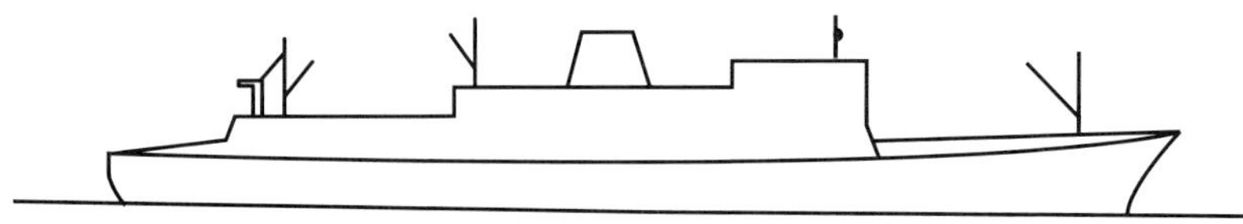

Whale Catcher

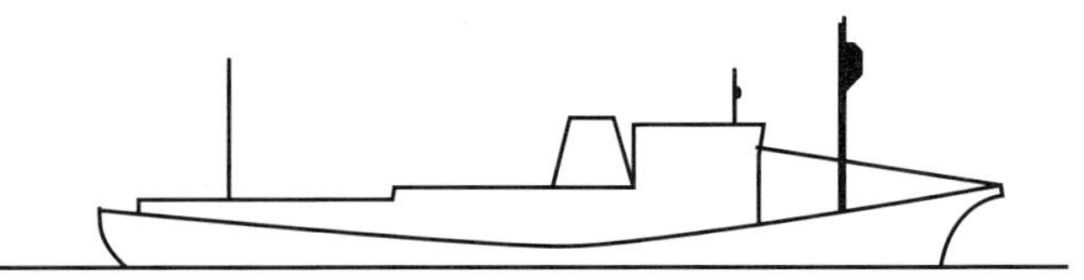

APPENDIX 1

Ship Profiles (Continued)

Offshore Supply Ship

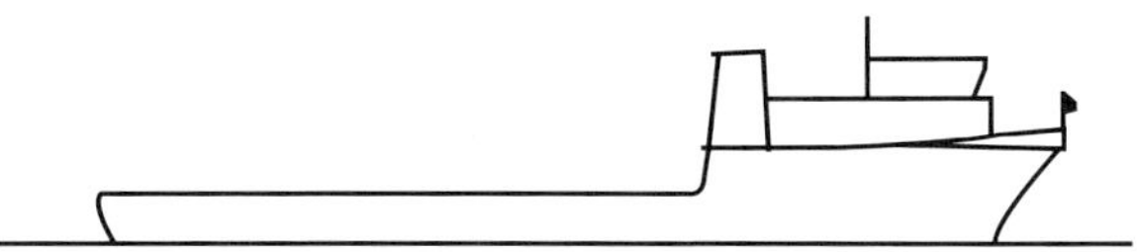

Offshore Support Ship

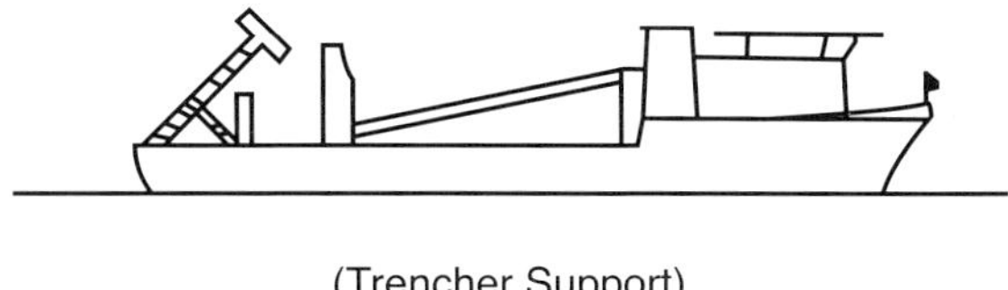

(Trencher Support)

Offshore Well Production Ship

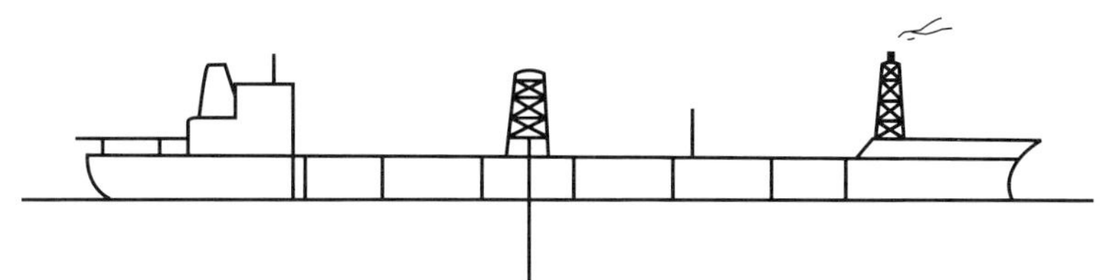

Drilling Ship

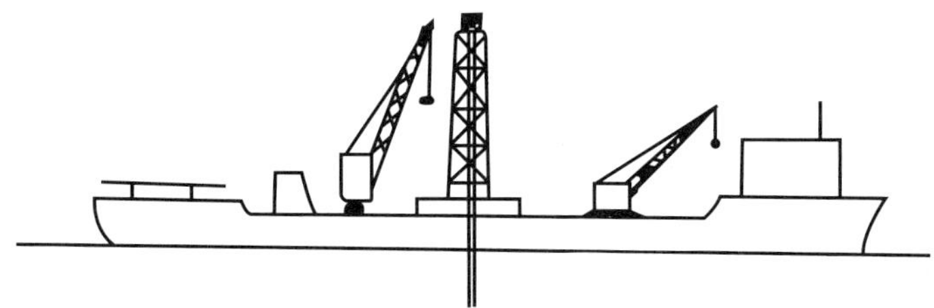

Pipe Laying Ship

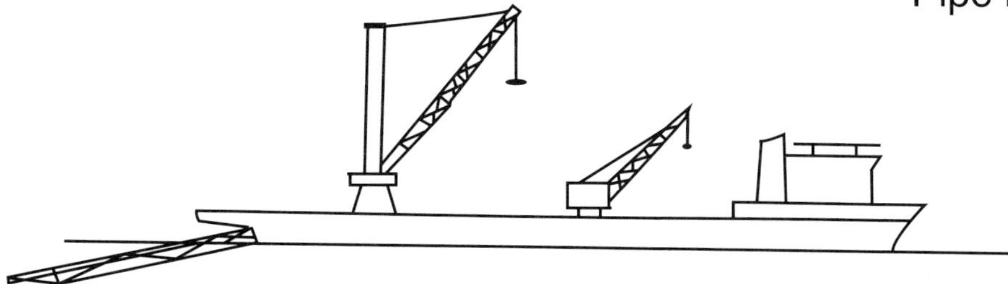

APPENDIX 1

Ship Profiles (Continued)

Crane Ship

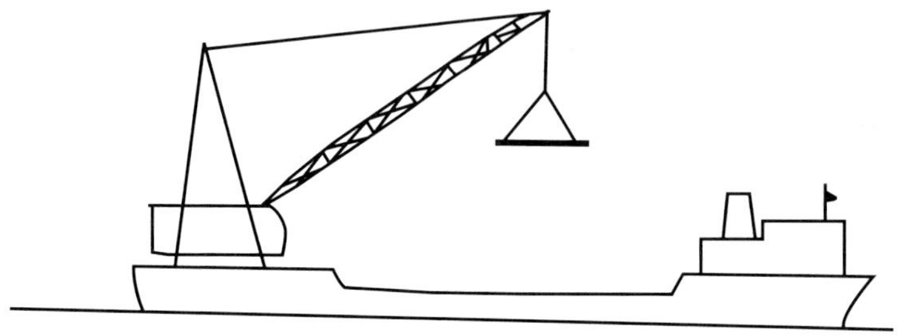

Cable Ship

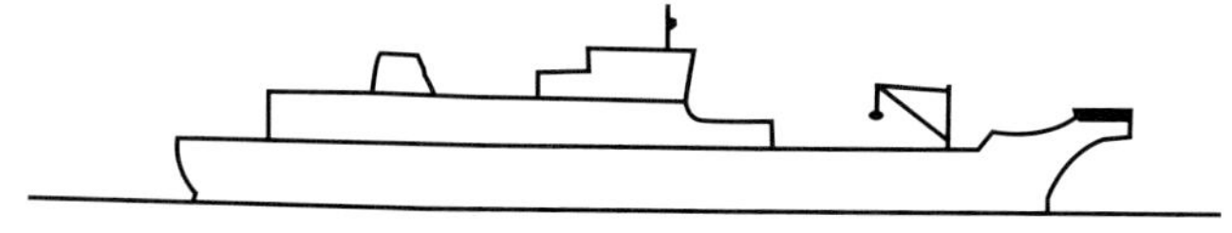

Ice Breaker

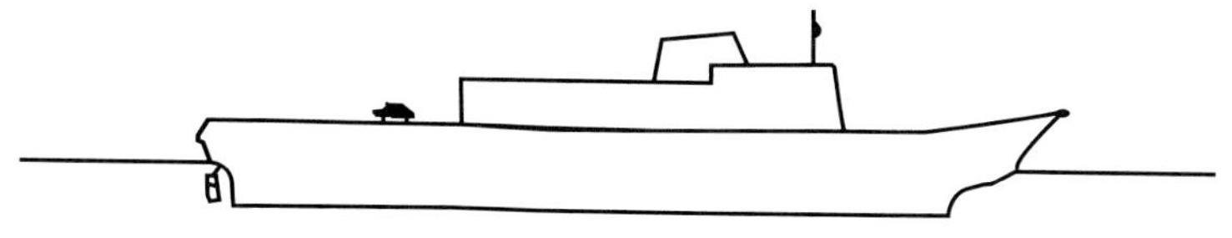

Tug

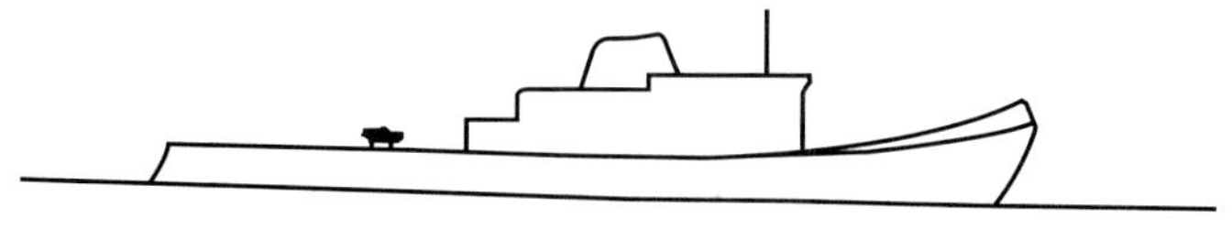

Pusher Tug

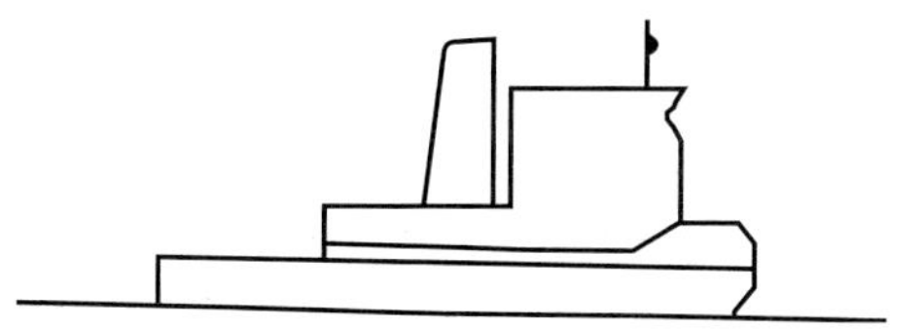

APPENDIX 1

Ship Profiles (Continued)

Dredger

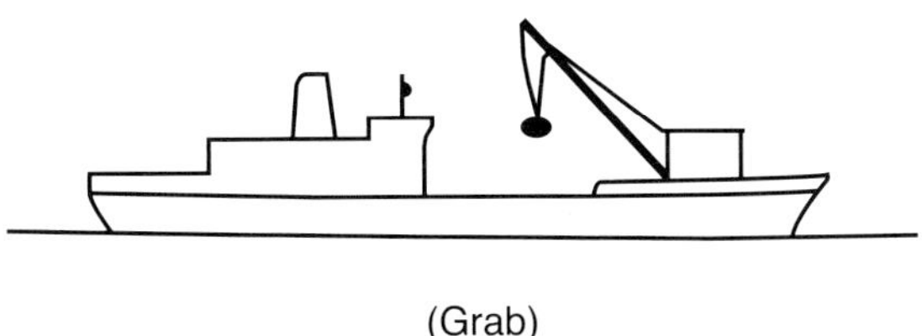

(Grab)

Hopper Dredger

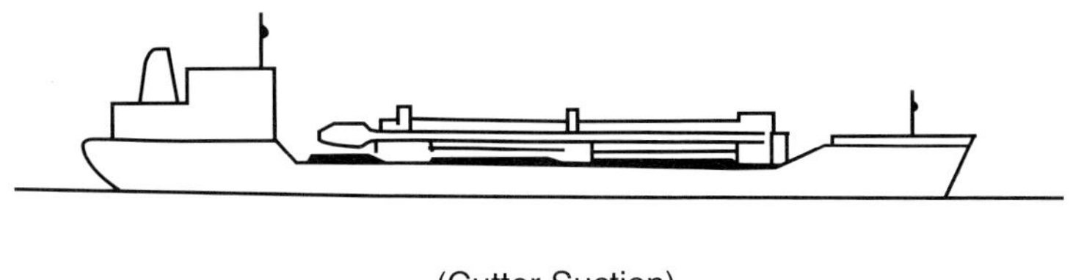

(Cutter Suction)

Hopper Ship

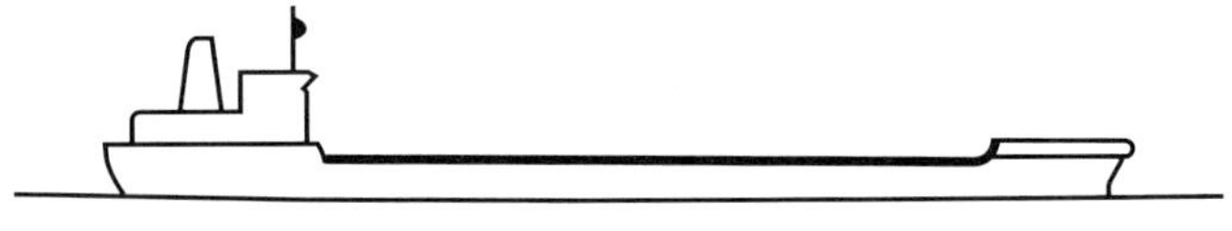

Sludge Carrier

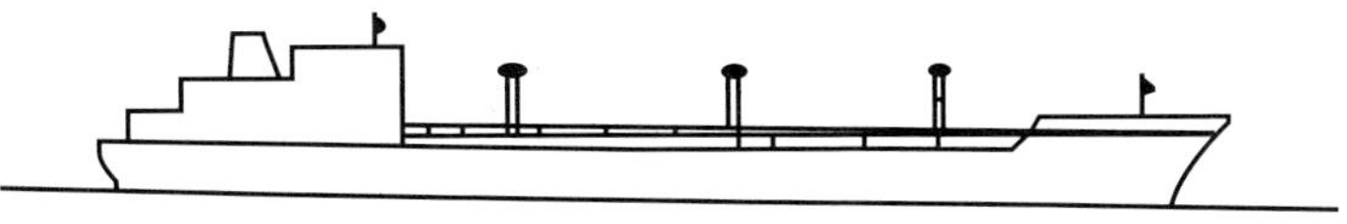

Incinerator Ship

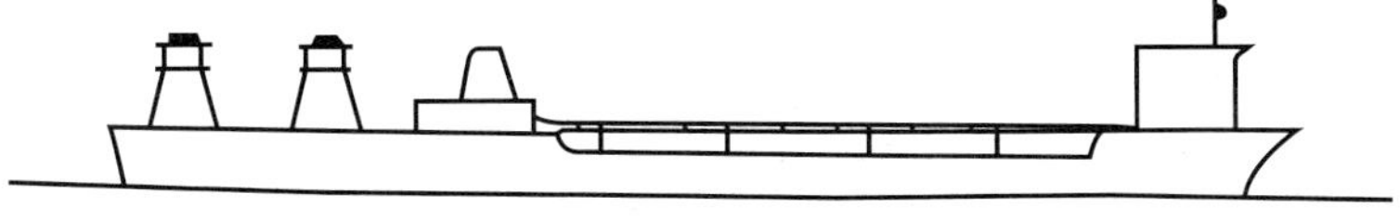

APPENDIX 1

Ship Profiles (Continued)

Landing Craft

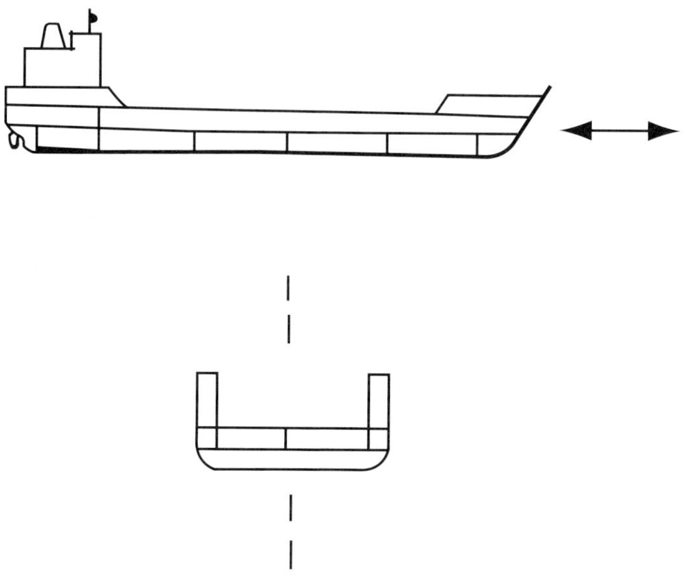

Deck Cargo Ship

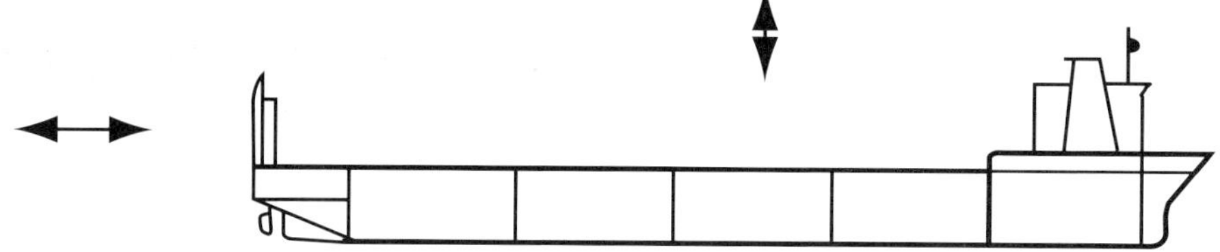

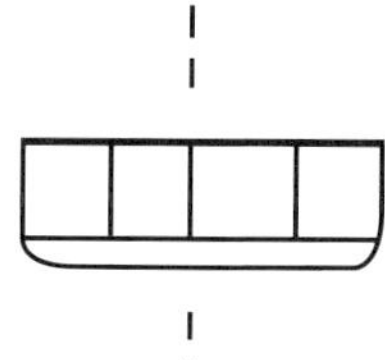

APPENDIX 1

Ship Profiles (Continued)

Deck Cargo Ship

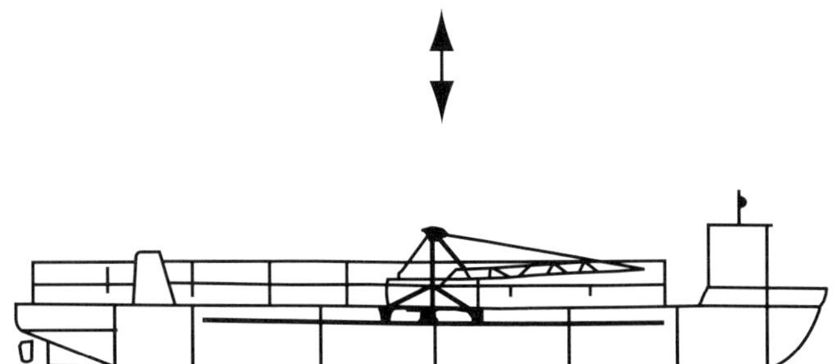

Semi-submersible Deck Cargo Ship

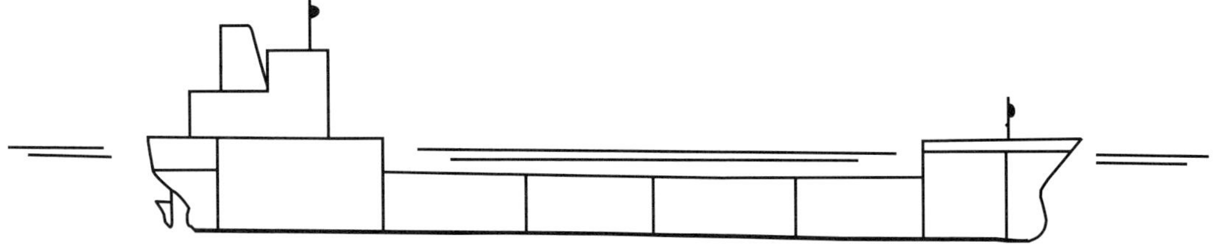

APPENDIX 1

Ship Profiles (Continued)

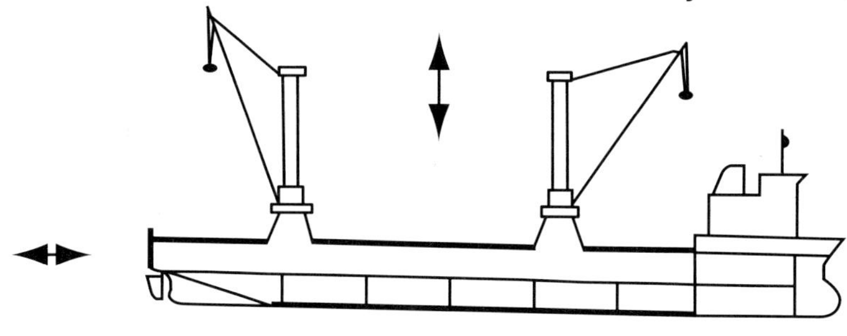

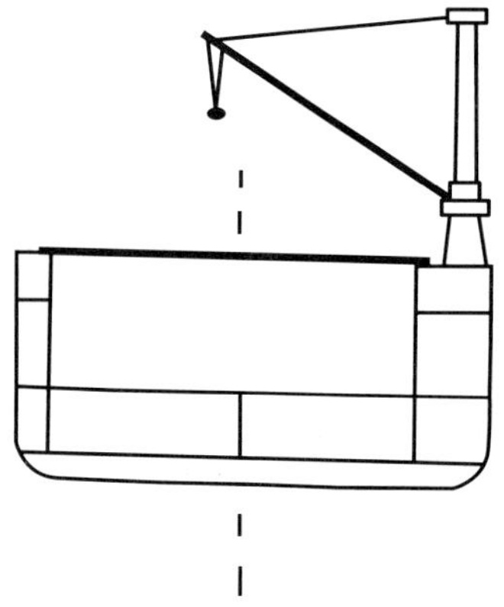

Semi-submersible Heavy Lift Cargo Ship

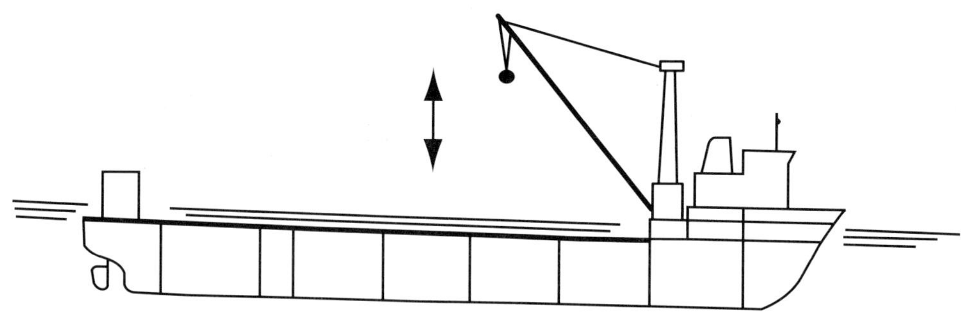

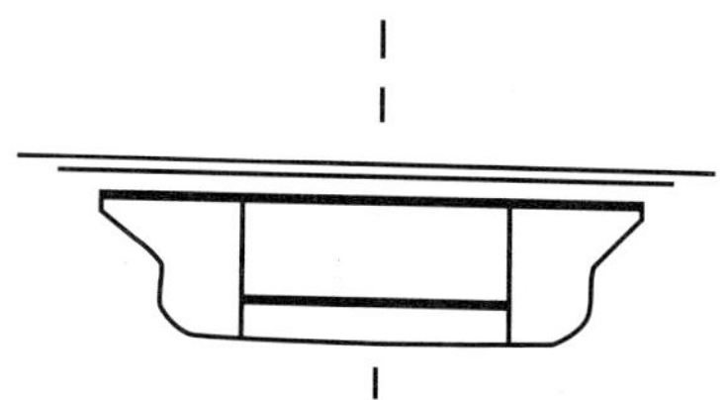

APPENDIX 1

Ship Profiles (Continued)

Barge Carrier

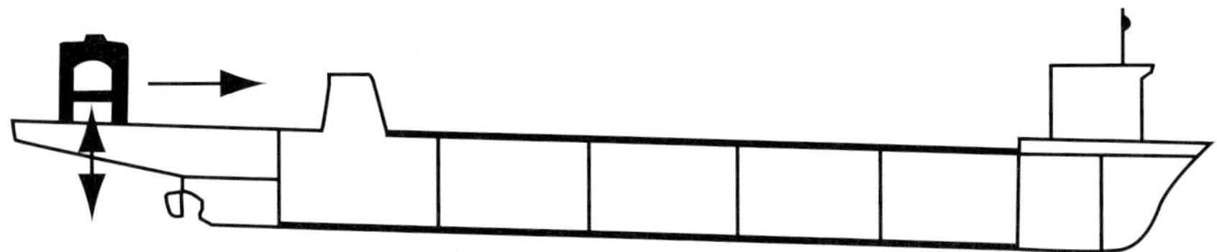

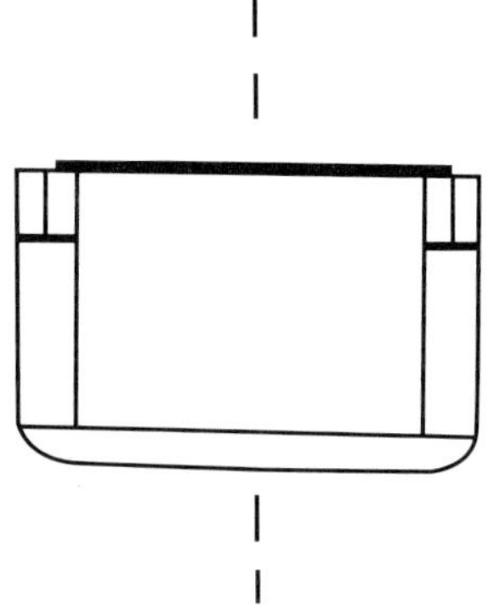

Semi-submersible Barge Carrier

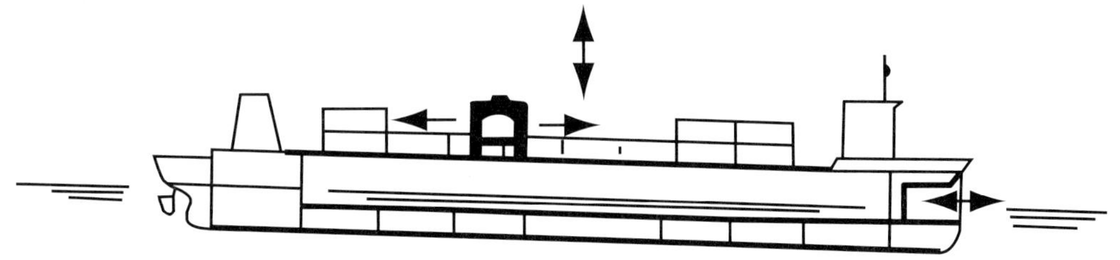

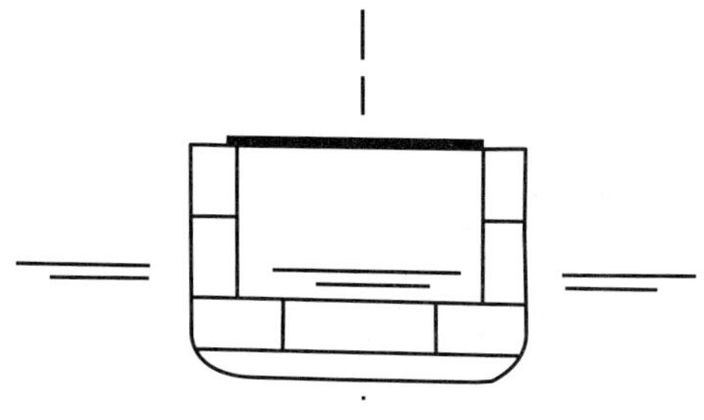

APPENDIX 2

General Arrangement Plan

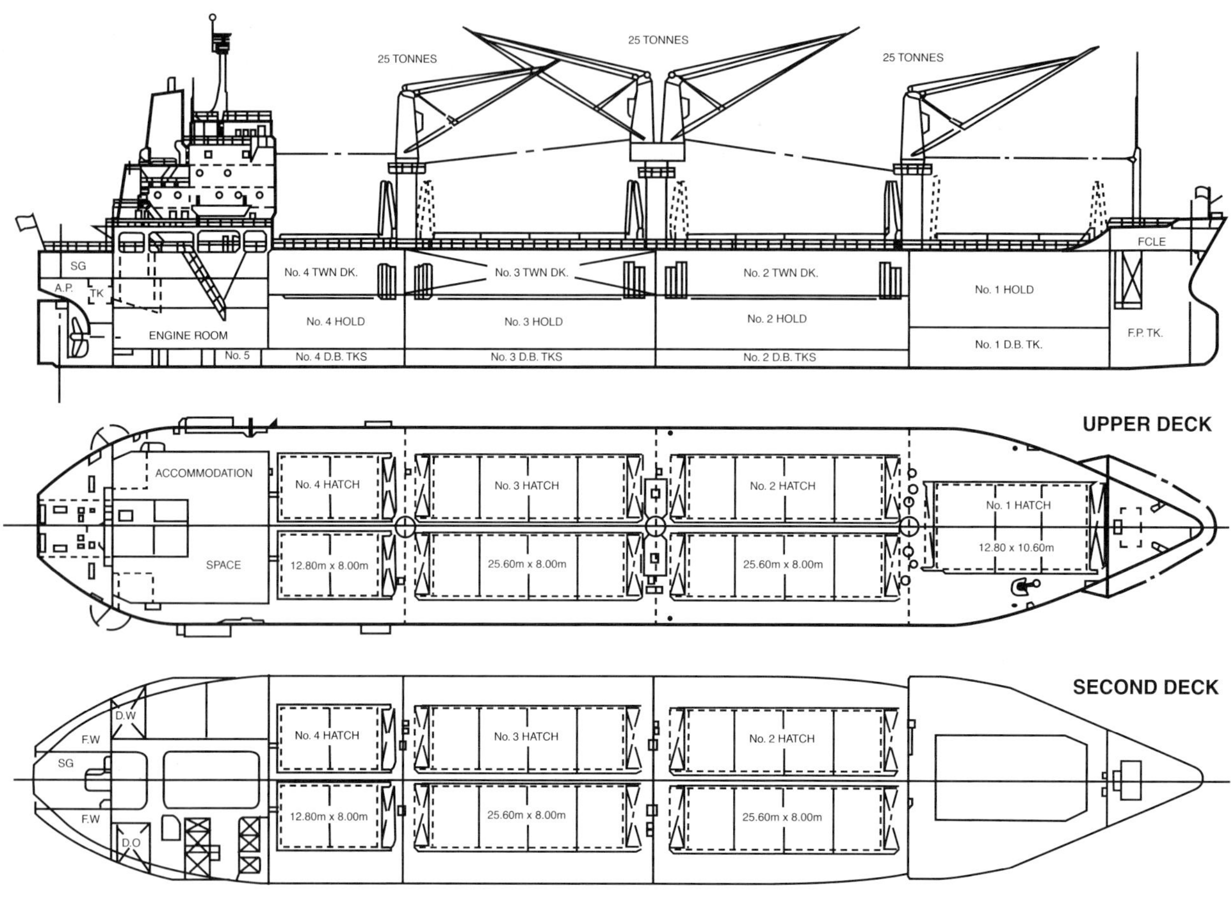

APPENDIX 3

British Registration Certificate

CERTIFICATE OF BRITISH REGISTRY

The Merchant Shipping Act 1995
The Merchant Shipping (Registration of Ships) Regulations 1993, as amended

PARTICULARS OF SHIP

Name Of Ship	YVONNE TEST			
Official Number	900078		*Radio Call Sign*	
IMO Number / HIN	1		*Port*	CARDIFF
Type Of Ship	PLEASURE YACHT			
Method Of Propulsion	SAIL & MOTOR			
Engine Make & Model	VOLVO PENTA			
Total Engine Power	33.57	*kW*		
Length	24.00	*metres*	*Breadth*	4.00 *metres*
Depth	3.00	*metres*		
Gross Tonnage	34.00		*Net Tonnage*	23.00
Registered Tonnage	0.00			
Year of Build	1997			
Name Of Builder	DAWKINS & DREW			
Country of Build	UNITED KINGDOM			

This Certificate was issued on 13 December 2000 *at* 15:03:12

This Certificate expires on 6 September 2004

Signed ....

For and on behalf of the Registrar, General of Shipping and Seamen

by the Maritime and Coastguard Agency, an Executive Agency of the Government of the United Kingdom

1/2 MSF 4700 REV 9/99

APPENDIX 3

British Registration Certificate (Continued)

For the purposes of registration there are 64 shares in a ship.

Name and address of owner(s)	No of shares
DAWKINS & DREW DUMMY ADDRESS *DAWKINS HOUSE, DAWKINS STREET, LLANDAFF, CARDIFF, CF5 3TU, WALES*	*64*

IMPORTANT INFORMATION

- A Certificate of Registry is not proof of ownership
- Details of registered mortgages are not shown.
- The Registry must be informed immediately:
  - *of any changes to the ships particulars or ownership;*
  - *if the vessel is lost.*
- The certificate must be surrendered to the Registry if the ship ceases to be a British registered ship.
- A duplicate must be obtained if the certificate is lost or becomes illegible.
- For further information contact the

Registry of Shipping and Seamen
PO Box 165
Cardiff
United Kingdom CF14 5FU
Telephone: 029 20747333
Fax: 029 20747877

DEPARTMENT OF THE ENVIRONMENT, TRANSPORT AND REGIONS

2/2

APPENDIX 4

History of Flags of Convenience

A BRIEF HISTORY OF THE DEVELOPMENT OF OPEN REGISTRIES

Period	Flag of Registry	Motivation
16th Century	Spanish	English merchants circumvented restrictions limiting non-Spanish vessels from West Indies trade.
17th Century	French	English fishermen in Newfoundland used French registry as a means to continue operation in conjunction with British registry fishing boats.
19th Century	Norwegian	British trawler owners changed registry to fish off Moray Firth.
Nepoleonic Wars	German	English shipowners in Massachusetts changed registry to avoid capture by the British.
1922	Panamanian	Two ships of United American Lines changed from US registry to avoid laws on serving alcoholic drink aboard US ships.
1920-1930	Panamanian/Honduran	US shipowners switched registry to reduce operating costs by employing cheaper shipboard labour.
1930s	Panamanian	Shipowners with German registered ships switched to Panamanian registry to avoid possible seizure.
1939-1941	Panamanian	With encouragement from the US Government, shipowners switched to Panamanian registry to assist the Allies without violating the Neutrality Laws. European shipowners also switched to Panamanian registry to avoid wartime requisitioning of their vessels.
1946-1949	Panamanian	More than 150 ships sold under the US Merchant Sales Act of 1946 were registered in Panama – as it offered liberal registration and taxation advantages.
1949-	Liberian	Low registration fees, absence of Liberian taxes, absence of operating and crewing restrictions made registry economically attractive.
1950 to present	Many FCOs	As registration in the developed world became increasingly costly and restrictive, many shipowners turned to open registers.

APPENDIX 5

Lloyd's Register Abbreviations

† for fuller explanation see the Key

Abbreviation	Column	Explanation
*	4 & 7	
•	4 & 7	
✠	4	
100	4	Character symbols, figures and letters
A	4	of class and equipment
1	4	See Key, Column 4
N	4	
T	4	
OU	4	
a	4, 5 & 7	aft
AB	4	American Bureau of Shipping
a.c.	7	alternating current
ACV	4	Air Cushion Vehicles
A dk	5	Awning deck
(AdV)	4	† Advancement of Special Survey
A. Fr	6	A-Frame
alt	5	altered
(alu)	6	aluminium
APBH	5	After Peak Bulkhead
APT	4	After Peak Tank
Aux	6	Auxiliary
AuxB	7	† Auxiliary Boiler(s)
B	4 & 5	Bridge
B	6	† Bale capacity (in cubic metres)
(BB)	5	† Bulbous Bow
BC	4	British Corporation
BH	5	Bulkhead(s)
bhp	7	† brake horsepower
BK	5	Bar Keel
Box K	5	Box Keel
Bow/CM	5	Distance from bow to centre manifold
B. P.	5	Between Perpendiculars
BR	4	Bulgarian Register of Shipping
BS	4	† Classification symbols of the British
BS (Comp)	4	Corporation
bth	6	† Passenger berths
btm	5	bottom
BV	4	Bureau Veritas
c	5 & 7	centre
(c)	7	† Burning coal
C	4	† Diameter of wrought iron cable in sixteenths of an inch (British Corporation Rules)
C	6	† Total carrying capacity of Containers
C	7	Compound expansion engines
CAS(HR) Level 1SS	6	† Condition Assessment Scheme
CAS(HR) Level 2SS	6	† Condition Assessment Scheme
CASPPR	4	Canadian Arctic Shipping Pollution Prevention Regulations
Cbn	6	† Passenger cabins
CBT	6	† Clean Ballast arrangements
CBT (LR)	6	
(cc)	4	† corrosion control
((cc))	4	
(CC)	7	Constant Current system
CCS	4	China Classification Society
CCS	4	† Centralised Control System
(CCS)	4	Approval of control engineering equipment temporarily suspended
ccy	6	conical cylindrical
C. Dk	6	† Containers carried on Deck
C. Ho	6	† Containers carried in Hold(s)
Cell. Ho.	6	† Cellular Hold(s)
CG	4	Cargo gear on ships
CL	4	Cargo Lifts
CM	4 & 6	Construction Monitoring
Cmd.	5	† Commissioned
(C.mn.stl)	6	Carbon manganese steel
Cmpl.	5	† Completed
Coll	5	Collision
Coll Rdr	1	Collision Radar
Comb.	5	Combined
comb.	6	combined
Comp.	6	Composite construction
Comp	7	Composite (oil & ex. g) fired
Cont	4	† Continuation of class
contr.	7	controllable
conv	5	converted/adapted (from)
COW	6	† Crude Oil Washing
COW (LR)	6	
(cr)	4	centre
Cr	6	† Cranes
CR	4	Cargo Ramps
CR	4 & 6	† Corrosion Resistant material
CRS	4	Hrvatski Registar Brodova (Croatia)
cs	6	† cargo segregation
CS	4	Continuous Survey of the Hull
CSD	6	Closed Shelter Deck Ship
CT	4	† Cubic Tonnage (British Corporation Rules)
Cy.	7	† Cylinders
cyl	6	cylindrical
D	6	† Drivers
D	7	Diagonal engines
DA	7	† Double Acting
db	7	† domestic boiler
DB	4 & 6	Double Bottom
d.c.	7	direct current
dcc	6	double cylindrical conical
dcy	6	double-lobe cylindrical
DD	6	Double Deck
D-E	6	Diesel-Electric
Der	6	† Derricks
Der/Cr	6	Derricks/Cranes
Df	1	Direction finder
Diam.	5	Diameter of manifold
disch.	6	discharge
dk	5 & 6	deck
Dk	5	Deck tank (for water ballast)
DK	5	Duct Keel
(d.o.)	7	† burning diesel oil
DP (AA)	4	Dynamic Positioning with fully redundant automatic control system
DP (AAA)	4	Dynamic Positioning with fully redundant automatic control system and emergency automatic control system
DP (AM)	4	Dynamic Positioning with automatic and centralised remote manual control system
DP (CM)	4	Dynamic Positioning with centralised remote manual control system
dr	7	double reduction (gearing)
DSRK	4	Deutsche Schiffs-Revision und Klassifikation GmbH
DSS	6	Double Skin Side
DT	4, 5 & 6	Deep Tank
DTs	4 & 5	Deep Tanks
E	7	† Engine(s)
e(ex. g)	7	exhaust gas economiser
econ	7	economiser
(EI)	4	† Equipment Incomplete (British Corporation Rules)
EL	4	† Equipment Letter
elec.	7	electric
Emy.	7	Emergency
ER	4 & 5	Engine Room
ER	6	† Engine Room
ES	6	† Enhanced Scantlings
Esd	1	Echo sounding device
ESP	4	Enhanced Survey Programme
ESQ	4	Extra Special Quality steel cable
(ex. g)	7	exhaust gas (boilers)
f	4, 5 & 7	forward
F	5	Forecastle
fbd	4	† freeboard
fcsa	6	freight container securing arrangements
FD	7	Forced Draught
FDA	4 & 6	† Fatigue Design Assessment
FN	4	† Fee Numeral
FP	4	Flash Point
FPT	4	Fore Peak Tank
FSWR	4	Flexible Steel Wire Ropes
FW	5	† Fresh Water
fwd	2, 5, 6 & 7	forward
G.	6	† Grain capacity (in cubic metres)
G./Cr	6	Gantry/Cranes
Gc	1	Gyro-compass
gen.	7	generator(s)
GL	4	Germanischer Lloyd AG
GT	6	Gas Turbine
GT-E	6	Gas Turbo-Electric
H	5	† Houses on deck
H	7	Horizontal engines
Ha	6	† Hatchway(s)
HCM	6	† Hull Condition Monitoring
HeCls. B	6	Heating Coils in Bunkers
HeCls. C	6	Heating Coils in Cargo Tanks
Ho	6	† Holds
Ho/Ta	6	Holds/Tanks
HP	7	High Pressure
HR	4	Hellenic Register of Shipping
hs	7	† heating surface (in square metres)
HSC	4	High Speed Craft
HSS	4	Hull Surveillance System
htr	7	heater
(hvf)	7	† Fitted for burning high viscosity fuel
HWH	7	Hot Water Heater
Hz	7	hertz
IBS	4	Integrated Bridge Navigation System
ICC	4	Integrated Computer Control
(i.f.o.)	7	intermediate fuel oil
IFP	4	Integrated Fire Protection
IGS	6	† Inert Gas System
IGS (LR)	6	
IGS	4	
(IGS)	4	Approval of inert gas system temporarily suspended
ihp	7	† indicated horsepower
In.	6	† Insulated capacity (in cubic metres)
incl.	5	including
IP	4	Integrated propulsion
IP	7	Intermediate Pressure
Irn	5	Iron
(Irn)	6	Iron
IRS	4	Indian Register of Shipping
*I.W.S.	4	Ship arranged for In Water Survey
JR	4	Jugoslavenski Registar Brodova
KI	4	Biro Klasifikasi Indonesia
kn	7	† knots
KR	4	Korean Register of Shipping
kW	7	† kilowatts
L	6	Ramp length
L	6	† Liquid capacity (in cubic metres)
LA	4	Lifting Appliance
Lake SS	4	Periodical survey of ship classed for Great Lakes service
Lch.	5	† Launched
LDC	4	Light Displacement Craft
len	5	lengthened
LI	4 & 6	Loading Instrument
Lloyd's RMC	4	† Refrigerated cargo installation class
(Lloyd's RMC)	4	Lloyd's RMC class temporarily suspended
Lloyd's RMC (LG)	4	† Class for refrigerating equipment for dealing with boil-off gas on a liquefied gas carrier
(Lloyd's RMC (LG))	4	Lloyd's RMC (LG) class temporarily suspended
LMA	4	Lloyd's Manoeuvring Assessment
LMC	4	† Machinery class
(LMC)	4	† Machinery class temporarily suspended
LP	7	Low Pressure
LR	4	Lloyd's Register
L.S.'O'.	4	Loading Sequence Accelerated
L.S.'T'.	4	Loading Sequence Normal
Lwr	6	Lower
lwr	6 & 7	lower
m	4 & 5	midship
M	4	† Modified Special Survey
M	6	Motorship
MBS	4	† Machinery class (British Corporation Rules)
MBS $^{E}_{B}$	4	
Mchy	6	Machinery
M.Cr	6	Mobile Crane
M.E.	7	Main Engine
MH	5	Height of manifold above upper deck
N	4	† Equipment not required
NAuxB	7	† New Auxiliary Boiler(s)
NAV	4	† Lloyd's Navigation Certificate
NAV1	4	† Lloyd's Navigation Certificate for Periodic One Man Watch
NB	7	† New Main Boiler(s)
ND	5	New Deck
ND	7	Natural Draught
ndb	7	† new domestic boiler(s)
NE	7	† New Engine(s)
(Ni.stl)	6	Nickel Steel
NK	4	Nippon Kaiji Kyokai
NNR	7	New Nuclear Reactor(s)
NR	7	Nuclear Reactor

APPENDIX 5

Lloyd's Register Abbreviations (Continued)

Abbreviation	Column	Explanation
NV	4	Det Norske Veritas Classification A/S
NWTB	7	† New Water Tube Main Boiler(s)
nwtdb	7	† new water tube domestic boiler(s)
(o.f.)	7	† oil fuel or oil-fired boilers
OSD	6	Open Shelter Deck Ship
OSD/CSD	6	† Open & Closed Shelter Deck Ship
p or (p)	6 & 7	port
P	5	Poop
P	6	† Passengers
P	6	Paddle
PBH	5	Partial Bulkhead
PC	4	Cranes on Platforms
PCR	4	Performance Capability Rating
PCWBT	6	† Protective Coatings in Water Ballast Tanks
pd	7	per day
Pfd	1	Position fixing device
PL	4	Passenger Lifts
PL	6	Protective Location
PM	4	Position Mooring
PMC	4	Position Mooring in Close Proximity
PM ,	4	Position Mooring with Thruster assist
PMC*	4	Position Mooring with Thruster assist in close Proximity
PMS	6	Approved Planned Maintenance Scheme
PMS(CM)	6	Approved Planned Maintenance Scheme based on machinery condition monitoring
PORT	4	Automation in port operations
pri	6	prismatic
PR	4	Polski Rejestr Statkow
Prom dk	5	Promenade deck
pt	2, 4, 5 & 6	part
pv	4	† pressure/vacuum relief valve
Q	6	Quadruple screw
Q	7	Quadruple expansion engines
R	5	† Riveted
RAD	5	Raised After Deck
RCB	4	Registro Cubano de Buques
rcv	7	receiver
R dk	5	Raised deck
Rdr	1	Radar
rec	6	rectangular
Recmd.	5	† Recommissioned
Ref	6	Ship fitted with refrigerated cargo installation
Rest	4	† Restoration of class
rf	5	† rise of floor (or deadrise)
RFD	5	Raised Fore Deck
RI	4	Registro Italiano Navale
RIB	4	Rigid Inflatable Boat
(r.l)	6	rubber lined
RNR	4	Registru Naval Roman
RoRo	6	Roll on-Roll off
RQD	5	Raised Quarter Deck
RP	4	Rinave Portuguesa
RS	4	Russian Maritime Register of Shipping
RSD	5	Raised Shelter Deck
RT	1	Radio-Telephone
RTm	1	Radio-Telephone (medium frequency)
RTh	1	Radio-Telephone (high frequency)
RTv	1	Radio-Telephone (very high frequency)
RW	5	† Riveted and Welded
s or (s)	6 & 7	starboard
S	4	† Diameter of steel cable in sixteenths of an inch (British Corporation Rules)
S	6	Steamship
S	7	Simple expansion engine(s)
SA	7	† Single Acting
SatCom	1	Satellite Communication
SatNav	1	Satellite Navigation
SB	7	Single-ended Main Boiler(s)
SBP	6	† Steady Bollard Pull
SBT	6	† Segregated Ballast Tanks
SBT(LR)	6	
SBT/PL	6	
SBT/PL(LR)	6	
SC	4	Service Craft
SCM	6	Screwshaft Condition Monitoring
sc.	7	screw
SDA	4 & 6	† Structural Design Assessment
S dk	5	Shelter Deck
SDS	6	SOLAS Damage Stability
SDS(LR)	6	
SEA	6	† Ship Event Analysis
SEA(R)	6	† Ship Event Analysis with Continuous Data Recording Capability
SERS	6	† Ship Emergency Response Service
SES	4	Surface Effect Ship
sg	7	steam heated steam generator(s)
SG	4	† Specific gravity (relative density)
shp	7	† Shaft horsepower
sph	6	spherical
SPM	4	Single Point Mooring
spt	7	† Superheater(s)
SQ	4	Special Quality steel cable
sr	7	single reduction (gearing)
SS	4	† Special Survey
SSC	4	Special Service Craft
(s.stl)	6	stainless steel
ST	5	Side Tank
stbd	4 & 7	starboard
(stl)	6	steel
Stl	5	Steel
Str.	6	Strengthened
STs	5	Side Tanks
S Turb	7	Steam Turbine(s)
S.W.B.M.	4	Still Water Bending Moment
SWL	6	Safe Working Load
SWR	4	Steel Wire Ropes
(Sy)	7	Synchronous system
t	5	tons (2240lb)
t	7	tonnes (1000kg)
T	4	Operation and equipment
T	5	Tonnes (1000kg)
T	6	Tapered hatchway, with narrower breadth
T	6	Twin Screw
T	7	Triple expansion engine
Ta	6	Tanks
T/cm	3	Tonnes per centimetre immersion
TCM	6	Main steam Turbine Condition Monitoring
T/hr	6	Tonnes per hour
T-E	6	Turbo-Electric
teak s	5	teak sheathed (decks)
TEU	6	Twenty-foot equivalent units
Thw.	7	Athwartship
TL	4	Turk Loydu
T.Mk	3	† Tonnage Mark
TOH	7	Thermal Oil Heater
Tr	6	Triple screw
tr	7	triple reduction (gearing)
TwD	4 & 5	'Tween Deck tank(s)
TwD	6	'Tween Deck space
U	7	Unaflow or Uniflow
U1	4	† Grades of chain cable
U2		
U3		
U4		
U dk	5	Upper deck
UMS	4	† Unattended Machinery Spaces
(UMS)	4	Approval of control engineering equipment temporarily suspended
UnDk	5	Underdeck tank(s)
Upr.	5 & 6	Upper
upr	7	upper
V	7	volt
VDR	4	Voyage Data Recorder System
veg.	4	vegetable
(w)	6	wood
W	6	Traversable width of ramp
W	6	† Winches
WB	5	Water Ballast
W dk	5	Weather deck
WI	4	Wrought Iron cable
(WL)	7	Ward Leonard system
ws	5	wood sheathed (decks)
WT	5	Watertight
WTAuxB	7	Water Tube Auxiliary Boiler(s)
WTB	7	Water Tube Main Boiler(s)
wtdb	7	water tube domestic boiler(s)

APPENDIX 6

Lloyd's Register Column Headings

REGISTO DE NAVIOS

1	2	3	4	5	6	7
LR No. de identificação	NOME DO NAVIO	TONELAGEM	CLASSIFICAÇÃO	CASCO	TIPO DE NAVIO/APARELHO DE CARGA	MÁQUINAS
Radio Distintivo No. Oficial Ajudas de Navegação	Nomes anteriores Armadores Administradores Porto de Registo Nacionalidade	Bruta Liquida Dead-weight Bruta Liquida Dead-weight	Casco Ultima reclassificação Máquinas Instalação frigorífica de carga Letra de equipamento Numero base dos honorarios	Data construção Estaleiros—Local de construção No. de construção Comprimento fora a fora Boca extrema Calado máximo Comprimento entre perpendiculares Boca na ossada Pontal ossada Superstruturas Convéses Cravado/Soldado Elevação Caverna Quilha (mm) Alterações Conversões Antepares Lastro de água	Propulsão Tipo navio Shelter Deck Passageiros No de porões e Comprimentos (m) Tanques de Carga e tipos Cereal/Liquido (m^3) Fardos (m^3) Espaços Isolados (m^3) Serpentinas de aquecimento Contentores e comprimentos (pés) Escotilhas e dimensões (m) Guinchos Gruas/Paus de carga (S.W.L. tons.)	No. e tipo de máquinas Diâmetro · Curso (mm) Potência [illegible] Fabricantes das máquinas Local de [illegible] Pressão caldeiras Superfície de aquecimento Fornalhas Geradores auxiliares eléctricos Hélices especiais Tanques de combustível (tonnes) Velocidad

SCHIFFSREGISTER

1	2	3	4	5	6	7
LR-NUMMER	SCHIFFSNAME	TONNAGE	SCHIFFSKLASSE	SCHIFFSRUMPF	SCHIFFSTYP/LADEEINRICHTUNGEN	MASCHINENANLAGE
Signal Reg.-Nr. Navigations-Instr.	Frühere Namen Reederei Korr.-Reeder Heimathafen Flagge	Brutto Netto *Tragfähigkeit Brutto Netto *Tragfähigkeit *(tonnen)	Schiffsrumpf Klassenbesichtigung Maschinenanlage Ladekühlanlage Ausrüstungsbuchstabe Gebührenkennzahl	Baudatum Bauwerft u. -ort Bau Nr. Länge über alles (m) Äußerste Breite (m) Größter Tiefgang (m) Länge zw. d. Loten (m) Breite auf Spanten (m) Seitenhöhe (m) Aufbauten (m) Decks Genietet/Geschweißt Aufkimmung (mm) Kiel (mm) Änderungen Schotte Ballastwasser Umbauten	Antrieb Schiffstyp Schutzdeck Passagiere Laderäume m. Längen (m)/Ladetanks & Art Getreide/Flüss. Ladung (m^3) Ballen (m^3) Isolierte Räume (m^3) Heizschlangen Container m. Längen (Fuß) Luken m. Größen (m) Winden Krane/Ladebäume (Nutzlast in t)	Motorentyp & -anzahl Zyl. Durchm. × Hub Leistung Bau[illegible] Hersteller Bauor[illegible] Kessel Druck Heizfläche Feuerraum Bordnetzgeneratorsätze & Leistung Spezialpropeller Brennstoffbunker (t) Geschwindigkeit

REGISTRO DE BUQUES

1	2	3	4	5	6	7
NUMERO DE LR	NOMBRE DEL BUQUE	TONELAJE	CLASIFICACION	CASCO	TIPO DE BUQUE/ MANIPULACION DE CARGA	MAQUINARIA
Señal distintivo Número oficial Ayudas navegacionales	Nombres anteriores Armador Naviero Puerto de matrícula Bandera	Bruto Neto *Peso muerto Bruto Neto *Peso muerto *(tonnes)	Casco Visita Especial Maquinaria Instalación para carga refrigerada Letra del equipo Numeral de tarifa	Fecha de construcción Constructores—Lugar de construcción No. de construcción Eslora total (m) Manga máxima (m) Calado máximo (m) Eslora entre perpendiculares (m) Manga de trazado (m) Puntal de trazado (m) Superestructuras (m) Cubiertas Remachado/Soldado Astilla muerta (mm) Quilla (mm) Alteraciones Mamparos Tanques de lastre Conversiones	Propulsión Tipo de buque "Shelter deck" Pasajeros Bodegas y longitudes (m)/Tanques de carga y tipos Grano/Líquido (m^3) Balas (m^3) Espacios aislados (m^3) Serpentines de calefacción Contenedores y longitudes (pies) Escotillas y dimensiones (m) Chigres Grúas/Puntales de carga (carga de trabajo en tonnes)	Número y tipo de motores Diámetro x carrera (mm) Potencia Diseño Constructores Lugar de construcción Calderas Presiones Superficie de caldeo Hornos Grupos electrógenos auxiliares y potencia Hélices especiales Capacidad de combustible (tonnes) Velocidad

REGISTER OF SHIPS

1	2	3	4	5	6	7
LR No.	SHIP'S NAME	TONS	CLASSIFICATION	HULL	SHIP TYPE/CARGO FACILITIES	MACHINERY
Call Sign Official No. Nav. aids	Former names Owners Managers Port of Registry Flag	Gross Net *Deadwt Gross Net *Deadwt *(tonnes)	Hull Special Survey Machinery Refrigerated cargo installation Equipment letter Fee Numeral	Date of build Shipbuilders—Place of build Yard Number Length overall (m) Breadth extreme (m) Draught maximum (m) Length B.P. (m) Breadth moulded (m) Depth moulded (m) Superstructures (m) Decks Riveted/Welded Rise of floor (mm) Keel (mm) Alterations Bulkheads Water ballast Conversions	Propulsion Ship type Shelter deck Passengers Holds & lengths (m)/Cargo tanks & types Grain/Liquid (m^3) Bale (m^3) Insulated spaces (m^3) Heating coils Containers & lengths (ft) Hatchways & sizes (m) Winches Cranes/Derricks (SWL tonnes)	No. & Type of engines Bore x stroke (mm) Power Design Enginebuilders Where manufactured Boilers Pressures Heating surface Furnaces Aux. electrical generating plant & output Special propellers Fuel bunkers (tonnes) Speed

APPENDIX 6

Lloyd's Register Column Headings (Continued)

REGISTRE DES NAVIRES

1 NUMERO LR	2 NOM DU NAVIRE	3 JAUGE	4 CLASSIFICATION	5 COQUE	6 TYPE DE NAVIRE ET MANUTENTION	7 MACHINES
Signal distinctif Numéro d'immatriculation Aides à la navigation	Anciens noms Armateur Gérant Port d'attache Pavillon	Brute Nette *Port en lourd Brute Nette *Port en lourd *(tonnes)	Coque Visite Spéciale Machines Installation pour fret réfrigéré Lettre d'armement Nombre guide	Date de construction Constructeurs—Lieu de construction No. de construction Longueur hors tout (m) Largeur au fort (m) Tirant d'eau maximum (m) Longueur entre PP (m) Largeur hors membres (m) Creux sur quille (m) Superstructures (m) Ponts Rivée/Soudée Relevé de varangue (mm) Quille (mm) Cloisons Lest liquide Modifications Conversions	Propulsion Type de navire Shelter deck Passagers Cales et longueurs (m)/citernes cargaison & types Grain/liquide (m³) Balles (m³) Espaces isothermes (m³) Serpentins de réchauffage Conteneurs & longueurs (pieds) Ecoutilles de chargement & dimensions (m) Treuils Grues/Mâts de charge (Charge maxi d'utilisation (tonnes))	Type de machines & nombre Alésage X course (mm) Puissance Licence Constructeurs Lieu de construction Chaudières Pressions Surface de chauffe Foyers Production d'électricité auxiliaire & puissance Propulseurs spéciaux Soutes à combustibles (tonnes) Vitesse

REGISTRO DELLE NAVI

1 No. di Identificazione LR	2 NOME DELLA NAVE	3 TONN.	4 CLASSIFICAZIONE	5 SCAFO	6 TIPO DELLA NAVE/SISTEMAZIONI PER IL CARICO	7 MACCHINA
Nomin. intern. No. di Registraz. nazionale Apper. di Navigazione	Nomi Precedenti ARMATORE Gestione Porto di Registro Bandiera	Stazza Lorda Stazza Netta *Portata Stazza Lorda Stazza Netta *Portata *(tonn.)	Scafo Notazione di Visita Speciale Macchine Impianto frigorifero per il carico Lettere d'Armam. Indice computo diritti	Data Costruz Costruttore—Luogo di Costruz Costruzione No. Lunghezza fuori tutto (m) Larghezza massima (m) Immersione estiva da s.c. (m) Lunghezza fra le Pp (m) Larghezza f.o. (m) Altezza di Costruzione (m) Sovrastrutture (m) Ponti Struttura chiodata/saldata Inclinazione lanciame fondo su L.C. (mm) Chiglia (m) Modifiche Paratie Acqua Zavorra Trasformazione	Propulsione Tipo della nave Shelter deck Passeggeri No. Stive per carico e lunghezza (m)/Cisterne (No. e tipi di carico) Grano/Liquidi (m³) Balle Cotone (m³) Spazi refrig. (m³) Serpentine riscald. Contenitori (numero e lunghezza in piedi) Boccaporte—No. e dimensioni (m) Verricelli da carico Gru/Picchi (Portata in tonn.)	No. e Tipo delle motrici Diametro x corsa (mm) Potenza Progetto Costruttore motrici Luogo di costruzione Caldaie Pressioni Superficie riscald. Forni Impianto elettrico ausiliario e potenza Propulsori di tipo speciale Capacità cisterne combustibile (tonn.) Velocità

SCHEPENLIJST

1 LR Identiteits No.	2 NAAM VAN HET SCHIP	3 TONNENMAAT	4 CLASSIFICATIE	5 CASCO	6 SCHEEPS-TYPE/LADING-FACILITEITEN	7 VOORTSTUWINGSINSTALLATIE
Roepletters Registratienummer Hulpmiddelen voor de navigatie	Vroegere namen EIGENAARS Reders Thuishaven Vlag	Bruto Netto Laadvermogen op zomermerk Bruto Netto Laadvermogen op zomermerk	Schip Laatst gehouden groot survey Machine Inrichting voor gekoelde lading Machinenummer Uitrustingsletter Tarief sleutel	Bouwdatum Werf-Bouwplaats Bouw Nr. Lengte over alles (m) Grootste breedte (m) Max. diepgang (m) Lengte L.L. (m) Breedte naar de mal (m) Holte naar de mal (m) Bovenbouw (m) Dekken Geklonken/gelast Vlaktilling (mm) Kiel (mm) Schotten Waterballast Veranderingen Ombouw	Voortstuwing Type schip Shelterdek Aantal passagiers Aantal ruimen & lengten (m)/Aantal ladingtanks & type Graan/Vloeistof (m³) Balen (m³) Geïsoleerde ruimen (m³) Verwarmingsspiralen Aantal containers & lengten (voeten) Luikhoofden-aantal/afmetingen (m) Aantal laadieren Kranen/laadbomen Aantal/veilige belasting	Machines-aantal/type Diameter x slag (mm) Vermogen Ontwerp Machinefabrikant Bouwplaats Ketels Werkdrukken Verwarmend oppervlak Vuurgangen Electrische hulpmachines & vermogen Bijzondere schroeven Brandstofbunkers (tonnen) Snelheid in knopen.

ΒΙΒΛΙΟΝ ΚΑΤΑΧΩΡΗΣΕΩΣ ΠΛΟΙΩΝ

1 ΑΡΙΘΜΟΣ ΚΑΤΑΧΩΡΗΣΕΩΣ ΝΗΟΓΝΩΜΟΝΟΣ	2 ΟΝΟΜΑ ΠΛΟΙΟΥ	3 ΧΩΡΗΤΙΚΟΤΗΣ	4 ΚΛΑΣΙΣ	5 ΣΚΑΦΟΣ	6 ΤΥΠΟΣ ΠΛΟΙΟΥ/ΜΕΣΑ ΦΟΡΤΩΣΕΩΣ	7 ΜΗΧΑΝΗΜΑΤΑ
[illegible] Ἀριθμοί Νηολογίου Ναυτιλιακά Ὄργανα	Προηγούμενα Ὀνόματα Πλοιοκτῆται Διαχειρισταί Λιμὴν Νηολογήσεως Σημαία	Ὀλική Καθαρά Νεκρόν Βάρος Ὀλική Καθαρά Νεκρόν Βάρος *(εἰς μετρικούς τόννους)	Σκάφος Εἰδική Ἐπιθεώρησις Μηχανή Ψυκτική Ἐγκατάστασις Φορτίου Δείκτης ἐξοπλισμοῦ	Ἔτος Κατασκευῆς Κατασκευασταί—Τόπος Ναυπηγήσεως Ἀριθμός Ναυπηγήσεως Μῆκος Ὁλικόν (εἰς μέτρα) Πλάτος Μέγιστον (εἰς μέτρα) Βύθισμα Μέγιστον (εἰς μέτρα) Μῆκος μεταξύ καθέτων (εἰς μέτρα) [illegible] Κοίλον ἢ ὕψος πλοίου (εἰς μέτρα) [illegible] (εἰς μέτρα) [illegible] [illegible] Τρόπις (εἰς χιλιοστά) [illegible] Θαλάσσιον Ἔρμα Ἀλλαγαί Μετατροπαί	[illegible] Τύπος πλοίου [illegible] Ἐπιβάται [illegible] (εἰς μέτρα)/[illegible] φορτίου & τύποι Σιτηρά/Ὑγρά (μ³) [illegible] (μ³) [illegible] (μ³) [illegible] [illegible] (πόδες) [illegible] (εἰς μέτρα) [illegible] (Φορτίον Ἀσφαλείας εἰς μετρικούς τόννους)	Ἀριθμός & τύπος [illegible] μηχανῶν [illegible] (χιλιοστά) Ἰσχύς [illegible] Κατασκευασταί Μηχανῆς [illegible] Λέβητες Πιέσεις [illegible] Ἐπιφάνεια [illegible] [illegible] Ἰσχύς [illegible] [illegible] (εἰς μετρικούς τόννους) Ταχύτης

APPENDIX 7

Copy of a Lloyd's Register Page

AMPHION

Register of Ships 2003-2004

7903328 *9HGD5* 5321 -	**AMPHION** *ex* Venita *-1996* *ex* Mega Venita *-1992* *ex* Venita *-1990* *ex* Diana *-1987* **Amphion Shipping Co. Ltd.** Paralos Maritime Corp. S.A. *Valletta* *Malta* SatCom: Inmarsat A MMSI: 249804000	**53,898** 23,425 87,549 T/cm 88.4	Class: NV (NK)	**1980**-07 **Sasebo Heavy Industries Co. Ltd.-Sasebo Yard, Sasebo** Yd No: 282 Loa 243.01 Br ex 42.04 Dght 12.722 Lbp 230.03 Br md 42.03 Dpth 19.82 Welded, 1 dk	**Crude Oil Tanker** COW IGS SBT Liq(Oil): 105,997 Cargo Heating Coils 3 Cargo Pumps Manifold: Bow/CM: 122m	**1 oil engine** *driving 1 CP propeller* Total Power: 11,700kW(15,906hp) 13.0kn MAN 12V48/60 1 x Vee 4 Stroke 12 Cy. 480 x 600 (new engine 1993) MAN B&W Diesel AG AuxGen: 1 x 560kW 450V 60Hz, 2 x 440kW 450V 60Hz Fuel: 281.0(d.o.) 2773.5(hvf) 53.0pd
8407890 *SXZP* 573 -	**AMPHION** *ex* Grischuna *-1999* **Panther Navigation Inc.** Andriaki Shipping Co. Ltd. *Andros* *Greece* MMSI: 239620000	**37,031** 24,287 64,442 T/cm 65.8	Class: AB	**1987**-10 **Hyundai Heavy Industries Co., Ltd.-Ulsan** Yd No: 359 Loa 225.03 (BB) Br ex 32.26 Dght 13.101 Lbp 215.65 Br md 32.21 Dpth 18.01 Welded, 1 dk	**Bulk Carrier** Str. heavy cargoes SERS(LR) Grain: 80,056 Compartments: 7 Ho, ER 7 Ha: ER	**1 oil engine** *driving 1 FP propeller* Total Power: 8,799kW(11,963hp) 15.0kn B&W 5L70MC 1 x 2 Stroke 5 Cy. 700 x 2,268 Hyundai Engine & Machinery Co., Ltd. AuxGen: 3 x 525kW 440V 60Hz Fuel: 99.5(d.o.) 1890.0(hvf) 36.0pd
7226093 *UZCZ* 712663 -	**AMPHITRITE** *ex* Sovetskiy Sever *-1998* *ex* Viktor Koryakin *-1993* **Joint Stock Co "Amphitrite" (A/O "Amphitrite")** - *Kherson* *Ukraine* MMSI: 272151000	**2,478** 917 3,135 T/cm -	Class: RS	**1972** **Sudostroitelnyy Zavod im. "Volodarskiy"-Rybinsk** Yd No: 61 Loa 113.90 Br ex 13.21 Dght 3.700 Lbp 108.01 Br md - Dpth 5.54 Welded, 1 dk	**General Cargo Ship** Ice strengthened Bale: 4,125 Compartments: 4 Ho, ER 4 Ha: (17.6 x 9.3) 3(18.1 x 9.3) ER	**2 oil engines** *driving 2 FP propellers* Total Power: 485kW(1,320hp) 10.5kn S.K.L. 6NVD48A-U 1 x 4 Stroke 6 Cy. 320 x 480 485kW(660bhp) VEB Schwermaschinenbau "Karl Liebknecht" (SKL) S.K.L. 1 x 4 Stroke 6 Cy. 320 x 480 485kW(660bhp) VEB Schwermaschinenbau "Karl Liebknecht" (SKL) AuxGen: 2 x 75kW, 1 x 50kW Fuel: 94.0(d.o.)
7224368 *XU7MZ* 0072334 -	**AMPLE HARVEST** *ex* Ample Route 1 *-2001* *ex* Jin Tai *-1999* *ex* Jia Fa *-1996* *ex* Ocean Mercury *-1986* *ex* Corona *-1986* *ex* Finnmaster *-1982* **Tian Hua Maritime Transportation Corp. Ltd.** - *Phnom-Penh* *Cambodia* SatCom: Inmarsat C	**4,275** 2,400 5,919 T/cm -	Class: (CC) (NV)	**1972** **Kleven Mek. Verksted AS -Ulsteinvik** Yd No: 23 Loa 106.80 Br ex 17.07 Dght 7.070 Lbp 100.36 Br md 17.00 Dpth 9.00 Welded, 2 dks	**General Cargo Ship** Grain: 8,546; Bale: 7,795 TEU 173 C.Ho 93/20' C.Dk 80/20'(40') Compartments: 2 Ho, ER, 2 TwDk 2 Ha: 2(27.4 x 13.3) ER Cranes: 2x12.5t, 2x10t	**1 oil engine** *driving 1 FP propeller* Total Power: 3,383kW(4,600hp) 14.0kn Werkspoor 8TM410 1 x 4 Stroke 8 Cy. 410 x 470 Stork-Werkspoor Diesel B.V. AuxGen: 3 x 174kW 380V 60Hz Fuel: 236.0(d.o.) 386.0(hvf) 14.0pd
9013177 *FQHN* 425434 -	**AMPORELLE** **Government of The Republic of France (Regie Departementale des Passages d'Eau de la Vendee)** - *Ile d'Yeu* *France* MMSI: 227004400	*345* *258* *100* *T/cm* -	Class: BV	**1991**-12 **Soc. Francaise de Cons. Nav. -Villeneuve—la—Garenne** Yd No: 869 Loa 38.00 Br ex - Dght 1.350 Lbp 33.50 Br md 7.75 Dpth 3.40 Welded, 1 dk	**Day-excursion Passenger Ship** Passengers: unberthed: 370	**2 oil engines** *with clutches, flexible couplings &sr geared to sc. shafts driving 2 Water jets* Total Power: 3,398kW(4,620hp) 28.0kn MWM TBD604BV16 2 x Vee 4 Stroke 16 Cy. 170 x 195 each-1,699kW(2,310bhp) Motoren Werke Mannheim AG (MWM) AuxGen: 2 x 60kW 380V 50Hz Fuel: 10.4(d.o.)
7102508 *XUSF7* 9870089 -	**AMR** *ex* Cherepovets *-1998* **Quantel Shipping Ltd.** Romalex Marine S.A.E. *Phnom-Penh* *Cambodia* MMSI: 514166000	**1,582** 708 1,857 T/cm -	Class: (RS)	**1970** **Santierul Naval Constanta S.A. -Constanta** Yd No: 339 Loa 80.27 Br ex 11.94 Dght 4.900 Lbp 71.49 Br md - Dpth 5.69 Welded, 1 dk	**General Cargo Ship** Ice strengthened Bale: 2,450 Compartments: 3 Ho, ER 3 Ha: (8.2 x 5.8) 2(8.2 x 7.9) ER Cranes: 3x5t	**1 oil engine** *driving 1 FP propeller* Total Power: 1,147kW(1,560hp) 12.0kn Sulzer 6TAD36 1 x 2 Stroke 6 Cy. 360 x 600 Tvornica Dizel Motora "Jugoturbina"
5015294 - - -	**AMRADO** **Government of The Republic of Ghana (Ports Authority)** - *Takoradi* *Ghana*	*201* - - *T/cm* -	Class: (LR) ✠ Classed LR until 10/48	**1948**-03 **Ferguson Bros. (Port Glasgow) Ltd.-Port Glasgow** Yd No: 384 Loa 32.67 Br ex 7.47 Dght 3.277 Lbp - Br md - Dpth - Welded,	**Tug**	**2 Steam Recip.** *driving 2 FP propellers* 2 x Steam Recip. Triple exp In-Line 6Cy. HP-(2) 283 IP1-(2) 445 & LP-(2) 737 x Stroke-559 Ferguson Bros. (Port Glasgow) Ltd.
5138058 *YKBS* 39/LA -	**AMREET** *ex* Al Schooner *-1992* *ex* Rim *-1988* *ex* Mona Star *-1978* *ex* Gullkrona *-1976* **Nazih Sidawi, Hussni Ammoun, Abdul Mouem Markabi & Mohi Eldin Kaak** Schooner Shipping *Lattakia* *Syria*	*999* *504* *1,408* *T/cm* -	Class: (LR) ✠ Classed LR until 7/1/83	**1958**-07 **Valmet Oy -Helsinki** Yd No: 191 Loa 69.19 Br ex 10.83 Dght 4.242 Lbp 62.62 Br md 10.80 Dpth 4.42 Welded, 1 dk	**General Cargo Ship** Ice strengthened Grain: 1,940; Bale: 1,743 2 Ha: (10.2 x 5.4) (16.2 x 6.0) ER Cranes: 2x3t	**1 oil engine** *driving 1 FP propeller* Total Power: 706kW(960hp) 11.0kn Alpha 498R 1 x 2 Stroke 8 Cy. 290 x 490 Alpha Diesel A/S Fuel: 71.0(d.o.)
9081746 *VVXL* 225 -	**AMRIT KAUR** **Government of The Republic of India (Coast Guard)** - *India* SatCom: Inmarsat C	**306** 91 - T/cm -	Class: (AB) (IR)	**1993**-03 **Goa Shipyard Ltd. -Goa** Yd No: 1150 Loa 45.95 Br ex - Dght - Lbp 43.50 Br md 7.50 Dpth 4.30 Welded, 1 dk	**Patrol Vessel** Search & Rescue	**2 oil engines** *sr geared to sc. shaft driving 1 FP propeller* Total Power: 2,960kW(4,024hp) 23.0kn M.T.U. 12V538TB82 2 x Vee 4 Stroke 12 Cy. 185 x 200 each-1,480kW(2,012bhp) MTU Friedrichshafen GmbH AuxGen: 3 x 80kW 415V 50Hz
7102211 *YBYO* 1172 -	**AMRITA I** **P.T. Pelayaran Lokal Karunrung** - *Jakarta* *Indonesia*	*173* *10* - *T/cm* -	Class: KI (GL)	**1971** **Handara Engineering & Shiprepairing Ltd.-Hong Kong** Yd No: 22 Loa 29.04 Br ex 7.73 Dght 3.210 Lbp 26.80 Br md 7.40 Dpth 3.41 Welded, 1 dk	**Tug**	**1 oil engine** *driving 1 CP propeller* Total Power: 588kW(800hp) 11.2kn Alpha 408-26VO 1 x 2 Stroke 8 Cy. 260 x 400 Alpha Diesel A/S
5207615 *ODBX* B2795 -	**AMRO Z** *ex* Rabunion V *-1992* *ex* Croesus *-1975* *ex* Berta *-1973* *ex* Libertas *-1972* **Amro Z Shipping Co. SARL** Zeido Group *Beirut* *Lebanon*	*396* *220* *1,315* *T/cm* -	Class: (LR) ✠ Classed LR until 1/1/95	**1958**-09 **E.J. Smit & Zoon's Scheepswerven N.V.-Westerbroek** Yd No: 746 Converted from: General Cargo Ship-1982 Loa 64.85 Br ex 9.91 Dght 4.560 Lbp 59.75 Br md 9.81 Dpth 5.80 Riveted/Welded, 2 dks	**Livestock Carrier** Ice strengthened Bale: 1,744 Compartments: 2 Ho, ER 2 Ha: (8.0 x 4.0) (12.1 x 4.0) ER Derricks: 2x6t, 4x3t; Winches: 6	**1 oil engine** *driving 1 FP propeller* Total Power: 552kW(750hp) 10.8kn Werkspoor TMAB396 1 x 4 Stroke 6 Cy. 390 x 680 N.V. Werkspoor AuxGen: 3 x 25kW 110V d.c.
8401755 *3FVN2* 14189-84CH -	**AMRTA JAYA I** **Admiral Three Star S.A.** P.T. Pelayaran Samudera "Admiral Lines" *Panama* *Panama* MMSI: 352112000	**5,464** 2,262 6,839 T/cm -	Class: NK	**1984**-05 **Higaki Zosen K.K. -Imabari** Yd No: 320 Loa 98.18 (BB) Br ex 18.01 Dght 7.544 Lbp 89.95 Br md 18.00 Dpth 13.01 Welded, 1 dk	**General Cargo Ship** Grain: 13,070; Bale: 12,097 Compartments: 2 Ho, ER 2 Ha: (22.2 x 9.8) (24.7 x 9.8) ER Cranes: 4x20t	**1 oil engine** *driving 1 FP propeller* Total Power: 2,427kW(3,300hp) 12.0kn Hanshin 6EL40 1 x 4 Stroke 6 Cy. 400 x 800 The Hanshin Diesel Works Ltd.
8401834 *YFUS* - -	**AMRTA JAYA II** **P.T. Pelayaran Samudera "Admiral Lines"** - *Jakarta* *Indonesia*	**5,498** 3,836 6,840 T/cm -	Class: NK	**1984**-08 **Nishi Zosen K.K. -Imabari** Yd No: 327 Loa 98.18 (BB) Br ex 18.04 Dght 7.544 Lbp 89.95 Br md 18.00 Dpth 13.00 Welded, 2 dks	**General Cargo Ship** Grain: 13,070; Bale: 12,096 Compartments: 2 Ho, ER 2 Ha: (22.2 x 9.8) (24.7 x 9.8) ER Derricks: 4x20t	**1 oil engine** *driving 1 FP propeller* Total Power: 2,427kW(3,300hp) 12.0kn Hanshin 6EL40 1 x 4 Stroke 6 Cy. 400 x 800 The Hanshin Diesel Works Ltd. AuxGen: 3 x 280kW a.c.
9003988 *3EKN8* 19238-90C -	**AMRTA VII** *ex* Orient Queen *-1997* **Admiral Three Star S.A.** P.T. Pelayaran Samudera "Admiral Lines" *Panama* *Panama* SatCom: Inmarsat M MMSI: 353116000	**5,473** 1,999 7,018 T/cm -	Class: NK	**1990**-10 **Murakami Hide Zosen K.K. -Hakata** Yd No: 318 Loa 99.92 (BB) Br ex - Dght 7.573 Lbp 89.95 Br md 18.00 Dpth 13.00 Welded,	**General Cargo Ship** Grain: 13,285; Bale: 12,611 Compartments: 2 Ho, ER, 2 TwDk 2 Ha: (21.7 x 9.8) (24.5 x 9.8) ER Derricks: 4x20t	**1 oil engine** *driving 1 FP propeller* Total Power: 2,427kW(3,300hp) 11.6kn Akasaka A41 1 x 4 Stroke 6 Cy. 410 x 800 Akasaka Tekkosho K.K., (Akasaka Diesels Ltd.) AuxGen: 4 x 167kW a.c.
9150080 *V2LF* - -	**AMRUM TRADER** *ex* Seaboard Unity *-1998* *launched as* Amrum Trader - **Dreiunddreissigste Grosse Bleichen Schiffahrtsgesellschaft mbH & Co. KG** Hermann Buss GmbH & Cie. *Leer* *Antigua & Barbuda*	**5,941** 2,777 8,081 T/cm -	Class: GL	**1997**-04 **Peterswerft Wewelsfleth GmbH & Co.-Wewelsfleth** Yd No: 659 Loa 132.30 (BB) Br ex 19.50 Dght 6.921 Lbp 123.40 Br md 19.20 Dpth 9.20 Welded, 1 dk	**Container Ship (Fully Cellular)** Grain: 9,259; Bale: 8,957 TEU 624 C.Ho 170/20' (40') C.Dk 454/20' (40') incl. 80 ref C. Compartments: 3 Cell Ho, ER 3 Ha: ER	**1 oil engine** *with flexible couplings & reductiongeared to sc. shaft driving 1 CP propeller* Total Power: 5,940kW(8,075hp) Wartsila 9R38 1 x 4 Stroke 9 Cy. 380 x 475 Stork-Wartsila Diesel B.V. AuxGen: 2 x 320kW 400V 50Hz Thrusters: 1 Thwart. FP thruster (f) Fuel: 120.0(d.o.) 560.0(i.f.o.) 25.0pd

APPENDIX 8

Copy of a Germanischer Lloyd Page

140 CAR SEESCHIFFE

Ship	Class / Type	Tonnage / Dimensions	Built / Shipyard	Engine	Generators
12799 CARIBE MS DBCC RO-RO-SCHIFF (03.'21) SVEA STAR, FREEPORT, FREEPORT 1 VOM STAPEL GELAUFEN ALS FREEPORT X Z TUV PR LA EK BREMER SCHIFFAHRTSGES. MBH & CO.KG BREMEN BR DEUTSCHLAND	LR	3308 125.31 4861 21.53 15000' 12.50 7.500	11.68 LUBECK ORENSTEIN & KOPPEL A.-G. 558 9 SCHO 2 0 DB 2PTK	68 HAMBURG OTTENSENER EISENWERK G.M.B.H. MH 2 MAT 2TE 11768- 500/ 237 (8000 PSe) - 16x 400 / 460 MAT ÜBER 2 GTR 2 UPROP 4378 KVA 440	2 DL 1330 30 2 DL 230 30
18311 CARIBIA EXPRESS MS DGCE X Z TUV PRO A EKS HAPAG-LLOYD AKTIENGESELLSCHAFT AK3 138 HAMBURG BR DEUTSCHLAND	⊕100A4 CONTAINERSCHIFF ⊕MC AUT-16/24 ⊕KAZ	27934 199.12 16853 30.66 23047' 15.60 10.008 156-20 240-22-	11.78(3.78) GDANSK STOCZNIA GDANSKA IM. LENINA 400/1-8 BA 20,70 10 SCHO 1 0 DB HSTKM TTKV 2PTK 8 LU 13,60x 8.15 PORTALKRAN 40T	75 POZNAN "H. CEGIELSKI" ZAKLADY PRZEMYSLU METALOWEGO 10RND90 MH 1 MAT 2TE 21330- 122 (29000 PSe) - 10x 900 /1550 1 PROP 4820 KVA 440 22	1 HI 7.0 82.0 1 HWA 7.0 826.0 2 DL 1000 30 1 DL 300 38 2 DL 400 7
15461 CARIBIC MS DAH8 X Z TUV PRO A EK BUGSIER- REEDEREI- UND BERGUNGS AG AK2 116 HAMBURG BR DEUTSCHLAND	⊕100A4 E1 SCHLEPPER ⊕MC E1 AUT-16/24	385 31.36 54 12.55 5.50 1.780	12.77(10.77) BREMERHAVEN SCHIFFSWERFT UND MASCHF. MAX SIEGHOLD 178 SPBA 25.50 4 SCHO 1 0 2TKV PROPO TOTHOLZ-HÜTTEN	77 KÖLN KLÖCKNER-HUMBOLDT-DEUTZ AG SBV6M540 MH 2 MAT 4TE 4413- 600/ 180 (6800 PSe) - 5x 373 / 400 MAT ÜBER 2 GTR 2 UPROP 1577 KVA 380/220 15	2 DL 1250 30 1 DL 63 30 1 DL 20 38 5 DL 50 230
12740 CARINA MS DNCW STOCKGUTFRACHTER TUV PR A EX PARTENREEDEREI KR HANS PETER WEGENER AK2 117 HAMBURG BR DEUTSCHLAND	⊕100A4 E2 EINGERICHTET FÜR CONTAINER- TRANSPORT ⊕MC E2 AUT-16/24	789 73.72 579 13.42 2580' 3.17 5.030 GE 4730' BLN 4415' 190-20	2.77(1.77) HAMBURG J.J. SIETAS SCHIFFSWERFT 782 PP 13.20 SRBA 59.40 3 SCHO 2 0 DB 2PTK 1 LU 50.42x10.13 LRL 53,80 DECKSHAUS ELASTISCH GELAGERT	76 KIEL MAK MASCHINENBAU GMBH 9MU453AK MH 1 MAT 4TE 1649- (2650 PSe) (470- 550/ 247 (1999 PSe)) 3x 320 / 420 MAT ÜBER 1 GTR 1 UPROP 619 KVA 380/220 13.73	1 DL 530 30 1 DL 125 30
12835 CARINA MS DUHU STOCKGUTFRACHTER T V PR A EX MS "CARINA" ROHDEN BEREEDERUNGS-AG AK2 114 ELSFLETH BR DEUTSCHLAND	⊕100A4 M E1 AMT 7480 2.582 ⊕MC E1 AUT-16/24	499 77.20 287 12.33 1510' 4.30 2.430 GE 3740' BLN 3170'	6.78(5.78) KÖLN KÖLNER WERFT GMBH & CO. SCHIFFBAU KG 816 PP 12.60 BA 3.40 4 SCHO 2 0 DB STKM 2PTK 1 LU 47.37x10.25 LRL 52.60	73 KÖLN KLÖCKNER-HUMBOLDT-DEUTZ AG SBA12M528 MH 1 MAT 4TE 1173- 750/ 250 (1300 PSe) (1096- 750/ 250 (1400 PSe)) 12x 220 / 280 MAT ÜBER 1 WGTR 1 PROP 254 KVA 380/220 11.80	2 DL 230 30 1 DL 40 5
04413 CARINA MS DADS STOCKGUTFRACHTER REGINE, CITY OF ANTWERP, REGINE T V PR A EX PARTENREEDEREI KR HANS PETER WEGENER AK2 21 HAMBURG BR DEUTSCHLAND	⊕100A4 E2 ⊕MC E2	52.51 10.52 5.35 499T 4.00 322 1.380 1140' GE 2480' BLN 2230' 400'	1.65(12.55) HAMBURG J.J. SIETAS SCHIFFSWERFT 540 BA 6.90 3 SCHO 2 0 DB 2PTK 1 LU 37.29x 7.80 LRL 42.60	35 KÖLN KLÖCKNER-HUMBOLDT-DEUTZ AG RBV8M545 MH 1 MAT 4TE 780- 347 (1000 PSe) (736- 347 (1000 PSe)) 3x 320 / 450 1 PROP 138 KVA 380/220 11	2 DL 500 30 1 DL 230 30

APPENDIX 9

Copy of a Bureau Veritas Page

REN

490

Identification	Classification	Dim	Coque/Hull	Propulsion
RENE 17 77 L 106 *Liquefied gas carrier* DERCA S.A. Belgium Anvers	I 3/3 E (4-78) • Liquefied gas carrier Small coasting trade Max serv press. 18 bars • MOT Ch 28 Q1	**835** 545 79.92 73.60 8.50 4.50 2.28 540 *2 815*	SCHEEPSW.VAN DUYVENDIJK **1947** *Lekkerkerk (HOL)* Steel - 7 compt. - 1 deck - Mchy. aft *4 tanks : 942 (m^3)* Cgo. handl. : 4 pp 360 m3/h	2 DIESELS *BAUDOUIN* 1971 *Marseille (F)* *515 kW (700 HP) at 1 800 rpm/470 rpm* (2) 4T - 8 cyl - 15 × 15 F 380 V/E 220 V - 50 Hz - 3 dg 215 kVA/334 HP 4 dg 4 kW/15 HP 2 Prop PF Ord 2 *10 kn - 20 mt*
RENEE R E 27 U 480 FUDM Kram-71 *Cargo ship* PHOCENNE D'ARMEMENT MARITIME (CIE) France Marseille	I 3/3 E (8-75) + Deep sea Ice + MOT CS Ch 35 HR	**499** 285 *1 440* *66.01* **63.90** *11.00* 8.56 4.80 1 963 *4 604*	ROLANDWERFT GMBH **1966** *Bremen Hemelingen (D)* Steel - 5 compt. - 2 decks - Mchy. aft 3 hatch. : 10.3X5.2 Cgo. handl. : 3-5t, 1-10t	1 DIESEL *M A K* 1966 *Kiel (D)* *882 kW (1 199 HP) at 325 rpm* (1) 4T - 8 cyl - 32 × 45 177 kW/344 HP 1 Prop LB 3 *12.4 kn - 111 mt*
RENOIR 33 N 362 FNDT *Multipurpose Roll on/off ship* COMPAGNIE GENERALE MARITIME & FINANCIERE France Dunkerque	I 3/3 E CS (1-78) + Roll on-Roll off Deep sea Container ship + MOT CS Ch 78 Q3	**13 828** 5 129 *19 669* 163.78 156.00 26.50 16.30 10.70 1 998 *55 952*	CH.DE L'ATLANTIQUE **1978** *Saint Nazaire (F)* *26* Steel - 4 compt. - 2 decks - Mchy. aft *4 holds : 28510(B) (m^3)* PORTE AR 8.5X4.5 CHARGE 50T Cgo. handl. : 2-25t; 2-40t	1 DIESEL *SEMT PIELSTICK* 1977 ALSTHOM ATLANTIQUE - *Montoir de Bretagne (F)* *17 222 kW (23 400 HP) at 520 rpm/130 rpm* (1) 4T - 18 cyl - 40 × 46 1 CHA 50 m^2/9 bars - 1 CHR 243 m^2/9 bars F 440 V/E 220 V - 60 Hz - 4 dg 4 027 kVA/4 320 HP 1 Prop PF LB 4 *20.7 kn - 3 008 mt*
REQUIN 16 N 112 *Bucket dredger* ROYAUME DU MAROC Morocco Casablanca	I 3/3 E (2-73) + Dredger Sheltered waters + MACH + CHAUD Ch 32	**442** 335 48.17 *9.70* 3.50 *1 596*	WERFT GUSTO **1931** *Schiedam (HOL)* Steel - 12 compt. - 1 deck	NON-PROPELLED ***WERF GUSTO-DRAGAGE*** WERF GUSTO - *Schiedam (HOL)* *331 kW (450 HP)* 2 CHC 256 m^2/12 bars 1 dg 120 kVA/152 HP *50 mt*
RESACA 23 B 277 *Bucket dredger* EXCAVACIONES SUBMARINAS Spain Sevilla	I 3/3 E (12-76) + Dredger + MACH + CHAUD Ch 30	**543** 32 *52.00* 10.00 3.75 1 250 *1 950*	AST. DE SEVILLA **1959** *Sevilla (E)* Steel - 17 compt. - 1 deck	NON-PROPELLED ***MA-DRAGAGE*** AST. DE SEVILLA - *Sevilla (E)* *294 kW (400 HP) at 150 rpm* 1 CHC 160 m^2/13 bars 24 kW/44 HP *70 mt*
REVENANT 75 X 024 Atlantic Gladiator-54, Rush *Yacht* SCHURCH M. Switzerland Stafa	13-4 R (1-75) + S M 50	**8** *8.85* 6.95 *1.86* 1.10 632 *14*	YACHTVARV **1968** *Kungsors (S)* Wood	NON-PROPELLED
REY FRUELA 30 W 886 *Cargo/Container ship* ASTUR ANDALUZA S.A. (NAVIERA) Spain Gijon	I 3/3 E (10-77) + Container ship Deep sea Heavy cargo + MOT CS Ch 58 Q2	**2 524** 1 518 90.50 82.53 13.50 7.20 5.02 1 178 *8 021*	MARITIMA DEL MUSEL **1972** *Gijon (E)* Steel - 5 compt. - 1 deck - Mchy. aft *2 holds : 4721(G) (m^3)* 2 hatch. : (19.5-25.9X10.6)	1 DIESEL *DEUTZ* 1972 *Vigo (E)* *2 163 kW (2 940 HP) at 375 rpm/201 rpm* (1) 4T - 8 cyl - 58 × 40 F 380 V/E 220 V - 3 dg 475 kVA/611 HP 1 at 75 kVA 1 Prop PF CC 4 *14 kn - 392 m^3*
REYES 26 R 235 Juanita de Chacartegui-69 *Cargo ship* ASON S.A.NAVIERA Spain Santander	I 3/3 S (5-75) + Deep sea + MOT CS Ch 33	742 581 *54.98* *9.24* 5.17 651 *2 626*	AST. LUZURIAGA **1964** *Pasajes (E)* Steel - 15 compt. - 1 deck - Mchy. aft *2 holds : 168 (m^3)* 2 hatch. : 13.2X5.0 Cgo. handl. : 4-2t	1 DIESEL *KRUPP M T M* 1962 *Barcelona (E)* *644 kW (875 HP) at 375 rpm* (1) 4T - 8 cyl - 29.5 × 42 130 kVA/145 HP 1 Prop CC 3 *11.9 kn*
REZA PAHLAVI 24 P 876 EPBN *Oil tanker* NATIONAL IRANIAN TANKER CO Iran Bandar Shahpour	I 3/3 E (10-79) + Oil tanker Deep sea + TURB CS + CHAUD Ch 80	**34 173** 21 004 *54 400* 237.46 228.50 31.10 18.16 12.47 3 730 *114 838*	CH.DE L'ATLANTIQUE **1961** *Saint Nazaire (F)* Steel - 18 compt. - 1 deck *36 tank. : 73342 (m^3)* Cgo. handl. : 4 pp 4520 m3/h	1 STEAM TURBINE *C E M* 1961 ***PARSONS*** CH.DE L'ATLANTIQUE - *Saint Nazaire (F)* *13 984 kW (19 000 HP) at 104 rpm* 2 CHP FOSTER WHEELER (2) 2 126 m^2/49 bars; F 440 V/E 115 V - 2 tg 1 300 kW/1 768 HP 1 dg 75 kW/145 HP 1 Prop PF LB 3 *17.1 kn - 6 223 m^3*
RHEA 33 J 680 *Bucket dredger* AMSTERDAMSE BALLAST BAGGER EN GROND B.V. Netherlands Amstelveen	I 3/3 . (8-77) + Dredger Deep sea + MOT	**722** 580 58.00 49.95 11.90 3.80 2.61 1 210 *2 256*	SCHEEPSW.DE LIESBOSCH **1977** *Nieuwegein (HOL)* *151* Steel - 7 compt. - 1 deck	NON-PROPELLED

APPENDIX 10

Norwegian Saleform 1987

MEMORANDUM OF AGREEMENT

Norwegian Shipbrokers' Association's Memorandum of Agreement for sale and purchase of ships. Adopted by The Baltic and International Maritime Council (BIMCO) in 1956.
Code-name
SALEFORM 1987
Revised 1966, 1983 and 1986

Dated:

hereinafter called the Sellers, have today sold, and

hereinafter called the Buyers, have today bought

Classification:
Built: by:
Flag: Place of Registration:
Call sign: Register tonnage:
Register number:
on the following conditions:

1. Price
Price:

2. Deposit
As a security for the correct fulfillment of this contract, the Buyers shall pay a deposit of 10%—ten per cent—of the Purchase Money within banking days from the date of this agreement. This amount shall be deposited with

and held by them in a joint account for the Sellers and the Buyers. Interest, if any, to be credited the Buyers. Any fee charged for holding said deposit shall be borne equally by the Sellers and the Buyers.

3. Payment
The said Purchase Money shall be paid free of bank charges to

on delivery of the vessel, but not later than three banking days after the vessel is ready for delivery and written or telexed notice thereof has been given to the Buyers by the Sellers.

4. Inspections
The Buyers shall have the right to inspect the vessel's classification records and declare whether same are accepted or not within

The Sellers shall provide for inspection of the vessel at/in

The Buyers shall undertake the inspection without undue delay to the vessel. Should the Buyers cause such delay, they shall compensate the Sellers for the losses thereby incurred.

The Buyers shall inspect the vessel afloat without opening up and without cost to the Sellers. During the inspection, the vessel's log books for engine and deck shall be made available for the Buyers' examination. If the vessel is accepted after such afloat inspection, the purchase shall become definite —except for other possible subjects in this contract—provided the Sellers receive written or telexed notice from the Buyers within 48 hours after completion of such afloat inspection. Should notice of acceptance of the vessel's classification records and of the vessel not be received by the Sellers as aforesaid, the deposit shall immediately be released, whereafter this contract shall be considered null and void.

5. Place and time of delivery
The vessel shall be delivered and taken over at/in

Expected time of delivery:

APPENDIX 10

Norwegian Saleform 1987 (Continued)

Date of cancelling (see clause 14):

The Sellers shall keep the Buyers well posted about the vessel's itinerary and estimated time and place of drydocking.

Should the vessel become a total or constructive total loss before delivery the deposit shall immediately be released to the Buyers and the contract thereafter considered null and void.

6. Drydocking

In connection with the delivery the Sellers shall place the vessel in drydock at the port of delivery for inspection by the Classification Society of the bottom and other underwater parts below the Summer Load Line. If the rudder, propeller, bottom or other underwater parts below the Summer Load Line be found broken, damaged or defective, so as to affect the vessel's clean certificate of class, such defects shall be made good at the Sellers' expense to 1)

satisfaction without qualification on such underwater parts. 2)

Whilst the vessel is in drydock, and if required by the Buyers or the representative of the Classification Society, the Sellers shall arrange to have the tail-end shaft drawn. Should same be condemned or found defective so as to affect the vessel's clean certificate of class, it shall be renewed or made good at the Sellers' expense to the Classification Society's satisfaction without qualification.

The expenses of drawing and replacing the tail-end shaft shall be borne by the Buyers unless the Classification Society requires the tail-end shaft to be drawn (whether damaged or not), renewed or made good in which event the Sellers shall pay these expenses.

The expenses in connection with putting the vessel in and taking her out of drydock, including drydock dues and the Classification Surveyor's fees shall be paid by the Sellers if the rudder, propeller, bottom, other underwater parts below the Summer Load Line or the tail-end shaft be found broken, damaged or defective as aforesaid or if the Classification Society requires the tail-end shaft to be drawn (whether damaged or not). In all other cases the Buyers shall pay the aforesaid expenses, dues and fees.

During the above mentioned inspections by the Classification Society the Buyers' representative shall have the right to be present in the drydock but without interfering with the Classification Surveyor's decisions.

The Sellers shall bring the vessel to the drydock and from the drydock to the place of delivery at their own expense.

7. Spares/bunkers etc.

The Sellers shall deliver the vessel to the Buyers with everything belonging to her on board and on shore. All spare parts and spare equipment including spare tail-end shaft(s) and/or spare propeller(s), if any, belonging to the vessel at the time of inspection, used or unused, whether on board or not shall become the Buyers' property, but spares on order to be excluded. Forwarding charges, if any, shall be for the Buyers' account. The Sellers are not required to replace spare parts including spare tail-end shaft(s) and spare propeller(s) which are taken out of spare and used as replacement prior to delivery, but the replaced items shall be the property of the Buyers. The radio installation and navigational equipment shall be included in the sale without extra payment, if same is the property of the Sellers.

The Sellers have the right to take ashore crockery, plate, cutlery, linen and other articles bearing the Sellers' flag or name, provided they replace same with similar unmarked items. Library, forms, etc., exclusively for use in the Sellers' vessels, shall be excluded without compensation. Captain's, Officers' and Crew's personal belongings including slop chest to be excluded from the sale, as well as the following additional items:

The Buyers shall take over remaining bunkers, unused lubricating oils and unused stores and provisions and pay the current market price at the port and date of delivery of the vessel.

Payment under this clause shall be made at the same time and place and in the same currency as the Purchase Money.

8. Documentation

In exchange for payment of the Purchase Money the Sellers shall furnish the Buyers with legal Bill of Sale of the said vessel free from all encumbrances and maritime liens or any other debts whatsoe-

APPENDIX 10

Norwegian Saleform 1987 (Continued)

ver, duly notarially attested and legalised by the consul together with a certificate stating that the vessel is free from registered encumbrances. On delivery of the vessel the Sellers shall provide for the deletion of the vessel from the Registry of Vessels and deliver a certificate of deletion to the Buyers. The deposit shall be placed at the disposal of the Sellers as well as the balance of the Purchase Money, which shall be paid as agreed together with payment for items mentioned in clause 7 above.

The Sellers shall, at the time of delivery, hand to the Buyers all classification certificates as well as all plans etc. which are onboard the vessel. Other technical documentation which may be in the Sellers' possession shall promptly upon the Buyers' instructions be forwarded to the Buyers. The Sellers may keep the log books, but the Buyers to have the right to take copies of same.

9. Encumbrances

The Sellers warrant that the vessel, at the time of delivery, is free from all encumbrances and maritime liens or any other debts whatsoever. Should any claims which have been incurred prior to the time of delivery be made against the vessel, the Sellers hereby undertake to indemnify the Buyers against all consequences of such claims.

10. Taxes etc.

Any taxes, fees and expenses connected with the purchase and registration under the Buyers' flag shall be for the Buyers' account, whereas similar charges connected with the closing of the Sellers' register shall be for the Sellers' account.

11. Condition on delivery

The vessel with everything belonging to her shall be at the Sellers' risk and expense until she is delivered to the Buyers, but subject to the conditions of this contract, she shall be delivered and taken over as she is at the time of inspection, fair wear and tear excepted.

However, the vessel shall be delivered with present class free of recommendations. The Sellers shall notify the Classification Society of any matters coming to their knowledge prior to delivery which upon being reported to the Classification Society would lead to the withdrawal of the vessel's class or to the imposition of a recommendation relating to her class.

12. Name/markings

Upon delivery the Buyers undertake to change the name of the vessel and alter funnel markings.

13. Buyers' default

Should the deposit not be paid as aforesaid, the Sellers have the right to cancel this contract, and they shall be entitled to claim compensation for their losses and for all expenses incurred together with interest at the rate of 12% per annum.

Should the Purchase Money not be paid as aforesaid, the Sellers have the right to cancel this contract, in which case the amount deposited together with interest earned, if any, shall be forfeited to the Sellers. If the deposit does not cover the Sellers' losses, they shall be entitled to claim further compensation for their losses and for all expenses together with interest at the rate of 12% per annum.

14. Sellers' default

If the Sellers fail to execute a legal transfer or to deliver the vessel with everything belonging to her in the manner and within the time specified in line 38, the Buyers shall have the right to cancel this contract in which case the deposit in full shall be returned to the Buyers together with interest at the rate of 12% per annum. The Sellers shall make due compensation for the losses caused to the Buyers by failure to execute a legal transfer or to deliver the vessel in the manner and within the time specified in line 38, if such are due to the proven negligence of the Sellers.

15. Arbitration

If any dispute should arise in connection with the interpretation and fulfilment of this contract, same shall be decided by arbitration in the city of 3)
and shall be referred to a single Arbitrator to be appointed by the parties hereto. If the parties cannot agree upon the appointment of the single Arbitrator, the dispute shall be settled by three Arbitrators, each party appointing one Arbitrator, the third being appointed by 4)

APPENDIX 10

Norwegian Saleform 1987 (Continued)

If either of the appointed Arbitrators refuses or is incapable of acting, the party who appointed him, shall appoint a new Arbitrator in his place.

If one of the parties fails to appoint an Arbitrator—either originally or by way of substitution—for two weeks after the other party having appointed his Arbitrator has sent the party making default notice by mail, cable or telex to make the appointment, the party appointing the third Arbitrator shall, after application from the party having appointed his Arbitrator, also appoint an Arbitrator on behalf of the party making default.

The award rendered by the Arbitration Court shall be final and binding upon the parties and may if necessary be enforced by the Court or any other competent authority in the same manner as a judgement in the Court of Justice.

This contract shall be subject to the law of the country agreed as place of arbitration.

1) *The name of the Classification Society to be inserted.*
2) *Notes, if any, in the Surveyor's report which are accepted by the Classification Society without qualification are not to be taken into account*
3) *The place of arbitration to be inserted. If this line is not filled in, it is understood that arbitration will take place in London in accordance with English law.*
4) *If this line is not filled in it is understood that the third Arbitrator shall be appointed by the London Maritime Arbitrators' Association in London.*

APPENDIX 10

Norwegian Saleform 1987 (Continued)

Appendix to Memorandum of Agreement code-name **SALEFORM 1987**–dated

---

APPENDIX 11

Norwegian Saleform

MEMORANDUM OF AGREEMENT

Norwegian Shipbrokers' Association's Memorandum of Agreement for sale and purchase of ships. Adopted by The Baltic and International Maritime Council (BIMCO) in 1956.
Code-name
SALEFORM 1993
Revised 1966, 1983 and 1986-87.

Dated:

hereinafter called the Sellers, have agreed to sell, and

hereinafter called the Buyers, have agreed to buy

Name:

Classification Society/Class:

Built: By:

Flag: Place of Registration:

Call Sign: Grt/Nrt:

Register Number:

hereinafter called the Vessel, on the following terms and conditions:

Definitions

"Banking days" are days on which banks are open both in the country of the currency stipulated for the Purchase Price in Clause 1 and in the place of closing stipulated in Clause 8.

"In writing" or "written" means a letter handed over from the Sellers to the Buyers or vice versa, a registered letter, telex, telefax or other modern form of written communication.

"Classification Society" or "Class" means the Society referred to in line 4.

1. Purchase Price

2. Deposit

As security for the correct fulfilment of this Agreement the Buyers shall pay a deposit of 10 % (ten per cent) of the Purchase Price within banking days from the date of this Agreement. This deposit shall be placed with

and held by them in a joint account for the Sellers and the Buyers, to be released in accordance with joint written instructions of the Sellers and the Buyers. Interest, if any, to be credited to the Buyers. Any fee charged for holding the said deposit shall be borne equally by the Sellers and the Buyers.

3. Payment

The said Purchase Price shall be paid in full free of bank charges to

on delivery of the Vessel, but not later than 3 banking days after the Vessel is in every respect physically ready for delivery in accordance with the terms and conditions of this Agreement and Notice of Readiness has been given in accordance with Clause 5.

4. Inspections

a)* The Buyers have inspected and accepted the Vessel's classification records. The Buyers have also inspected the Vessel at/in on and have accepted the Vessel following this inspection and the sale is outright and definite, subject only to the terms and conditions of this Agreement.

b)* The Buyers shall have the right to inspect the Vessel's classification records and declare whether same are accepted or not within

The Sellers shall provide for inspection of the Vessel at/in

The Buyers shall undertake the inspection without undue delay to the Vessel. Should the Buyers cause undue delay they shall compensate the Sellers for the losses thereby incurred.

APPENDIX 11

Norwegian Saleform (Continued)

The Buyers shall inspect the Vessel without opening up and without cost to the Sellers. During the inspection, the Vessel's deck and engine log books shall be made available for examination by the Buyers. If the Vessel is accepted after such inspection, the sale shall become outright and definite, subject only to the terms and conditions of this Agreement, provided the Sellers receive written notice of acceptance from the Buyers within 72 hours after completion of such inspection.
Should notice of acceptance of the Vessel's classification records and of the Vessel not be received by the Sellers as aforesaid, the deposit together with interest earned shall be released immediately to the Buyers, whereafter this Agreement shall be null and void.

* *4a) and 4b) are alternatives; delete whichever is not applicable. In the absence of deletions, alternative 4a) to apply.*

5. Notices, time and place of delivery

a) The Sellers shall keep the Buyers well informed of the Vessel's itinerary and shall provide the Buyers with , , and days notice of the estimated time of arrival at the intended place of drydocking/underwater inspection/delivery. When the Vessel is at the place of delivery and in every respect physically ready for delivery in accordance with this Agreement, the Sellers shall give the Buyers a written Notice of Readiness for delivery.

b) The Vessel shall be delivered and taken over safely afloat at a safe and accessible berth or anchorage at/in

in the Sellers' option.

Expected time of delivery:

Date of cancelling (see Clauses 5 c), 6 b) (iii) and 14):

c) If the Sellers anticipate that, notwithstanding the exercise of due diligence by them, the Vessel will not be ready for delivery by the cancelling date they may notify the Buyers in writing stating the date when they anticipate that the Vessel will be ready for delivery and propose a new cancelling date. Upon receipt of such notification the Buyers shall have the option of either cancelling this Agreement in accordance with Clause 14 within 7 running days of receipt of the notice or of accepting the new date as the new cancelling date. If the Buyers have not declared their option within 7 running days of receipt of the Sellers' notification or if the Buyers accept the new date, the date proposed in the Sellers' notification shall be deemed to be the new cancelling date and shall be substituted for the cancelling date stipulated in line 61.

If this Agreement is maintained with the new cancelling date all other terms and conditions hereof including those contained in Clauses 5 a) and 5 c) shall remain unaltered and in full force and effect. Cancellation or failure to cancel shall be entirely without prejudice to any claim for damages the Buyers may have under Clause 14 for the Vessel not being ready by the original cancelling date.

d) Should the Vessel become an actual, constructive or compromised total loss before delivery the deposit together with interest earned shall be released immediately to the Buyers whereafter this Agreement shall be null and void.

6. Drydocking/Divers Inspection

a)** The Sellers shall place the Vessel in drydock at the port of delivery for inspection by the Classification Society of the Vessel's underwater parts below the deepest load line, the extent of the inspection being in accordance with the Classification Society's rules. If the rudder, propeller, bottom or other underwater parts below the deepest load line are found broken, damaged or defective so as to affect the Vessel's class, such defects shall be made good at the Sellers' expense to the satisfaction of the Classification Society without condition/recommendation*.

b)** (i) The Vessel is to be delivered without drydocking. However, the Buyers shall have the right at their expense to arrange for an underwater inspection by a diver approved by the Classification Society prior to the delivery of the Vessel. The Sellers shall at their cost make the Vessel available for such inspection. The extent of the inspection and the conditions under which it is performed shall be to the satisfaction of the Classification

APPENDIX 11

Norwegian Saleform (Continued)

Society. If the conditions at the port of delivery are unsuitable for such inspection, the Sellers shall make the Vessel available at a suitable alternative place near to the delivery port.

(ii) If the rudder, propeller, bottom or other underwater parts below the deepest load line are found broken, damaged or defective so as to affect the Vessel's class, then unless repairs can be carried out afloat to the satisfaction of the Classification Society, the Sellers shall arrange for the Vessel to be drydocked at their expense for inspection by the Classification Society of the Vessel's underwater parts below the deepest load line, the extent of the inspection being in accordance with the Classification Society's rules. If the rudder, propeller, bottom or other underwater parts below the deepest load line are found broken, damaged or defective so as to affect the Vessel's class, such defects shall be made good by the Sellers at their expense to the satisfaction of the Classification Society without condition/recommendation*. In such event the Sellers are to pay also for the cost of the underwater inspection and the Classification Society's attendance.

(iii) If the Vessel is to be drydocked pursuant to Clause 6 b) (ii) and no suitable dry-docking facilities are available at the port of delivery, the Sellers shall take the Vessel to a port where suitable drydocking facilities are available, whether within or outside the delivery range as per Clause 5 b). Once drydocking has taken place the Sellers shall deliver the Vessel at a port within the delivery range as per Clause 5 b) which shall, for the purpose of this Clause, become the new port of delivery. In such event the cancelling date provided for in Clause 5 b) shall be extended by the additional time required for the drydocking and extra steaming, but limited to a maximum of 14 running days.

c) If the Vessel is drydocked pursuant to Clause 6 a) or 6 b) above

(i) the Classification Society may require survey of the tailshaft system, the extent of the survey being to the satisfaction of the Classification surveyor. If such survey is not required by the Classification Society, the Buyers shall have the right to require the tailshaft to be drawn and surveyed by the Classification Society, the extent of the survey being in accordance with the Classification Society's rules for tailshaft survey and consistent with the current stage of the Vessel's survey cycle. The Buyers shall declare whether they require the tailshaft to be drawn and surveyed not later than by the completion of the inspection by the Classification Society. The drawing and refitting of the tailshaft shall be arranged by the Sellers. Should any parts of the tailshaft system be condemned or found defective so as to affect the Vessel's class, those parts shall be renewed or made good at the Sellers' expense to the satisfaction of the Classification Society without condition/recommendation*.

(ii) the expenses relating to the survey of the tailshaft system shall be borne by the Buyers unless the Classification Society requires such survey to be carried out, in which case the Sellers shall pay these expenses. The Sellers shall also pay the expenses if the Buyers require the survey and parts of the system are condemned or found defective or broken so as to affect the Vessel's class*.

(iii) the expenses in connection with putting the Vessel in and taking her out of drydock, including the drydock dues and the Classification Society's fees shall be paid by the Sellers if the Classification Society issues any condition/recommendation* as a result of the survey or if it requires survey of the tailshaft system. In all other cases the Buyers shall pay the aforesaid expenses, dues and fees.

(iv) the Buyers' representative shall have the right to be present in the drydock, but without interfering with the work or decisions of the Classification surveyor.

(v) the Buyers shall have the right to have the underwater parts of the Vessel cleaned and painted at their risk and expense without interfering with the Sellers' or the Classification surveyor's work, if any, and without affecting the Vessel's timely delivery. If, however, the Buyers' work in drydock is still in progress when the Sellers have completed the work which the Sellers are required to do, the additional docking time needed to complete the Buyers' work shall be for the Buyers' risk and expense. In the event that the Buyers' work requires such additional time, the Sellers may upon completion of the Sellers' work tender Notice of Readiness for delivery whilst the Vessel is still in drydock and the Buyers shall be obliged to take delivery in accordance with Clause 3, whether the Vessel is in drydock or not and irrespective of Clause 5 b).

* Notes, if any, in the surveyor's report which are accepted by the Classification Society without condition/recommendation are not to be taken into account.

APPENDIX 11

Norwegian Saleform (Continued)

** *6 a) and 6 b) are alternatives; delete whichever is not applicable. In the absence of deletions, alternative 6 a) to apply.*

7. Spares/bunkers, etc.

The Sellers shall deliver the Vessel to the Buyers with everything belonging to her on board and on shore. All spare parts and spare equipment including spare tail-end shaft(s) and/or spare propeller(s)/propeller blade(s), if any, belonging to the Vessel at the time of inspection used or unused, whether on board or not shall become the Buyers' property, but spares on order are to be excluded. Forwarding charges, if any, shall be for the Buyers' account. The Sellers are not required to replace spare parts including spare tail-end shaft(s) and spare propeller(s)/propeller blade(s) which are taken out of spare and used as replacement prior to delivery, but the replaced items shall be the property of the Buyers. The radio installation and navigational equipment shall be included in the sale without extra payment if they are the property of the Sellers. Unused stores and provisions shall be included in the sale and be taken over by the Buyers without extra payment.

The Sellers have the right to take ashore crockery, plates, cutlery, linen and other articles bearing the Sellers' flag or name, provided they replace same with similar unmarked items. Library, forms, etc., exclusively for use in the Sellers' vessel(s), shall be excluded without compensation. Captain's, Officers' and Crew's personal belongings including the slop chest are to be excluded from the sale, as well as the following additional items (including items on hire):

The Buyers shall take over the remaining bunkers and unused lubricating oils in storage tanks and sealed drums and pay the current net market price (excluding barging expenses) at the port and date of delivery of the Vessel.
Payment under this Clause shall be made at the same time and place and in the same currency as the Purchase Price.

8. Documentation

The place of closing:

In exchange for payment of the Purchase Price the Sellers shall furnish the Buyers with delivery documents, namely:

a) Legal Bill of Sale in a form recordable in (the country in which the Buyers are to register the Vessel), warranting that the Vessel is free from all encumbrances, mortgages and maritime liens or any other debts or claims whatsoever, duly notarially attested and legalized by the consul of such country or other competent authority.

b) Current Certificate of Ownership issued by the competent authorities of the flag state of the Vessel.

c) Confirmation of Class issued within 72 hours prior to delivery.

d) Current Certificate issued by the competent authorities stating that the Vessel is free from registered encumbrances.

e) Certificate of Deletion of the Vessel from the Vessel's registry or other official evidence of deletion appropriate to the Vessel's registry at the time of delivery, or, in the event that the registry does not as a matter of practice issue such documentation immediately, a written undertaking by the Sellers to effect deletion from the Vessel's registry forthwith and furnish a Certificate or other official evidence of deletion to the Buyers promptly and latest within 4 (four) weeks after the Purchase Price has been paid and the Vessel has been delivered.

f) Any such additional documents as may reasonably be required by the competent authorities for the purpose of registering the Vessel, provided the Buyers notify the Sellers of any such documents as soon as possible after the date of this Agreement.

At the time of delivery the Buyers and Sellers shall sign and deliver to each other a Protocol of Delivery and Acceptance confirming the date and time of delivery of the Vessel from the Sellers to the Buyers.

APPENDIX 11

Norwegian Saleform (Continued)

At the time of delivery the Sellers shall hand to the Buyers the classification certificate(s) as well as all plans etc., which are on board the Vessel. Other certificates which are on board the Vessel shall also be handed over to the Buyers unless the Sellers are required to retain same, in which case the Buyers to have the right to take copies. Other technical documentation which may be in the Sellers' possession shall be promptly forwarded to the Buyers at their expense, if they so request. The Sellers may keep the Vessel's log books but the Buyers to have the right to take copies of same.

9. Encumbrances

The Sellers warrant that the Vessel, at the time of delivery, is free from all charters, encumbrances, mortgages and maritime liens or any other debts whatsoever. The Sellers hereby undertake to indemnify the Buyers against all consequences of claims made against the Vessel which have been incurred prior to the time of delivery.

10. Taxes, etc.

Any taxes, fees and expenses in connection with the purchase and registration under the Buyers' flag shall be for the Buyers' account, whereas similar charges in connection with the closing of the Sellers' register shall be for the Sellers' account.

11. Condition on delivery

The Vessel with everything belonging to her shall be at the Sellers' risk and expense until she is delivered to the Buyers, but subject to the terms and conditions of this Agreement she shall be delivered and taken over as she was at the time of inspection, fair wear and tear excepted.
However, the Vessel shall be delivered with her class maintained without condition/recommendation*, free of average damage affecting the Vessel's class, and with her classification certificates and national certificates, as well as all other certificates the Vessel had at the time of inspection, valid and unextended without condition/recommendation* by Class or the relevant authorities at the time of delivery.
"Inspection" in this Clause 11, shall mean the Buyers' inspection according to Clause 4 a) or 4 b), if applicable, or the Buyers' inspection prior to the signing of this Agreement. If the Vessel is taken over without inspection, the date of this Agreement shall be the relevant date.

* Notes, if any, in the surveyor's report which are accepted by the Classification Society without condition/recommendation are not to be taken into account.

12. Name/markings

Upon delivery the Buyers undertake to change the name of the Vessel and alter funnel markings.

13. Buyers' default

Should the deposit not be paid in accordance with Clause 2, the Sellers have the right to cancel this Agreement, and they shall be entitled to claim compensation for their losses and for all expenses incurred together with interest.
Should the Purchase Price not be paid in accordance with Clause 3, the Sellers have the right to cancel the Agreement, in which case the deposit together with interest earned shall be released to the Sellers. If the deposit does not cover their loss, the Sellers shall be entitled to claim further compensation for their losses and for all expenses incurred together with interest.

14. Sellers' default

Should the Sellers fail to give Notice of Readiness in accordance with Clause 5 a) or fail to be ready to validly complete a legal transfer by the date stipulated in line 61 the Buyers shall have the option of cancelling this Agreement provided always that the Sellers shall be granted a maximum of 3 banking days after Notice of Readiness has been given to make arrangements for the documentation set out in Clause 8. If after Notice of Readiness has been given but before the Buyers have taken delivery, the Vessel ceases to be physically ready for delivery and is not made physically ready again in every respect by the date stipulated in line 61 and new Notice of

APPENDIX 11

Norwegian Saleform (Continued)

Readiness given, the Buyers shall retain their option to cancel. In the event that the Buyers elect to cancel this Agreement the deposit together with interest earned shall be released to them immediately.
Should the Sellers fail to give Notice of Readiness by the date stipulated in line 61 or fail to be ready to validly complete a legal transfer as aforesaid they shall make due compensation to the Buyers for their loss and for all expenses together with interest if their failure is due to proven negligence and whether or not the Buyers cancel this Agreement.

15. Buyers' representatives

After this Agreement has been signed by both parties and the deposit has been lodged, the Buyers have the right to place two representatives on board the Vessel at their sole risk and expense upon arrival at on or about
These representatives are on board for the purpose of familiarisation and in the capacity of observers only, and they shall not interfere in any respect with the operation of the Vessel. The Buyers' representatives shall sign the Sellers' letter of indemnity prior to their embarkation.

16. Arbitration

a)* This Agreement shall be governed by and construed in accordance with English law and any dispute arising out of this Agreement shall be referred to arbitration in London in accordance with the Arbitration Acts 1950 and 1979 or any statutory modification or re-enactment thereof for the time being in force, one arbitrator being appointed by each party. On the receipt by one party of the nomination in writing of the other party's arbitrator, that party shall appoint their arbitrator within fourteen days, failing which the decision of the single arbitrator appointed shall apply. If two arbitrators properly appointed shall not agree they shall appoint an umpire whose decision shall be final.

b)* This Agreement shall be governed by and construed in accordance with Title 9 of the United States Code and the Law of the State of New York and should any dispute arise out of this Agreement, the matter in dispute shall be referred to three persons at New York, one to be appointed by each of the parties hereto, and the third by the two so chosen; their decision or that of any two of them shall be final, and for purpose of enforcing any award, this Agreement may be made a rule of the Court.
The proceedings shall be conducted in accordance with the rules of the Society of Maritime Arbitrators, Inc. New York.

c)* Any dispute arising out of this Agreement shall be referred to arbitration at , subject to the procedures applicable there.

The laws of shall govern this Agreement.

* *16 a), 16 b) and 16 c) are alternatives; delete whichever is not applicable. In the absence of deletions, alternative 16 a) to apply.*

By kind permission of The Norwegian Shipbrokers Association

APPENDIX 12

Nipponsale 1999

Issued Dec. 16, 1965
Amended Jul. 13, 1971
Amended Mar. 16, 1977
Amended Sep. 9, 1993
Amended Nov. 2, 1999

The Documentary Committee of The Japan Shipping Exchange, Inc.

MEMORANDUM OF AGREEMENT

Place and Date of Agreement	Code Name: **NIPPONSALE 1999** (Part I)
1. Sellers (Preamble)	2. Buyers (Preamble)
3. Vessel's name (Preamble)	4. Flag/Registry (Preamble, Cl. 3 (a) (ii))
5. Class (Preamble, Cl. 6 (b))	6. Built (year and builder's name) (Preamble)
7. Gross register tonnage (Preamble)	8. Summer deadweight tonnage (Preamble)
9. [illegible]ace/Da[illegible] of superficial i[illegible]pection (Prea[illegible] Cl. 5 (a), Cl. [illegible]	10[illegible]ace/[illegible] of cla[illegible]ecords examinati[illegible] (Preamb[illegible]
11. Purch[illegible]ice (Cl[illegible]	
12. Place of closing (Cl. 3 (c))	
13. Delivery range (Cl. 4 (a), Cl. 6 (e)(i), (f))	
14. Delivery period (Cl. 4 (a)) and Cancelling Date (Cl. 4 (a), (d), (e))	
15. Places (Cl. 2 (a), Cl. 4 (c))	
16. Liquidated damages, per day (Cl. 7 (c))	The additional clauses, if any, numbered from 16 to shall be deemed to be fully incorporated into this Agreement.

It is mutually agreed that this Agreement shall be performed in accordance with the terms and conditions contained herein.

Signature (Sellers) Signature (Buyers)

APPENDIX 12

Nipponsale 1999 (Continued)

NIPPONSALE 1999

(Part II)

IT IS THIS DAY MUTUALLY AGREED between the Sellers referred to in Box 1 ("the Sellers") and the Buyers referred to in Box 2 ("the Buyers") that the Sellers shall sell and the Buyers shall buy the Vessel named in Box 3 with particulars as referred to in Boxes 4 - 8 ("the Vessel"), which has been accepted by the Buyers following their superficial inspection of the Vessel and examination of her class records as referred to in Boxes 9 and 10 respectively on the following terms and conditions.

1. PURCHASE PRICE

The purchase price of the Vessel ("the Purchase Price") shall be as stated in Box 11.

2. PAYMENT

(a) As security for the fulfilment of this Agreement, the Buyers shall remit a deposit of ten (10) per cent of the Purchase Price ("the Deposit") to a bank nominated by the Sellers within three (3) banking days (being days on which banks are open for the transaction of business in the place stated in Box 15 ("Banking Days")), from the date of this Agreement, in the names of both the Sellers and the Buyers. Any interest earned on the Deposit shall be credited to the Buyers. Bank charges on the Deposit shall be borne equally by the Sellers and the Buyers. The Deposit shall be paid to the Sellers as a part of the Purchase Price in the same manner as the balance of the ninety (90) per cent of the Purchase Price as provided for hereunder.

(b) The Buyers shall remit the balance of the Purchase Price by telegraphic transfer to the said bank immediately after the Notice of Readiness for Delivery is tendered by the Sellers as per Clause 7 of this Agreement. The balance shall be paid to the Sellers together with the Deposit against the Protocol of Delivery and Acceptance being duly signed by a representative of each party at the time of delivery of the Vessel.

3. DOCUMENTATION

(a) At the time of delivery of the Vessel, the Sellers shall provide the Buyers with the following documents:

(i) the Bill of Sale, duly notarized by a Notary Public, specifying that the Vessel is free from all debts, encumbrances, mortgages and maritime liens; and

(ii) a letter from the Sellers undertaking to supply a Deletion Certificate from the Registry stated in Box 4 as soon as practicable after the Vessel's delivery; and

(iii) such other documents as may be mutually agreed.

(b) Upon delivery the Buyers and the Sellers shall execute and exchange a Protocol of Delivery and Acceptance, thereby confirming the date and time of delivery of the Vessel.

(c) Closing shall take place at the place stated in Box 12.

4. DELIVERY PLACE AND TIME

(a) The Sellers shall ensure that the Vessel is ready for delivery within the Delivery Range stated in Box 13 not before and not later than the dates stated in Box 14, the latter date being the Cancelling Date.

(b) The Sellers shall keep the Buyers informed of the Vessel's itinerary and give the Buyers thirty (30), fifteen (15), seven (7) and three (3) days notice of the expected date and place of readiness for delivery.

(c) In the event that the Vessel is not ready for delivery on or before the Cancelling Date, the Buyers shall have the option of cancelling this Agreement, provided such option shall be exercised in writing within two (2) Working Days (which shall be the days not falling on Saturdays, Sundays, or Public holidays in the place stated in Box 15) from the Cancelling Date. However, if the failure to deliver the Vessel is caused by any event over which the Sellers have no control, then the Cancelling Date shall be extended by the corresponding time lost due to such event but in no case shall such extension be for a period of more than thirty (30) days.

(d) In the event the Buyers do not elect to exercise the option to cancel this Agreement in accordance with sub-clause (c) above, they shall have the right to designate a new date for delivery of the Vessel, provided such right is exercised in writing within two (2) Working Days from the Cancelling Date, and such designated date shall be the new Cancelling Date as if stated in Box 14. However if no new Cancelling Date is designated by the Buyers in accordance with this sub-clause there shall be no further Cancelling Date and the Sellers shall deliver the Vessel as soon as practicable.

(e) Notwithstanding the exercise of due diligence by them, if the Sellers anticipate that the Vessel will not be ready for delivery by the Cancelling Date, (whether it be the first agreed Cancelling Date or any subsequent Cancelling Date as provided for in sub-clause (d) above), then the Sellers may notify the Buyers in writing stating the date when they anticipate that the Vessel will be ready for delivery and proposing that that date shall be the new Cancelling Date. Upon receipt of such notification the Buyers shall have the option to cancel this Agreement, provided such option is exercised in writing within two (2) Working Days from the receipt of the aforesaid notification from the Sellers. If the Buyers do not exercise the option to cancel this Agreement, the date proposed by the Sellers shall be the new Cancelling Date as if stated in Box 14.

5. DELIVERY CONDITION

(a) The Sellers shall deliver the Vessel to the Buyers in substantially the same condition as when the Vessel was inspected by the Buyers at the place stated in Box 9, fair wear and tear excepted, but free from outstanding recommendations and average damage affecting her present class and with all her class, national and international trading certificates clean and valid at the time of delivery.

(b) Upon the Vessel being delivered to and accepted by the Buyers in accordance with this Agreement the Sellers shall have no liability whatsoever for any fault or deficiency in their description of the Vessel or for any defect in the Vessel regardless of whether such defect was apparent or latent at the time of delivery.

6. UNDERWATER INSPECTION

(a) The Sellers may deliver the Vessel without drydocking, subject to the following provisions.

(b) Prior to delivery of the Vessel the Buyers shall have the right to have divers approved by a classification society referred to in Box 5 ("the Classification Society"), carry out an inspection of the Vessel's underwater parts below the summer load line in the presence of a surveyor of the Classification Society arranged by the Sellers. Such inspection, if any, is to be at the Buyers' arrangement, risk and expense and is not to interfere with the Vessel's operation and delivery schedule.

(c) The Buyers shall give a written notice of their intention to have an underwater inspection carried out within two (2) days from the receipt of the seven (7) days notice stipulated in sub-clause (b) of Clause 4. If the Buyers fail to give such a written notice within two (2) days, they shall lose their right to have an underwater inspection.

(d) Upon receipt of the Buyers' notice the Sellers shall arrange with the Classification Society to carry out an underwater inspection. The cost of the underwater inspection shall be borne by the Buyers unless damage affecting the class is found, in which case the Sellers shall bear the cost.

(e) Should any damage affecting the class be found by such divers' inspection the following shall apply:

(i) where the damage is of such nature that repairs are not required prior to the next scheduled drydocking by the Classification Society, then the Sellers and the Buyers shall each select a reputable shipyard in the Delivery Range stated in Box 13 or near thereto and obtain from such shipyard a quotation for the cost of repairs of the damage. Each quotation is to be for the direct repair costs of the damage only and is not to include the cost of

APPENDIX 12

Nipponsale 1999 (Continued)

NIPPONSALE 1999

(Part II)

dockage and general service expenses. The Sellers shall then have the option to either repair the damage prior to delivery of the Vessel or deliver the Vessel without the damage being repaired with a reduction from the Purchase Price of the estimated cost of repairs. The estimated cost of repairs shall be defined as the average of the two quotations obtained from the two shipyards;

(ii) where the damage is of such nature that repairs are required prior to the next scheduled drydocking by the Classification Society, then the Sellers shall repair the damage at their cost and expense and to the Classification Society's satisfaction.

(f) In the event that the Vessel is drydocked to effect repairs of damage in accordance with sub-clause (e) hereof, the Sellers shall have the right to designate the drydock place as the new delivery place if such drydock place is within the Delivery Range stated in Box 13. In such event the Buyers shall have the right to clean and paint the underwater parts of the Vessel at their risk and expense and without interfering with the work of the Sellers and a surveyor of the Classification Society and without affecting the Vessel's delivery schedule. However if the Buyers' work in drydock is still in progress when the Sellers have completed their work, then the additional docking period necessary for completing such work shall be at the Buyers' risk and expense, in which event the Sellers shall have the right to tender a Notice of Readiness for Delivery on or after completion of their work.

(g) If repairs are required in accordance with sub-clause (e) hereof, then the Cancelling Date shall be extended by the corresponding time lost to effect such repairs provided that such extension shall not in any event exceed thirty (30) days.

7. NOTICE OF READINESS AND LIQUIDATED DAMAGES

(a) When the Vessel becomes ready for delivery, the Sellers shall tender to the Buyers a Notice of Readiness for Delivery.

(b) The Buyers shall take over the Vessel within three (3) Banking Days from the day of receipt of such Notice of Readiness for Delivery.

(c) In the event the Buyers do not take delivery of the Vessel within the period specified above, the Buyers shall pay to the Sellers for each day of the delay up to the tenth (10th) day of the delay the liquidated damages as stated in Box 16. If the delay exceeds ten (10) days then the Sellers shall have the right to cancel this Agreement and claim damages for their losses flowing therefrom.

8. TOTAL LOSS AND FORCE MAJEURE

Should, before delivery, the Vessel become an actual, constructive or compromised total loss (not being a result of an act or omission of the Sellers committed with the intent to cause such total loss or recklessly and with knowledge that such total loss would probably result therefrom), or should the Vessel not be able to be delivered before the Cancelling Date through the outbreak of war, the restraint of Governments, Princes or People, political reasons or any other cause over which the Sellers have no control, then this Agreement shall be null and void and neither party shall be liable to the other. In such event the Deposit together with interest accrued thereon, if any, shall be immediately released in full to the Buyers.

9. TRANSFER OF TITLE AND RISK

Title and risk to the Vessel, together with everything belonging to her, shall pass to the Buyers upon both payment of the Purchase Price and delivery of the Vessel having occurred. Delivery of the Vessel shall be deemed to take place at the date and time specified in the Protocol of Delivery and Acceptance.

10. BELONGINGS AND BUNKERS

The Sellers shall deliver to the Buyers the Vessel with everything belonging to her at the time of the superficial inspection referred to in the Box 9 including all spare parts, stores and equipment, on board or on shore, used or unused, except such things as are in the normal course of operations used during the period between the superficial inspection and delivery. The Sellers shall provide the Buyers with an inventory list at the time of delivery. Forwarding charges, if any, shall be for the Buyers' account. The Buyers shall take over and pay the Sellers for the remaining bunkers and unused lubricating oils at the last purchased prices evidenced by supporting vouchers. Payment under this clause shall be made on or prior to delivery of the Vessel in the same currency as the Purchase Price.

11. EXCLUSION FROM THE SALE

The Sellers have the right to take ashore all crockery, cutlery, linen and other articles bearing the Sellers' flag or name, provided the Sellers substitute the same for an equivalent number and type of similar unmarked items. Books, cassettes and forms etc., exclusively for use by the Sellers on the Vessel, shall be taken ashore before delivery. Personal effects of the Master, Officers and Crew including slop chest and hired equipment, if any, are excluded from this sale and shall be removed by the Sellers prior to delivery of the Vessel.

12. CHANGE OF NAME ETC.

The Buyers undertake to change the name of the Vessel and alter the funnel markings upon delivery of the Vessel.

13. ENCUMBRANCES ETC.

The Sellers shall deliver to the Buyers the Vessel free from all debts, encumbrances, mortgages and maritime liens. The Sellers hereby undertake to indemnify the Buyers against all claims of whatever nature made against the Vessel in respect of liabilities incurred prior to the time of delivery.

14. DEFAULT AND COMPENSATION

(a) Should the Buyers default in the payment of the Deposit or the balance of the Purchase Price in the manner and within the time herein specified, or the Buyers otherwise fail to perform their obligations under this Agreement and such failure is not remedied within seven (7) days following receipt of a notice of default from the Sellers to the Buyers, then the Sellers shall have the right to cancel this Agreement. In such event the Deposit if already paid, together with interest accrued thereon, if any, shall be forfeited to the Sellers. If the Deposit has not yet been paid the Sellers shall have the right to receive the amount equivalent to the Deposit from the Buyers. If the Deposit or the amount equivalent to the Deposit does not cover the Sellers' losses, the Sellers shall have the right to claim further compensation from the Buyers to recover such losses.

(b) Should the Sellers default in the delivery of the Vessel with everything belonging to her in the manner and within the time herein specified, or the Sellers otherwise fail to perform their obligations under this Agreement and such failure is not remedied within seven (7) days following receipt of a notice of default from the Buyers to the Sellers, then the Buyers shall have the right to cancel this Agreement. In such event the Buyers shall have the right to be paid the amount equivalent to the Deposit by the Sellers and the Deposit, if already paid, together with interest accrued thereon, if any, shall be released to the Buyers. If the amount equivalent to the Deposit does not cover the Buyers' losses the Buyers shall have the right to claim further compensation from the Sellers to recover such losses.

15. ARBITRATION

Any and all disputes arising out of or in connection with this Agreement shall be submitted to arbitration held in Tokyo at the Tokyo Maritime Arbitration Commission ("TOMAC") of The Japan Shipping Exchange, Inc. in accordance with the Rules of TOMAC and any amendments thereto, and the award given by the arbitrators shall be final and binding on both parties.

APPENDIX 13

BIMCO "Salescrap"

1. Place and Date of Contract		THE BALTIC AND INTERNATIONAL MARITIME COUNCIL (BIMCO) STANDARD CONTRACT FOR THE SALE OF VESSELS FOR DEMOLITION CODE NAME: "SALESCRAP 87" PART I	
2. Sellers/Place of Business (full name, address & telex number)		3. Buyers/Place of Business (full name, address & telex number)	
4. Name of Vessel (also state ex. name)	5. Type of Vessel	6. Built (year and builder's name)	7. Flag
8. Class	9. Register Number	10. Place of Registration	11. GRT/NRT
12. Light Displacement Tonnage (Lightweight) (state whether in metric tons or long tons) (Cl.3)		13. Working Propeller(s) (state number and material)	14. Spare Propeller(s) (state number and material)
15. Spare Tail End Shaft (state no.)	16. Main Engine (type and number)	17. Generator(s) (state number and type)	
18. Purchase Price (in figures and letters) (state both lump sum price <u>and</u> equivalent price per ton lightweight; also state currency in which purchase price is payable) (Cl. 4) (a) Lump sum price (b) Equivalent price per ton lightweight (c) Currency in which purchase price payable			
19. Deposit (state amount, name and place of bank to which the deposit shall be paid) (Cl. 5)			
20. Letter of Credit (Cl. 6) (a) Number of banking days for establishing Letter of Credit (sub-clause 6.1. of Cl. 6) (b) Opening Bank (name and place) (sub-clause 6.2. of Cl. 6) (c) Advising Bank (name and place) (sub-clause 6.2. of Cl. 6) (d) Expiry Date of Letter of Credit (sub-clause 6.5. of Cl. 6)			

APPENDIX 13

BIMCO "Salescrap" (Continued)

(continued) **"SALESCRAP 87" STANDARD CONTRACT FOR THE SALE OF VESSELS FOR DEMOLITION** **PART I**

21. Vessel's present position (if trading state "now trading"; if laid up state "in lay-up" and place where) (Cl. 7)	22. Voyage (state whether under own power or under tow, as agreed) (Cl. 8)
23. Place of Delivery (also state approximate arrival draft fore and aft in metres or feet) (Cl. 9) (a) Place of delivery (sub-clause 9.1. of Cl. 9) (b) Approximate arrival draft fore and aft in metres or feet (sub-clause 9.1. of Cl. 9)	24. Time of Delivery/Cancelling Date (Cl. 10) (a) Expected to be ready for delivery between (two dates to be given) (sub-cl. 10.1. of Cl. 10) (b) Cancelling date (sub-cl. 10.1. of Cl. 10)
25. Advance Notices of Arrival and Delivery (state number of days definite notice of delivery) (Cl. 11)	
26. Financial Documentation and Payment (Cl. 13)	27. Buyers' Representative(s) (state no. of Representative(s)) (Cl. 19)
(a) state by whom Bill of Sale shall be legalised (sub-cl. 13.1.(i) of Cl. 13)	28. Buyers' Default (state rate of interest per annum) (Cl. 22)
(b) state number of Commercial Invoice (sub-cl. 13.1.(iv) of Cl. 13)	29. Sellers' Default (state rate of interest per annum) (Cl. 23)
30. Law and arbitration (state 24.1., 24.2. or 24.3. of Cl.24, as agreed; if 24.3. agreed also state place of arbitration) (if Box 30 not filled in 24.1. shall apply) (Cl. 24)	
31. Names and Addresses for Notices and other Communications to be given by the Sellers (Cl. 25)	32. Names and Addresses for Notices and other Communications to be given by the Buyers (Cl. 25)
33. Numbers of additional clauses covering special provisions, if agreed	

It is mutually agreed between the party named in Box 2 (hereinafter referred to as "the Sellers") and the party named in Box 3 (hereinafter referred to as "the Buyers") that on the date of this Contract the Sellers have sold and the Buyers have bought the Vessel described in PART I hereof and as may be further described in Appendix "A" (hereinafter referred to as "the Vessel") on the terms and conditions contained in this Contract consisting of PART I including additional clauses, if any agreed and stated in Box 33, and PART II as well as APPENDIX "A" as annexed hereto. In the event of a conflict of conditions, the provisions of PART I shall prevail over those of PART II and APPENDIX "A" to the extent of such conflict but no further.

Signature (Sellers)	Signature (Buyers)

APPENDIX 13

BIMCO "Salescrap" (Continued)

PART II
"SALESCRAP 87" Standard Contract

1. Vessel

On the date of this Contract the Vessel shall be of the description set out in PART I and, if required, as further described in Appendix "A".

2. Outright Sale

2.1. The Vessel has been accepted by the Buyers without inspection and the sale is, therefore, outright and definite and not subject to subsequent inspection.

2.2. The Vessel is sold with all materials, tackle, apparel, stores and spare parts belonging to her as on board at the date of this Contract but excluding items listed in Appendix "A" annexed to this Contract.

2.3. Unless otherwise agreed, any remaining bunkers on board at the time of delivery shall become the Buyers' property.

2.4. The Sellers shall, at the time of delivery, hand to the Buyers all plans, specifications and certificates, or photocopies hereof, as available and whether valid or invalid.

2.5. The Sellers shall have the right to take ashore without compensation the following items: crockery, plate, cutlery, linen and other articles bearing the Sellers' flag or name, as well as library, forms, etc., exclusively for use in the Sellers' vessels. Captain's, Officers' and Crew's personal belongings including slop chest to be excluded from the sale.

2.6. The Sellers are not required to replace such material, spare parts or stores including spare propeller(s) (if any) which may be consumed or taken out of spare and used as replacement prior to delivery, but all replaced spares shall be retained on board and shall become the property of the Buyers.

3. Light Displacement Tonnage (Lightweight)

The Vessel's Light Displacement Tonnage (Lightweight) as stated in Box 12 shall be evidenced by the Builder's capacity plan incorporating deadweight scale (or an authenticated copy hereof) or, in the Sellers' option, a letter from the Builders (or an authenticated copy hereof) or, subject to Buyers' approval, any equivalent evidence of present lightweight of the Vessel confirming same. Such proof shall be delivered by the Sellers to the Buyers latest 10 days after the date of this Contract but latest on delivery whichever is the earlier.

4. Purchase Price

The Purchase Price is the lump sum stated in Box 18 (a) payable in the currency indicated in Box 18 (c), based upon a price per ton lightweight as stated in Box 18 (b) calculated on the basis of the Vessel's lightweight as stated in Box 12. In the event the Vessel's lightweight as stated in Box 12 differs from the evidence as delivered by the Sellers according to Clause 3 hereof, the lump sum stated in Box 18 (a) shall be adjusted with the amount as stated in Box 18 (b) so as to reflect the difference.

5. Deposit

5.1. As a security for the correct fulfilment of this Contract, the Buyers shall pay a Deposit of 10 (ten) per cent. of the Purchase Price with the bank stated in Box 19 in the joint names of the Sellers and Buyers.

5.2. Such Deposit shall be made latest within 3 banking days from the date of this Contract.

5.3. Interest, if any, on such Deposit shall be credited the Buyers.

5.4. Any fees or charges for establishing and holding such Deposit shall be borne equally by the Sellers and the Buyers.

6. Letter of Credit

6.1. The Buyers shall establish by a fully detailed cable or telex a Confirmed Irrevocable At Sight Letter of Credit in a form satisfactory to the Sellers for the full amount of the Purchase Price latest within the number of banking days from the date of this Contract as stated in Box 20(a).

6.2. Such Letter of Credit shall be established by the Buyers with a first class Bank as named in Box 20(b) (hereinafter referred to as "the Opening Bank") under advice to the Bank nominated by the Sellers as named in Box 20(c) (hereinafter referred to as "the Advising Bank").

6.3. Such Letter of Credit shall contain a provision that if the Opening Bank has not within 3 banking days confirmed by telex or cable to the Advising Bank that Notice of Readiness for Delivery has been tendered according to Clause 12.1., the full amount of the Letter of Credit shall be released to the Sellers immediately upon the Sellers' presentation to the Advising Bank of a copy of the Notice of Readiness for Delivery together with the documents listed in sub-clause 13.1.

6.4. All bank charges in connection with the Confirmed Irrevocable Letter of Credit shall be for the Buyers' account except for Advising Bank negotiating charges.

6.5. The expiry date of the Letter of Credit shall not be earlier than the date stated in Box 20(d).

7. Vessel's Present Position

The Vessel's present position is as indicated in Box 21.

8. Voyage

8.1. The Vessel shall proceed to the Place of Delivery either under her own power or under tow, as agreed in Box 22.

8.2. The Sellers shall have the right either to let the Vessel proceed in ballast to the Place of Delivery or, in their option, to proceed thereto with cargo on board up to the Vessel's full capacity, via port or ports whether en route or not.

9. Place of Delivery

9.1. The Vessel shall be delivered by the Sellers to the Buyers safely afloat, free of cargo and (except for tank vessels) with hatches closed and with the approximate arrival draft stated in Box 23(b) at the place stated in Box 23(a) (hereinafter referred to as "the Place of Delivery").

9.2. If, on the Vessel's arrival, the Place of Delivery is inaccessible for any reason whatsoever including but not limited to port congestion, the Vessel shall be delivered and taken over by the Buyers as near thereto as she may safely get at a safe and accessible berth or at a safe anchorage which shall be designated by the Buyers always provided that such berth or anchorage shall be subject to the approval of the Sellers and the Master. Such approval shall not be unreasonably withheld. If the Buyers fail to nominate such place within 24 hours of arrival, the place at which it is customary for vessels to wait shall constitute the Place of Delivery.

9.3. The delivery of the Vessel according to the provisions of sub-clause 9.2. shall constitute a full performance of the Sellers' obligations according to sub-clause 9.1. and all other terms and conditions of this Contract shall apply as if delivery had taken place according to sub-clause 9.1.

10. Time of Delivery/Cancelling Date

10.1. The Vessel is expected to be ready for delivery between the dates (both inclusive) stated in Box 24 (a) but latest on the date stated in Box 24 (b) (hereinafter referred to as "the cancelling date").

10.2.(i). Should the Sellers anticipate with reasonable certainty that the Vessel will not be ready for delivery by the cancelling date, they shall notify the Buyers hereof without delay stating the probable date of the Vessel's readiness for delivery. Upon receipt of such notification the Buyers shall have the option either to cancel the Contract according to Clause 23 or to postpone the cancelling date.

10.2.(ii). If the Buyers decide to maintain the Contract and postpone the cancelling date or if the Buyers do not within 4 working days of receipt of the Sellers' notification declare their option to cancel the Contract according to Clause 23, the fourth running day after the new date of readiness for delivery indicated in the Sellers' notification shall be regarded as a new cancelling date and shall be substituted for the cancelling date stipulated in Box 24(b).

10.3. If the Buyers elect to maintain the Contract, all the terms and conditions of this Contract including the notification procedures laid down in Clause 12 shall remain in full force and effect.

11. Advance Notice of Arrival and Delivery

The Sellers shall keep the Buyers fully informed about the Vessel's position and about any alteration in expected time of arrival and shall also give to the Buyers the number of days definite notice of delivery as agreed in Box 25.

12. Notice of Readiness for Delivery

12.1. When the Vessel is ready for delivery, the Sellers or their Agents shall give to the Buyers and to the Opening Bank a written Notice of Readiness for Delivery. Such Notice of Readiness for Delivery shall be countersigned by Lloyd's Agents at the Place of Delivery.

12.2. In the event of the Vessel being a tank vessel, the Notice of Readiness for Delivery shall be accompanied by a valid Certificate issued by a competent authority or person acceptable to the Buyers certifying that all cargo tanks, cofferdams and pump rooms are gas-free, safe for men and fire, and substantially free of residues, slops and sludges and such Certificate shall be deemed to be a full compliance and discharge of the Sellers' obligations with respect to the cargo tanks, cofferdams and pump rooms. Such Certificate shall be provided by the Sellers at their cost.

13. Financial Documentation and Payment

13.1. The Sellers shall furnish the Advising Bank with the following documents:

(i) Legal Bill of Sale stating that the said Vessel is free from all encumbrances and maritime liens or any other debts whatsoever, duly notarially attested and legalised by the Consul or other competent authority stated in Box 26(a);

(ii) Certificate of Ownership issued by the competent authorities of the Flag State of the Vessel;

(iii) Certificate stating that the Vessel is free from registered encumbrances;

(iv) Commercial Invoice in the number stated in Box 26(b) signed by the Sellers, setting out the Vessel's particulars;

(v) Certificate of Deletion of the Vessel from the Vessel's Registry or, in the Sellers' option, a Written Undertaking by the Sellers to promptly, and latest within four weeks after the Purchase Sum has been fully paid and the Vessel has been delivered, to effect deletion from the Vessel's Registry and that a Certificate of Deletion will thereupon be furnished to the Buyers;

(vi) A written authorization from the Sellers to release to the Buyers the Deposit established by the Buyers according to Clause 5;

(vii) A Written Undertaking by the Sellers to instruct the Master or their Agents by cable or telex to release and physically deliver the Vessel to the Buyers.

13.2. Immediately upon the tendering of Notice of Readiness for Delivery according to Clause 12.1., the Opening Bank shall confirm by telex or cable to the Advising Bank that the Notice of Readiness for Delivery has been received whereafter the full amount of the Letter of Credit shall be released to the Sellers provided that the Advising Bank has been furnished with the documents listed in sub-clause 13.1.

If such confirmation by telex or cable has not been given by the Opening Bank to the Advising Bank within 3 banking days after the Sellers' Notice of Readiness of Delivery has been tendered, the full amount of the Letter of Credit shall be released to the Sellers immediately upon the Sellers' presentation to the Advising Bank of a copy of the Notice of Readiness for Delivery and the documents listed in sub-clause 13.1.

14. Condition on Delivery

14.1. The Vessel with everything belonging to her shall be at the Sellers' risk and expense until she is delivered to the Buyers.

14.2. Notwithstanding the provisions of sub-clause 14.1., the Vessel with everything belonging to her shall be delivered and taken over by the Buyers substantially in the same condition as she was on the date of this Contract after which the Sellers shall have no responsibility for possible faults or deficiencies of any description.

APPENDIX 13

BIMCO "Salescrap" (Continued)

PART II
"SALESCRAP 87" Standard Contract

15. Funnel Mark, etc.

As soon as possible after delivery the Buyers undertake to obliterate the name of the Vessel and funnel mark.

16. Encumbrances and Maritime Liens, etc.

The Sellers warrant that the Vessel, at the time of delivery, is charter-free and free from all encumbrances and maritime liens or any other debts whatsoever. Should any claims which have been incurred prior to the time of delivery be made against the Vessel, the Sellers hereby undertake to indemnify the Buyers against all consequences of such claims.

17. Taxes, Dues and Charges, etc.

17.1. All taxes, dues, duties (including import duties) and charges imposed upon the Vessel at the Place of Delivery and notarial and/or consular and/or other charges or expenses connected with the purchase and import of the Vessel at the Place of Delivery shall be borne by the Buyers.

17.2. All taxes, dues, duties and charges, including notarial and/or consular and/or other charges, or expenses connected with the closing of the Sellers' Register, shall be for the Sellers' account.

18. Deratisation Exemption Certificate

The Vessel shall be delivered by the Sellers with a valid Deratisation Exemption Certificate.

19. Buyers' Representative(s)

The Sellers agree to allow the Buyers to place the number of Representative(s) stated in Box 27 on board the Vessel on her arrival at the Place of Delivery.

Whilst on board the Vessel, such Representative(s) shall be at the sole risk, liability and expense of the Buyers and the Buyers shall indemnify the Sellers for any claims and damage in this respect. The Buyers' Representative(s) must not interfere with the operation of the Vessel.

20. Purpose of Sale

20.1. The Vessel is sold for the purpose of breaking-up only and the Buyers undertake that they will neither trade the Vessel for their own account nor sell the Vessel to a third party for any purpose other than breaking-up. The Buyers shall procure that this obligation is made a term of any and every subsequent agreement for the resale of the Vessel.

20.2. Non-compliance with the provisions contained in sub-clause 20.1. shall amount to a breach of the contract and the Buyers shall be liable to pay to the Sellers 20 (twenty) per cent. of the Purchase Price as liquidated damages resulting from such a breach.

20.3. The Buyers shall, in due course, furnish the Sellers with a Certificate stating that the Vessel has been totally demolished.

21. Exemptions

The Sellers shall be under no liability to the Buyers if the Vessel should become an actual, constructive or compromised total loss before delivery, or if delivery of the Vessel by the cancelling date should otherwise be prevented or delayed due to outbreak of war, restraint of Government, Princes, Rulers or People of any Nation or the United Nations, Act of God, or any other cause beyond the Sellers' control. If damage is sustained by the Vessel before delivery for any cause whatsoever or howsoever arising and if the estimated cost of repairs to enable the Vessel to proceed to the Place of Delivery would exceed 10 (ten) per cent. of the Purchase Price stated in Box 18, the Sellers shall not be bound to repair the Vessel but shall be entitled to treat delivery as having thereby been prevented and shall similarly be under no liability to the Buyers. Where delivery shall become impossible or prevented as aforesaid the Deposit as well as the Letter of Credit, if established, shall be returned to the Buyers forthwith.

22. Buyers' Default

22.1. Should the Deposit not be paid in accordance with the provisions of Clause 5, the Sellers shall have the right to cancel this Contract, and they shall be entitled to claim compensation for their losses and for all expenses incurred together with interest at the rate per annum stated in Box 28.

22.2. If the Buyers fail to establish the Letter of Credit in accordance with the provisions of Clause 6 or should the Purchase Sum not be paid in the manner provided for in this Contract, the Sellers shall have the right to cancel this Contract, in which case the amount deposited together with interest earned, if any, shall be forfeited to the Sellers. If the Deposit does not cover the Sellers' losses, they shall be entitled to claim further compensation for their losses and for all expenses together with interest at the rate per annum stated in Box 28.

23. Sellers' Default

If the Sellers fail to execute a legal transfer or to deliver the Vessel with everything belonging to her in the manner and at the latest on the date specified in Box 24(b), the Buyers shall have the right to cancel this Contract, in which case the Deposit in full together with the Letter of Credit, if established, shall be returned to the Buyers together with interest at the rate per annum stated in Box 29. The Sellers shall make due compensation for the losses caused to the Buyers by failure to execute a legal transfer or to deliver the Vessel in the manner and at the latest on the date specified in Box 24(b), if such are due to the proven negligence of the Sellers.

24. Law and Arbitration

*) 24.1. This Contract shall be governed by English law and any dispute arising out of this Contract shall be referred to arbitration in London, one arbitrator being appointed by each party, in accordance with the Arbitration Acts 1950 and 1979 or any statutory modification or re-enactment thereof for the time being in force. On the receipt by one party of the nomination in writing of the other party's arbitrator, that party shall appoint their arbitrator within fourteen days, failing which the decision of the single Arbitrator appointed shall apply. If two Arbitrators properly appointed shall not agree they shall appoint an umpire whose decision shall be final.

*) 24.2. This Contract shall be governed by U.S. Law and all disputes arising out of this Contract shall be arbitrated at New York in the following manner:

One arbitrator is to be appointed by each of the parties herein and a third by the two so chosen. Their decision or that of any two of them shall be final, and for the purpose of enforcing any award, this agreement may be made a rule of the court. The Arbitrators shall be commercial men. Such Arbitration is to be conducted in accordance with the rules of the Society of Maritime Arbitrators, Inc., New York, as currently amended.

A sole arbitrator may be appointed, if so desired by both parties.

Either party may call for arbitration by service of notice upon the other. If the other party does not appoint its arbitrator within fourteen days of such written notice, then the first moving party shall have the right, without further notice, to appoint a second arbitrator, with the same force and effect as if said second arbitrator had been appointed by the other party.

*) 24.3. Any dispute arising out of this Contract shall be referred to arbitration at the place indicated in Box 30, subject to the law and procedures applicable there.

24.4. If Box 30 in Part I is not filled in, sub-clause 24.1. of this Clause shall apply.

**) 24.1., 24.2. and 24.3. are alternatives; indicate alternative agreed in Box 30.*

25. Names and Addresses for Notices and Other Communications

All notices and communications shall be in writing or by cable, telex or telegram and shall, unless otherwise provided for in this Contract, be made by the Sellers, respectively the Buyers, to the addresses stated in Boxes 31 and 32.

APPENDIX 13

BIMCO "Salescrap" (Continued)

Appendix "A" to Standard Contract for the Sale of Vessels for Demolition
Code Name: "SALESCRAP 87" – dated

(i) Further description of the Vessel (if required):

(ii) Items excluded from the sale:

APPENDIX 14

"Fairplay" Market Report

Markets

Demolition

Scrapping slow after busy week

THE demolition market is finally showing signs of weakening after a busy week for brokers.

The largest vessel to be sold for demolition was the very large crude carrier ***Kudos***. This 1975-built 233,352 dwt 35,527 ldt tanker headed for Bangladesh beaches at a rate of $144 per ldt.

Moving down in size, the 1977-built 132,285 dwt 21,733 ldt tanker ***Romina G*** was also sold to Bangladesh breakers for a healthy price of $150 per ldt, as was the 1975-built, 89,644 dwt, 16,732 ldt ***Coral Sea II***.

More specialist tonnage, in the form of the 1977-built 127,209 dwt, 20,462 ldt ore-oiler ***Peregrine VIII***, was sold on as "as is" basis at her last location in Portugal for a price of $66 per ldt, a price reflective of her condition.

Another vessel sold on as "as is" basis was the 1971-built, 38,930 dwt, 14,055 ldt gas carrier ***Havast***. Her location was Fujairah and she was sold to Indian breakers for a price in the region of $153 per ldt.

The 1979-built, 5,657 dwt reefer ***Syros Reefer*** and the 1977-built, 14,678 dwt, 6,082 ldt general cargoship ***Tasmia*** were sold for demolition, but the full details of the price and the final destination for both remain hazy.

Bulk carriers have been on the shopping list for Indian breakers, as the purchase of the 1970-built, 45,206 dwt, 9,844 ldt ***Marinaki*** for $152 per ldt illustrates.

The previously reported sale of the 1973-built, 31,295 dwt, 7,240 ldt tanker ***Sant III*** has been finalised and she is making her final voyage for Indian scrapyards for an undisclosed sum.

A larger vessel that has also been purchased at an auction by Indian demolition yards is the 1970-built, 40,610 dwt, 10,266 ldt general cargoship ***Med Salvador*** for $146 per ldt.

Staying with Indian breakers, a further bulk carrier has been purchased. The 1977-built, 19,027 dwt, 4,807 ldt ***Tenedos*** received $152 per ldt.

Owners of a bulk carrier with recent engine problems have decided to give up the vessel for demolition. The 1975-built, 16,534 dwt, 4,217 ldt ***Ege K*** had a malfunction in her engine at the end of March and was towed to Mina Saqr. Now her final destination will be to Indian beaches, although the details of the price she received were not forthcoming.

The 1977-built 3,501 dwt, 2,939 ldt ro-ro ***Fast Alexandria*** has been sold on an "as is" basis in Portugal. The price of $66 per ldt reflects her crankshaft damage.

Meanwhile, the 1973-built, 8,265 dwt, 3,500 ldt general cargoship ***Dubai Orient*** was said to have been sold to Indian interests under private terms, while the 1975-built 16,618 dwt, 6,382 ldt 'tween decker ***Galina II*** was reported sold to Indian breakers for $167 per ldt.

Further to an earlier report, details of the demolition of the 1976-built, 53,341 dwt, 10,551 ldt ***Mentese*** have now materialised. She was sold to a Chinese scrapyard for $120 per ldt.

In amendments to previously reported items, three tankers received differing prices. The ***Monte Chiaro*** achieved a price of $167 per ldt, the ***Franca D'Alesio*** sale finalised at $123 per ldt and the ***Petro Mersey*** was purchased for $167 per ldt.

Also of interest are the figures that indicate China has increased its buying activity in the demolition market this year. Annualised figures suggest the country is 106% ahead, with 2.9m dwt of tonnage dismantled so far this year. India however, remains the largest breakers' yard with 3.5m dwt of tonnage scrapped, an annualised rise of 25% compared with 1999, according to Clarkson data.

This year, Allied Shipbroking reports, 71 tankers, total 8.515m dwt, and 72 dry bulk carriers, total 2.5m dwt, have been scrapped. The total number scrapped this year is 174 of 11.581m dwt.

APPENDIX 15

Lloyd's List Market Report

Ship Sales

Container and Multi-purpose

ASTRA LIFT (Heavy Lift): sold by Carsten Rehder, Germany to undisclosed interests, $1.15M. *1978. 3,861 DWT, 3,038 GT. Built CN Solimano, Nohab, 4,200bhp/15kt.*

BOL (Multi-Purpose) *Tbn-Galina IV*: sold by Jadroplov, Croatia to Koalbye Shipping, Ukraine, $1M. *1980. 14,930 DWT, 12,327 GT, 388 TEU. Built Kherson Shipyard, B&W, 10,600bhp/18kt.*

CHALLENGER K (Ro-Ro) *ex-Kirk Challenger*: sold by Kirk Line, US to undisclosed interests, $1.006M. *1979. 2,823 DWT, 5,945 GT, 260 TEU. Built Elsinore Shipbuilding, Mak, 4,500bhp/15kt.*

ETTRICKBANK (Multi-Purpose) *ex-Gregor*: sold by Ormos, Greece to undisclosed interests, $1.3M. *1977. 18,632 DWT, 13,542 GT, 545 TEU. Built Mitsubishi HI, Sulzer, 9,900bhp/14kt.*

GASTELLO (General Cargo), en-bloc with NOGLIKI, SLAVNOE & TOMARI *Tbn-Alexandria*: sold by ASP-Seascot, UK to undisclosed interests, $2.8M each. *1992* (GASTELLO 1993). *4,168 DWT, 3,972 GT, 224 TEU. Built Sedef Gemi, B&W, 4,563bhp/13.1kt.*

RICKMERS DALIAN (Multi-Purpose): sold by Rickmers-Linie, Germany to Middle East Interests, $2.25M. *1978. 24,080 DWT, 16,930 GT, 536 TEU. Built Aker, B&W, 13,100bhp/18kt.*

Sold recently by Rickmers Linie to Middle East interests following the company's sale by Hapag-Lloyd, the 24,080 DWT Rickmers Dalian *is not a pretty sight according to our picture. Hardly surprising when it has switched names at least 11 times indicating several different operators during its 22 years. The latest sale price was just $2.25M (photo Ralf Witthohn)*

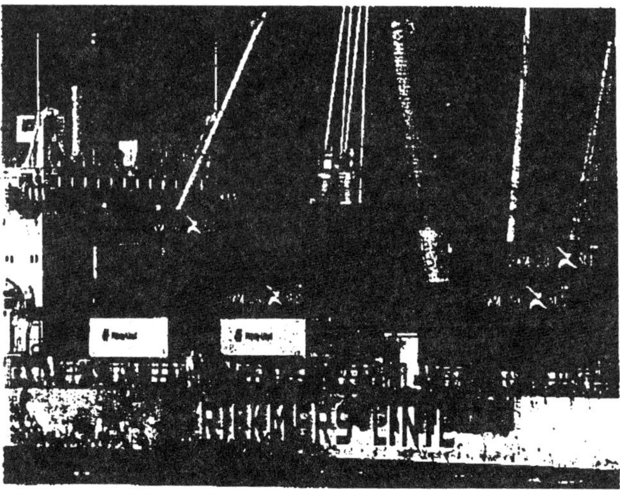

Bulkers

EVGENIA (Ore Strenghtened): sold by Leandros, Greece to Tsakos, Greece, $4.5M. *1981. 68,427 DWT, 37,939 GT, 1,064 TEU. Built Kasado Dockyard, B&W, 14,013bhp/15kt.*

HYDROBULK: sold by Sonderjysk Erhvervsinvstg, Denmark to Hans Torkelsen, Norway, $1.8M. *1986. 4,319 DWT, 3,088 GT, 130 TEU. Built Svendborg Repair Yard, Mak, 2,450bhp/12.8kt.*

KANARIS en bloc with PELOPIDAS: sold by Safety Management Overseas, Greece to undisclosed interests, $2.65M each. *1977. 39,800 DWT, 22,473 GT. Built Mitsubishi HI, Sulzer, 12,000bhp/15kt.*

Tankers

BRUCE SMART (Crude Oil): en bloc with J DENNIS BONNEY & JOHN YOUNG: sold by Chevron Transport, US to General Maritime, US. BRUCE SMART: $28.5M. *1991. 157,632 DWT, 90,369 GT. Built Ishibras, Sulzer, 21,000bhp/15kt.* J DENNIS BONNEY: $28.5M. *1991. 157,584 DWT, 90,369 GT. Built Ishibras, Sulzer, 21,000bhp/16kt.* JOHN YOUNG: $28M. *1990. 155,547 DWT, 88,946 GT. Built IHI, Sulzer, 21,000bhp/15kt.* Ships to be operated by Universe Tankships, US.

DANUBE (Products) *Tbn-Harting* en bloc with TRENT: sold by OMI Corp, US to Ga Chau, Hong Kong, $21M. DANUBE $10.5M. *1991. 29,998 DWT, 17,018 GT. Built Szczecinska, B&W, 8,845bhp/14kt.* TRENT $10.50M, Last sale: 1999, $11M. *1991. 29,998 DWT, 17,018 GT. Built Szczecinska, B&W, 9,908bhp/14kt.* Both ships to be operated by Denholm, UK.

LEON (Crude Oil) *ex-Maritza*: sold by Olympic Gulf Tankers, Greece to Middle East interests, $1M. Last sale: 1998, $1.1M. *1977. 16,540 DWT, 10,791 GT. Built Baltiyskiy Zavod, B&W, 9,000bhp/14kt.*

NOL PAVO (Crude Oil) *ex-Neptune Pavo*: sold by Neptune Iota Lines, Singapore to Brave Maritime, Greece, $5.3M. *1981. 86,417 DWT, 51,967 GT. Built IHI, Semt-Pielstick, 15,000bhp/14.7kt.*

PETRO VISTA: sold by Petroships, Singapore to undisclosed interests, $0.87M. *1976. 5,640 DWT, 3,454 GT. Built Tokushima Zosen, Hanshin, 3,800bhp/10.5kt.*

Scrapped

BRITISH RANGER (Crude Oil Tanker): sold by BP Amoco, UK to Chinese breakers, $4.62M ($125 per LDT). *1976, 269,881 DWT, 130,145 GT. Built Mitsubishi HI, Mitsubishi, 34,000bhp/15kt*

GEORGE (Multi-Purpose) *ex-Alkaios*: sold by Aegeus, Greece to Indian breakers, $0.78M ($140 per LDT). Last sale: 1980, $8.25M. *1977, 16,875 DWT, 11,420 GT, 192 TEU. Built Sunderland Shipbuilding, Doxford, 10,800bhp/17kt*

MEGA BAY (Crude Oil Tanker) *ex-Hansa Visby*: sold by Mega Tankers, Hong Kong to Bangladeshi breakers, $3.29M ($140 per LDT). Last sale: 1989, $21.50M. *1976, 139,209 DWT, 71,107 GT. Built Mitsui Eng & Shipbuilding, B&W, 27,326bhp/15kt*

NISHA (Bulk Carrier Ore Strengthened) *ex-Jag Vishnu*: sold by Great Eastern Shipping, India to Indian breakers, $1.01M ($152 per LDT). *1977, 27,481 DWT, 16,731 GT. Built Osaka Zosensho, Sulzer, 11,550bhp/15kt*

OILINVEST PRIMA (Crude Oil Tanker) *ex-Oilinvest*: sold by Nameseco Holland, Netherlands to Bangladeshi breakers, $3.08M ($147 per LDT). Last sale: 1991, $14.80M, *1975, 134,999 DWT, 75,215 GT. Built Oresundsvarvet, B&W, 27,326bhp/14kt*

PROFESOR K BOHDANOWICZ (Chemical/Oil Tanker): sold by Zegluga Polska, Poland to Indian breakers, $0.57M ($142 per LDT). *1974, 9,694 DWT, 6,688 GT. Built Lodose Varf, MWM, 3,000bhp/14kt*

RAS TINA (Container) *ex-Isla de Fuerteventura*: sold by Flimex, Canary Islands to unknown breakers, price unknown. *1960, 1,956 DWT, 1,576 GT, 91 TEU. Built Juliana Gijonesa, MTM, 2,349bhp/12kt*

STANDARD ENDEAVOUR (Bulk Carrier Ore Strengthened) *ex-Chalmette*: sold by Standard Bulk Trans, Greece to Indian breakers, $1.67M ($147 per LDT). Last sale: 1984, $4.6M. *1972, 69,408 DWT, 32,140 GT. Built NKK, Sulzer, 15,000bhp/16kt*

WESER ORE (Ore/Oil Carrier) *ex-Tarafala*: sold by Associated Maritime Co, Hong Kong to Chinese breakers, price unknown. *1974, 278,734 DWT, 134,366 GT. Built Uljanik Brodogradiliste, B&W, 40,000bhp/16.5kt*

All details given in good faith but without guarantee

APPENDIX 16

Bill of Sale

BILL OF SALE

1. Seller(s) (state full name, description and address)		2. Buyer(s) (state full name, description and address)	
3. Name of Vessel	4. Type of Vessel	5. Port of Registry	6. Call Signs
7. Gross Register Tonnage	8. Net Register Tonnage	9. Date of Memorandum of Agreement	
10. Purchase Sum (in figures and in letters)			
11. Details of subsisting or outstanding Mortgage(s) or other encumbrances, if any; also state other details, if any, relevant to the sale and transfer of the Vessel			

The Seller(s), named in Box 1, who is (are) the Owner(s) of the Vessel described in Boxes 3 to 8, both inclusive, hereby confirm(s) having sold and handed over the said Vessel with everything belonging to her to the Buyer(s), named in Box 2, for the Purchase Sum, as stated in Box 10.
Unless otherwise stated in Box 11, the Seller(s) warrant(s) that the Vessel is free from encumbrances, debts and maritime liens of any kind whatsoever and confirm(s) that the sale and transfer of the Vessel is effected in accordance with Memorandum of Agreement dated as indicated in Box 9.
In consideration of the said Purchase Sum, paid to the Seller(s) by the Buyer(s), the Seller(s) hereby transfer(s) the Vessel to the Buyer(s) so that the Vessel shall hereinafter become his (their) legal property.
IN WITNESS whereof this Bill of Sale has been issued and signed at the place and on the date stated in Box 12 in the presence of the Witness(es) as indicated in Box 13 whose signature(s) has (have) been certified (if required) by the person indicated in Box 14.

*

12. Place and date and signature of Seller(s)
13. The undersigned Witness(es) hereby certifies(y) the correctness of the Seller(s)' signature(s) to this Bill of Sale and the date hereof (state full name, title and address of Witness(es))
14. The undersigned Consul (General) hereby certifies the correctness of the Witness(es)' signature(s) as stated in Box 13

MOCK EXAMINATION

DO NOT turn to the next page until you have followed the suggestions set out below.

Overleaf is a sample examination paper. In your own interest do not look at it yet but instead, do the same revision of the course as you would for any examination.

On completing your revision, put away your notes, have pens and papers ready and set aside three hours when you will not be interrupted, in other words create, as near as possible, examination room conditions.

It is recommended that you hand write this mock examination. You will have to write the actual examination and many students find that it is difficult to write legibly for three hours without practice. If your handwriting is illegible you will lose marks. Examiners cannot mark what they cannot read.

Carry out the instructions on the question paper and send your answers to your tutor for marking. (Note your start and finish times on the front answer paper).

THE INSTITUTE OF CHARTERED SHIPBROKERS

MOCK EXAMINATION

SHIP SALE AND PURCHASE

Time allowed – Three hours

Answer any FIVE questions – all questions carry equal marks

1. Your ship-owning company has agreed terms to purchase a second-hand Bulk Carrier and has successfully secured a Time-Charter for this ship commencing at the Port of Delivery immediately after purchase. Prepare a plan of action in the correct order of occurrence of the tasks and procedures that your company will have to perform during the period from the day of signing the MOA for this ship right up to the day the ship is handed over to the new Time Charterers.

2. In the context of the second-hand market, comment upon the significance of the following:-

   (i) "Subject Board Approval"

   (ii) The importance of exact tonnage certificate to a ship-owner

   (iii) Buyer Beware

   (iv) "The Buyers shall inspect the vessel without opening it"

3. The Documentation Clause of the 1993 NSF sets out the documents to be provided by the Sellers in exchange for payment of the purchase price. The Clause itemises several standard documents that will almost always be needed but a prudent Buyer will also negotiate by way of an addendum to the printed terms various additional documents to be presented by the Seller at the time of delivery, covering both ashore and on board ship. Using a ship type of your choice, comment on the documents in the printed Clause itself along with all possible additional documentation that this Buyer may have incorporated into the MOA.

   In respect of the documentation issued by the Seller, how can a Buyer seek protection against fraudulent paperwork?

4. There are certain types of insurance policies associated with the sale and purchase of the ships in respect of the new-building, second-handed and demolition markets. What are these and what precisely are these policies designed to cover. For each policy, who pays the premium?

5. In the family of tankers, the Aframax is known as "the workhorse" of the industry. Selecting either a clean or dirty product trading Aframax give a full description of this tanker with particular attention to the characteristics that relate to the products being carried. Detail these products along with their main trading routes.

   Compliment your answer with a comprehensive drawing of both the ship and a world map showing the trading routes.

6. When selling a ship for further trading, the NSF provides an essential Clause which covers the items to be included in the purchase price and those, unless otherwise agreed, that must be paid for by the Buyer as extra items.

   Explain in full the terms of this Clause making particular reference to each of the following:-

   (i) Spares on order and forwarding charges, if any

(ii) Spares taken out of spare parts and spare equipment and used as a replacement prior to delivery

(iii) Radio installation and navigational equipment

(iv) Payment under the terms of the Clause

7. Analyse the different methods of ship finance for the purchase of a second-hand ship for further trading. To what extent would this differ if the purchase were for demolition?

8. 2003 saw historical high freight rates in the cape size dry bulk market. Analyse the reasons for these record high daily rates and what possible effects do such rates have on the cape-size new-building, second-hand and demolition markets.

THE PURPOSE AND SCOPE OF THIS BOOK COURSE GUIDE

THE SHIP

Thoroughly understand that the knowledge of ship design and construction required of a Sale & Purchase Broker is that which is necessary to communicate effectively with a potential Buyer. Think in terms of the sort of information that a successful car dealer or real estate agent need in their respective trades.

Thoroughly understand the fundamental differences between dry bulk cargo ships, general-purpose ships, liners (container, break-bulk and Ro-Ro) and tankers, including Ore/Oil and Ore/Bulk/Oil carriers. (Students are expected to be able produce fairly detailed sketches).

Understand that Tankers sub-divide into several categories including carriers for crude oil, petroleum products, chemicals, liquid gases, vegetable oils etc.

Be aware of size ranges of bulk carriers including Capesize, Panamax, Handy-size.

Understand the purpose also basic design and construction features of decks, holds, hatches, derricks, winches cranes and other cargo handling gear. Be aware of ballasting and ballast systems.

Understand the terminology of measuring ships including:

Displacement	TEU lane metres
DWCC	LOA
DWAT	LBP
GT	Moulded Depth
NT	Draft
Bale & Grain Cube	Air draft

Understand other dimensions used in ships including freeboard, draft, moulded depth, length overall, length between perpendiculars, beam extreme breadth.

Thoroughly understand the importance of displacement (especially light displacement) tonnage in ship sales for demolition.

Understand what information is contained in General Arrangement Plans.

Thoroughly understand the basic characteristics of a ship's propulsion machinery also other machinery and equipment that may feature in ship sale negotiations.

Understand the trends in ship development especially those which are affected by legislation and/or international convention (e.g. double skinned tankers). Be aware of perceptions of future developments which may affect a purchaser's thinking.

GEOGRAPHY

Understand the location of the main areas of current shipbuilding; be aware of the size, capabilities and specialisation of the major yards. Understand the location of the major Buyers of tonnage for demolition.

Understand cargoes, trade routes and meteorological phenomena to the extent that these may influence the types and sizes of ships to be employed.

REGISTRATION AND CLASSIFICATION

Thoroughly understand the need for a ship to be **registered.**

Thoroughly understand the differences between registration in the Owner's own country (flag state) and registration in another country (offshore registration). Understand the differences between flags of convenience and "open registers" operated by traditional maritime nations.

Understand the advantages and disadvantages of each form of registration.

Be aware of the advantages both real and hoped-for arising out of the introduction of tonnage tax.

Be aware of the manner in which an S & P Broker may become involved in changing a ship's registration

Thoroughly understand the need for a ship to be **classified** and what classification entails.

Understand the role and function of classification societies and the names of the principle societies. Understand what membership of the International Association of Classification Societies (IACS) entails. Be aware of the considerable number of real and quasi-classification societies which do not qualify for membership of IACS.

Be aware of the manner in which an S & P Broker may become involved in changing a ship's classification.

THE PARTIES INVOLVED

Understand how an S & P Broker must be able to differentiate among the different types of Shipowners – the Buyers and the Sellers – including individual entrepreneurial Owners; limited companies large and small; divisions in conglomerates; investment groups which may purchase for immediate bareboat charter to an Operator; shipping pools. Understand how their attitude in S & P negotiations may differ.

Understand the role and function of other major players in the S & P market including other Brokers; ship breakers; Charterers (for example a ship may be sold with an existing charter commitment); bankers and other financiers.

Understand the role and function of those who may become involved at the time of completion of a sale including lawyers; notaries; consuls; registrars; classification society representatives.

Be aware of the structure of a typical S & P Broker's office and the importance of record-keeping.

MARKETS

Thoroughly understand the differences and interrelationships between the markets for newbuildings, second hand tonnage and demolition. Be aware of how the information each requires differs in emphasis.

Understand what factors influence the state (firmness or weakness) of the S & P Market generally and what factors influence each of these markets particularly.

Understand what factors influence the chartering market and how these directly impinge on the second hand market and indirectly on the demolition market and how current views on the future of world economy affect the newbuilding market.

Understand the influence on markets of external factors including natural catastrophes; political crises; environmental disasters; aid programmes.

Be aware of the markets for tramps, liners and tankers and how different countries may react to different factors.

Understand the skill required to prepare and to interpret market reports including both statistical and written reports.

CONTRACTS AND DOCUMENTATION

Thoroughly understand the basic anatomy of an agreement to sell a ship and the essential differences depending upon whether it is for a newbuilding, a second hand ship or a ship destined for scrap.

Understand the existence of all the standard Memorandums of Agreement in current use. Thoroughly understand the most widely used namely **Norwegian Saleform.**

Understand that there are two Norwegian Saleforms in current use, the 1987 version and the 1993 version. NB. Because many practitioners prefer the tried and trusted to the new and improved, students should be able to compare the two versions.

Understand the intention of each clause in a saleform, be aware of the Clause numbers of the more crucial clauses.

Understand the practicalities of the inspection and dry-docking clauses and when these are customarily carried out.

Understand how to compile additional clauses when these are desirable to supplement or replace those in the printed form.

Understand the role and function of all other documentation which Buyers and Sellers normally must produce at the time of completing the sale and the legal transfer of the ship. Including safety and other compliance certificates. Be aware of the issuing authorities for these documents. Be aware of representatives of other parties whose presence or electronic contact may be required at time of handover.

NEGOTIATION

Thoroughly understand the basics of firm offer and counter offer in the negotiating process and the manner in which it is customary for the two parties each having their respective Brokers. Understand the importance of time limits in offers.

Understand how to draft an opening offer encompassing all the Principal's requirements including the wording of any clauses not covered by the printed form and which may have to be specifically compiled.

Understand how the negotiating process leads to a conclusion necessitating a recapitulation together with a completion agenda. Be aware of the various "subjects" particularly "subject inspection" which have to be lifted before the sale is finally complete

Understand the manner in which a ship's particulars are usually compiled when placing a ship on the market for sale. Thoroughly understand that such primary information is given on a "believed to be correct but not guaranteed" basis.

Be aware of the etiquette and ethics customary among S & P Brokers including the commitment to clients when certain information has been requested and given.

FINANCE AND INSURANCE

Thoroughly understand the different ways a Buyer may raise the funds to finance the purchase.

Understand the sources of such funds and the type of information such financiers will require.

Thoroughly understand the role and function of a mortgage when used as security for a loan to finance the purchase.

Understand the procedures of leasing and bareboat chartering as methods of acquiring tonnage.

Be aware of the effect of interest rates, foreign currency and currency fluctuation on the raising of finance and servicing the loan.

Understand the manner in which the Seller's and Buyer's insurable risk changes as the negotiations progress and the importance of ensuring cover is obtained at the correct time. Be aware of the providers of insurance including the role of a P & I Club.

VALUATIONS

Thoroughly understand the duties of a valuer in ship sale and purchase be aware of the reasons for and types of bodies requiring valuations.

Understand the legal liabilities upon and protection needed by valuers. Understand how a valuation is presented with particular attention to appropriate caveats.

Understand the information upon which a valuation is based and the method of assessing a value. Be aware that it does not involve physically surveying the actual vessel.

LEGAL ASPECTS OF SALE AND PURCHASE

Thoroughly understand the legal position of the Broker in S & P and the relationship with the Principal.

Understand the principle of the Broker acting under the specific authority of the Principal and the liability likely to arise if this authority is not acted upon meticulously.

Understand what is involved in breach of warranty of authority both with and without negligence.

Understand what is implied with the words "free of all encumbrances and maritime liens".

Understand the importance of a valid Notice of Readiness and of the ship arriving within her cancelling date.

Be aware of the principle areas of dispute including alleged misrepresentation in the description of the vessel, condition of the vessel on delivery, quantity of bunkers on delivery, alleged absence of items of equipment on delivery.

Be aware that the Buyer is not obliged to give any reason for declining a ship on inspection.

Understand the Broker's right to a commission and the manner of ensuring this right is protected.

Be aware of the effect of international conventions and legislation on existing and new ships.

Order Form – TutorShip

This voucher entitles the student to a £10 discount off the price of *The Ships Atlas*. This offer is only available through Shipping Guides Ltd. Please contact us at the address below to find out the current price or visit our website www.portinfo.co.uk.

Company:

Address:

Post/Zip Code: Country:

VAT No. (EC only)

Contact: Title:

Tel No: Fax:

Email:

SHIPPING GUIDES LIMITED
75 Bell Street, Reigate, Surrey,
RH2 7AN, United Kingdom
Tel: +44 1737 242255
Fax: +44 1737 222449
Email: sales@portinfo.co.uk
Telex: 917070 Shipg G
VAT Registration Number
GB 243 9546 43

Nature of business

○ Ship master ○ Ship owner/operator/manager ○ Ship broker/agent
○ Ship charterer ○ Legal services ○ Financial services ○ Other

If other, please specify:

Required Products

Product Name	Quantity	Price
The Ships Atlas		
	Subtotal	
	Postage	
	VAT	
Please note that prices may be subject to VAT	Total	

Order Details

○ Please send a (proforma) invoice ○ We have arranged direct payment to your bank ○ We wish to pay by cheque/bank draft/credit card
(Delete as applicable)

The amount of £ Customers within the EU should quote their VAT numbers where appropriate

Please note that prices may be subject to VAT

Amex ○ Mastercard ○ Visa ○ Delta ○ Switch ○

Cardholder's Name:

Card Number:

Expiry Date: /

Signature: Date: / /

Method of payment

1. Sterling bank draft drawn on a bank in the UK made payable to Shipping Guides Ltd.
2. Credit card (complete section left).
3. Direct payment in Pounds Sterling to our bank (details below). Payment to be made in full
   - All charges to your account
   - All direct payments to state company name and complete address

Our Bank Details
Barclays Bank plc,
90 - 92 High Street, Crawley,
West Sussex, RH10 1BP, UK.

Account Number: 30079332
Sort Code: 20-23-97
IBAN No: GB32 BARC 202397 30079332
Swiftcode: BARCGB22